COVERS GEN I, II, AND III ENGINES

FORD Coyote Engines

REVISED EDITION

How to Build MAX PERFORMANCE

Jim Smart

CarTech®

CarTech®

CarTech, Inc.
6118 Main Street
North Branch, MN 55056
Phone: 651-277-1200 or 800-551-4754
Fax: 651-277-1203
www.cartechbooks.com

1st Edition Published 2016

Edit by Bob Wilson
Layout by Monica Seiberlich

ISBN 978-1-61325-798-2
Item No. SA545

Library of Congress Cataloging-in-Publication Data Available

Written, edited, and designed in the U.S.A.
Printed in China
10 9 8 7 6 5 4 3 2

DISTRIBUTION BY:

Europe
PGUK
63 Hatton Garden
London EC1N 8LE, England
Phone: 020 7061 1980 • Fax: 020 7242 3725
www.pguk.co.uk

Australia
Renniks Publications Ltd.
3/37-39 Green Street
Banksmeadow, NSW 2109, Australia
Phone: 2 9695 7055 • Fax: 2 9695 7355
www.renniks.com

Canada
Login Canada
300 Saulteaux Crescent
Winnipeg, MB, R3J 3T2 Canada
Phone: 800 665 1148 • Fax: 800 665 0103
www.lb.ca

CONTENTS

S-A DESIGN

ACKNOWLEDGMENTS

A book of this depth happens only with help from many valuable people in the industry and close friends who have been making it happen for me for a lifetime. Mike Delahanty, formerly of Ford Performance Parts, provided a complete box stock Gen II 5.0L Ti-VCT DOHC Coyote V-8 and most of the parts necessary to conduct dyno testing and prove this engine repeatedly. Ford Performance Parts offered the opportunity to take the high-tech Coyote and prove it out in an independent dynamometer lab.

Mike also invited me to Detroit for a close look at how Ford Performance Aluminator crate engines are planned out and built by Performance Assembly Solutions (PAS) in Livonia, Michigan. Crate engines have long had a well-deserved bad rap over quality issues. However, the Aluminator Coyote crate engine is a huge exception to this belief because standards are very high and OEM in scope. These are world-class engines that are mass produced in an intimate environment where every engine and every step experiences strict accountability. The staff members talk with each other, and problems are discussed and rectified immediately.

Mike Goodwin of Ford Performance Parts provided a Gen III Coyote crate engine to play with and explore for this book effort as well as editorial content for magazines and websites. He also invited me to Performance Assembly Solutions for a fresh look at how Ford Performance crate Coyotes are made today. The quality and attention to detail in these Coyote crates have never been better. Mike, I'm grateful for your support. John Torvinen, Frank Hoffman, and Will Clendenin of PAS have been endlessly supportive during the update of this book. As Mike Delahanty did years ago, these gentlemen invited me to PAS to cover Gen III builds.

Dennis Corn of Roush Performance invited me to the company's vast Livonia, Michigan, facility for an intimate look at how Roush has grown from a modest race shop to a huge research and development as well as manufacturing operation from aftermarket parts and engines to valuable OEM engineering support. Founder and President Jack Roush came from humble beginnings to create what is easily one of the most respected race-oriented operations in the world. Roush Performance offers the enthusiast Ti-VCT Coyote crate engine performance in a variety of upscale Coyote Aluminator packages from Ford Performance.

Jim Grubbs of JGM Performance Engineering in Valencia, California, decided to take on this project and became very committed to its success. He and then associate Jeff Latimer spent weeks preparing JGM's SuperFlow 901 dyno for our testing. The thrill on Jim's face as we have tested this high-tech V-8 has been nothing short of remarkable. Ray Herron at Ford Performance Racing Parts' tech support department has been very supportive to our efforts in California. I call. He advises.

Ray McClelland of Full Throttle Kustomz in Fillmore, California, has been kind enough to come to JGM Performance Engineering to custom tune our Coyote test mule as I've made modifications. With Ray's knowledge and extraordinary tuning abilities, more than 100 hp was gained with simple bolt-on modifications in a naturally aspirated package.

Tim Gilpin at BBK Performance has been supportive to this effort by providing performance parts and technical support. Trent Goodwin at Comp Cams supported my efforts more times than I can count through the years by providing cam kits, valvetrain components, and performance parts. What's more is that Trent has provided incredible technical support.

Another great support system through the years has been Ron Rotunno, formerly of Federal-Mogul (Speed Pro, Sealed Power, and Fel-Pro). Ron provided technical support and OEM-caliber product for at least two decades. Finally, there's Derek Ranney of L&R Custom Engine Building in Sante Fe Springs, California, who has been instrumental in showing how a Coyote should be planned and built. L&R has been family owned and operated since it opened its doors decades ago.

Gentlemen, I never could have produced this book without you nor without the support of my favorite cohort in crime: Bob Wilson at CarTech. I'm grateful for your friendships and unending support through the years. Thank you!

CHAPTER 1

INTRODUCTION TO THE COYOTE ENGINE

Ford's new 5.0L/5.2L Ti-VCT (Twin Independent Variable Cam Timing) Coyote and 5.2L Voodoo DOHC V-8s can easily be described as the two greatest V-8 engines ever produced in the company's history. Originally project code named "Coyote" within the company as early as 2007, the Ti-VCT V-8 was developed and engineered to be a true high-performance double overhead cam V-8 conceived specifically for the Mustang. In fact, the Coyote is considered the first Mustang-specific engine conceived in the marque's more than half-century history.

Those of us fortunate enough to be there when Ford was birthing this engine initially believed Ford would never be able to do any better than the all-new Coyote double-overhead-cam V-8. It was perfect in so many ways. However, a critical eye could find items that needed improvement. Improvement came in 2015 with the Gen II Coyote and later with the 2018 Gen III.

Ford engineers and product planners, led by Mike Harrison, looked at what they liked and didn't like about the venerable 4.6L and 5.4L overhead cam Modular engine family and applied it to the Coyote's development. Although the Coyote and Modular engines resemble each other, there is no interchangeability between the two engine families. The Coyote is a totally new DOHC Modular V-8 engine.

When it was in the rumor mill, the 5.0L DOHC Ti-VCT was believed to be the gallant return of the legendary 5.0L engine that made late-model Fox body and SN-95 Mustangs so notorious. There was street chatter about it being a push-rod engine on par with the classic small-block Ford V-8. However, nothing could have been further from the truth. Ford was moving forward, not backward, with a real

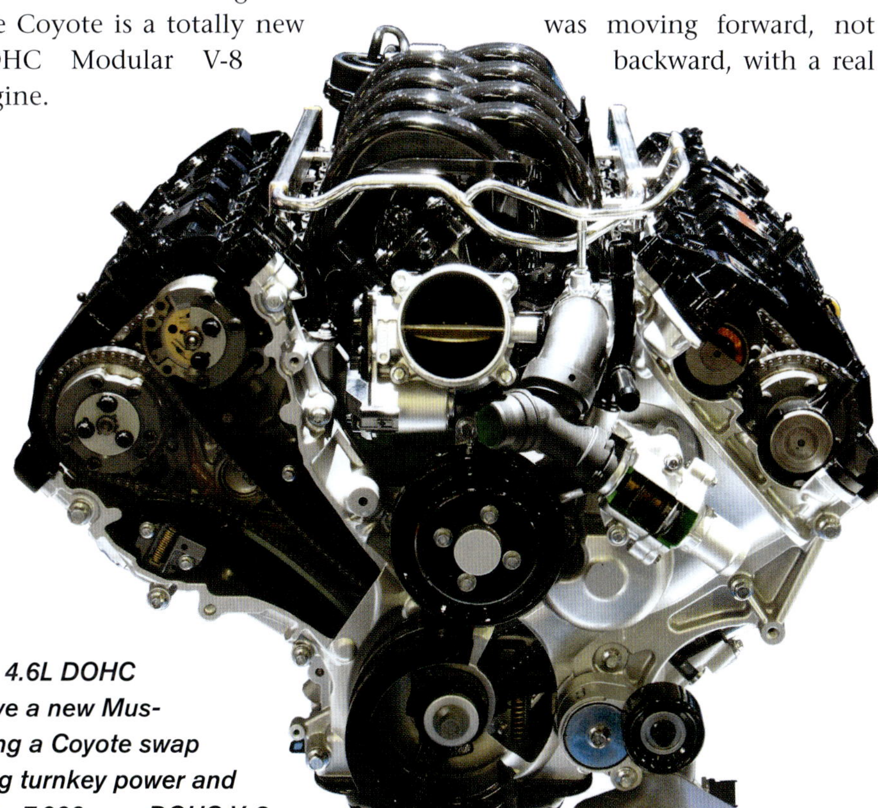

Head on, the Coyote is similar to the 4.6L DOHC engine it replaces. Whether you have a new Mustang or F-Series truck or are planning a Coyote swap into your vintage Ford, you're getting turnkey power and incredible fuel economy out of a 7,000-rpm DOHC V-8.

This inside look at the 5.0L Ti-VCT DOHC Coyote V-8 yields a close look at what makes this the most advanced Ford V-8 in history. Conceived as a Detroit-born high-performance V-8, the Coyote makes in excess of 400 hp out of the box. In addition, it is capable of 500 without extensive modifications.

purpose-born high-performance double overhead cam V-8.

In 2007, Ford knew it needed to conceive and build a world-class high-performance V-8 engine that could compete with tougher world-class competition from not only GM and Chrysler, but Europe and Japan. Ford's handpicked design and engineering team consisting of racers and manufacturing experts looked closely at how power was made and wasted. Team Coyote looked at thermal and volumetric efficiency along with frictional loss issues. It also looked at the limitations of the 4.6L and 5.4L Modular V-8 architecture to help set a course toward success.

The 5.0L Ti-VCT Coyote engine was born to be a true high-performance V-8, a factory-born racing engine for the street. All the traditional corporate roadblocks were cleared to get an eye-opening DOHC powerhouse to market quickly.

The first step toward the Ti-VCT 5.0L V-8 was the Hurricane engine, which ultimately became the production 6.2L SOHC iron-block Modular for Raptor and F-150 trucks. Though the 6.2L engine provided plenty of torque, it was not suitable for the Mustang in terms of size and power. It really was a completely different standalone Modular engine. Ford had taken the 4.6L, 5.4L, and 6.2L Modular engine family as far as it could.

Engine Specifications

The Coyote engine has been produced in three basic versions between 2011 and 2016. From 2011 to 2014, induction is conventional. From 2015 and on, the Coyote is fitted with Charge Motion induction and cylinder heads. The Shelby 5.2L Voodoo is a standalone Coyote-based engine.

2011–2014 5.0L (Gen I) Ti-VCT

- 5.0L Ti-VCT DOHC V-8: 302 ci or 4,951 cc
- Code-named "Coyote" by Ford, but not officially named
- Bore: 3.630 inches (92 mm)
- Pistons: Hypereutectic (high-silicon cast)
- Stroke: 3.650 inches (93 mm)
- Connecting Rods: Powdered metal, forged
- Crankshaft: Forged steel with eight-bolt flange
- Horsepower: 412 at 6,500 rpm
- Torque: 390 ft-lbs at 4,250 rpm
- Redline: 7,000 rpm
- Compression: 11.0:1 naturally aspirated; 9.0:1 supercharged
- Block: Aluminum with steel cylinder liners
- Heads: Aluminum hemispherical four-valve
- Timing: Variable valve, composite intake/exhaust cams
- Manufacture: Essex, Ontario, Canada
- Intake Manifold: Composite, 16.5-inch runners
- Fuel Injection: Returnless electronic
- Ignition: Coil-on-plug electronic
- Headers: Shorty tubular stainless steel
- Oil Capacity: 8 quarts with filter change

2015–2017 5.0L (Gen II) Ti-VCT

- 5.0L Ti-VCT DOHC V-8: 302 ci or 4,951 cc
- Code-named "Coyote" by Ford, but not officially named
- Bore: 3.630 inches (92 mm)
- Pistons: Hypereutectic (high-silicon cast)
- Stroke: 3.650 inches (93 mm)

Engine Specifications

- Connecting Rods: Powdered metal, forged
- Crankshaft: Forged steel with eight-bolt flange
- Horsepower: 435 at 6,500 rpm
- Torque: 400 ft-lbs at 4,250 rpm
- Redline: 7,000 rpm
- Compression: 11.0:1 naturally aspirated; 9.0:1 supercharged
- Block: Aluminum with steel cylinder liners
- Heads: Aluminum hemispherical four-valve
- Timing: Variable valve, composite intake/exhaust cams
- Manufacture: Essex, Ontario, Canada
- Intake Manifold: Composite, 16.5-inch runners
- Flap Valves: Charge motion for improved low-end torque and idle quality
- Fuel Injection: Returnless electronic
- Ignition: Coil-on-plug electronic
- Headers: Shorty tubular stainless steel
- Oil Capacity: 8 quarts with filter change

2015–2020 5.2L Shelby GT350 Voodoo

- 5.2L DOHC V-8: 315 ci, or 5,163 cc
- Code-named "Voodoo" by Ford, but not officially named
- Bore: 3.700 inches (94 mm)
- Pistons: Hypereutectic (high-silicon cast)
- Stroke: 3.660 inches (93 mm)
- Connecting Rods: Powdered metal, forged
- Crankshaft: Forged steel with eight-bolt flange
- Horsepower: 526 at 7,500 rpm
- Torque: 429 ft-lbs at 4,750 rpm
- Redline: 8,000-rpm
- Compression: 12.0:1 naturally aspirated
- Cylinder Liners: Plasma transferred wire arc, sprayed-on
- Heads: Aluminum hemispherical four-valve
- Timing: Variable valve, composite intake/exhaust cams
- Manufacture: Essex, Ontario, Canada
- Intake Manifold: Composite, 16.5-inch runners, 87-mm throttle body
- Flap Valves: Charge motion for improved low-end torque and idle quality
- Fuel Injection: Returnless electronic
- Ignition: Coil-on-plug electronic
- Headers: Shorty tubular stainless steel
- Oil Capacity: 8 quarts with filter change

2018–2023 5.0L (Gen III) Ti-VCT

- Larger cylinder bores to accommodate larger valves
- Plasma transferred wire arc (PTWA) cylinder walls borrowed from the Shelby GT350 5.2L block
- Larger intake and exhaust valves
- Revised lift intake and exhaust cams
- Stiffer valve springs to allow for higher maximum revs of 7,500 rpm
- New stronger cylinder head castings, including revised ports from the Gen II, resulting in better flow experienced from the CNC-ported GT350's 5.2L Voodoo
- Sinter-forged connecting rods carried over from the 2012–2013 Boss 302 engine and Gen II Coyote
- Greater compression (12.0:1) from domed pistons with deeper cutouts to clear larger valves
- Improved balanced forged steel crankshaft for higher-RPM operation
- A fresh revised intake manifold with the same charged motion (CMCV) from the Gen II
- Dual fuel induction with both direct and port fuel injection. This allows for higher compression and clean intake valve faces to maximize performance and fuel efficiency.
- On the intake side, variable camshaft timing with mid-lock phasers carried over from the Gen II. Exhaust cam phasers migrate to an in-head oil-control valve with spring return for better control at all speeds and loads.
- Additional oil return passage in the block for diverted oil from the oil-filter adapter
- Greater camshaft lift (14 mm) over the Gen II
- Exhaust cam #1 journal is larger to accommodate seals, which prevent oil leakage from the phaser
- Gen III chain drive uses Gen II intake phasers, primary chains, secondary chains, and crank sprocket
- Exhaust phasers (watch-spring style) are new for the Gen III (no interchangeability with Gen I and Gen II) and are attached with a single bolt. The Gen III chain driver kit is M-6004-A5018.
- Gen III valve springs employ a greater pressure and installed height than Gen II.
- Bridge cooling holes in Gen III head gaskets due to greater compression and cylinder pressures. ■

Though the Coyote design team wanted to create a completely new high-performance overhead cam V-8, the basics of Modular engine architecture had to remain due to cost and factory tooling considerations. The new Modular engine had to be produced from the same production lines and from the same machinery in order to keep cost in line. The 4.6L and 5.4L engines had limited potential for extreme performance. Conceiving the Coyote was an enormous challenge.

Development of Ford's 5.0L Coyote DOHC V-8 began in earnest in 2008 with Ford's vision being a true high-performance Mustang engine. Though the Coyote has also arrived in Ford's popular F-Series trucks, it was originally developed for the Mustang. Ford's direct injection and Ecoboost turbocharging technology were real considerations for the Ti-VCT V-8, yet not practical or necessary for this engine early in the going. This alone gave the Coyote an economic advantage. Lots of power from a naturally aspirated engine.

The objective was to make the Coyote as compact as possible while keeping block dimensions close to the same size as the 4.6L. The Coyote also had to be an engine that would make at least 400 hp, or 80 hp per liter. These expectations were huge and had to be met to realize the goal of exceeding the capabilities of the 4.6L engine. The Ti-VCT had to do what no Ford production engine had ever been asked to do.

Ford's goal for the Ti-VCT Coyote was a much stronger block to contain and deliver the kind of power expected. It had to be able to do what the 4.6L and 5.4L engines could do, without a raised deck. It wasn't just the factory 400/400-hp and torque goal, but also the kind of power enthusiasts wanted once the 2011 Mustang GT hit the streets. The Coyote was going to have to be a 7,000-rpm redline engine right off the production line.

Project planners knew they had to look far ahead into this engine's future at not only what performance enthusiasts would do with it, but also what Ford had planned in terms of direct injection and turbocharging. The objective was to engineer the block to a satisfactory point so that the engineers didn't have to come back and do it again later.

Where the Ti-VCT Coyote V-8 shines is its completely new cylinder head design and function; it has maximum flow into each cylinder and greatly reduced valvetrain friction and weight. Larger cylinder head bolts and improved sealing technology help contain much higher 11.0:1 compression.

Because the Coyote development timeline was tight, the team had to fast track this engine through development, prototyping, testing, certification, and into production. The traditional three-year development window to get this thing turning and burning was not an option. Existing Modular mule engines had to be used to work and test Coyote engine parts for durability. A lot of scrap that didn't measure up went into the recycle bin.

To get the Ti-VCT where Team Coyote wanted it necessitated a lot of back and forth between hardware people in engine building and dyno rooms and software geeks who compared information and made adjustments as necessary. It was a great combination of hard-core seat-of-the-pants engine experimentation and high-tech computer design. Engines were thrashed, tortured, and trashed via hundreds of hours of dyno lab testing. Any weak links were revised or eliminated.

By January 2009, Ti-VCT engine dyno testing was in full swing with those first prototype mule engines going under unspeakable loads at high RPM and throttled until they were worn out. Ford engineers disassembled used-up mules and inspected them for wear. Much to their amazement, the Ti-VCT held up very well with minimal abnormal wear issues.

Engine testing transcends hard full-throttle pulls on a dyno and in test vehicles. It must also pass tough corporate muster and federal emissions standards. Those first few prototype engines made it through testing and certification with very few changes. Field-testing in mule vehicles in extreme heat and cold was the final frontier where the Ti-VCT proved its worth. It performed flawlessly.

By the time the Coyote reached mass production in 2010, it had been tested, tortured, and abused unlike any Ford engine before. It was put through greater extremes than any Ford engine ever had to ascertain its integrity. The team wanted an engine that would deliver fuel efficiency, durability, and longevity. It wanted an engine that could handle both the daily commute and the racetrack without complaint.

The Ti-VCT Coyote was conceived during one of the most trying financial times in modern automotive history. Faced with a potential Ford bankruptcy, Ford CEO Alan Mulally saw the value in investing in product and people, and without government assistance. It paid off handsomely in a new generation of vehicles and powertrains. Mustang was among the first carlines to witness the payoff with the most advanced V-8 in its half-century production history.

The gold nugget in the Coyote was and still is its wonderful simplicity. It is an easy engine to understand and build because it is produced in only one North American plant (Essex, Ontario, Canada) with basically one block and head casting type, although I fully expect more variations in the future as this engine grows to meet demand. The confusion of two engine plants with different approaches and parts that existed with the 4.6L and 5.4L engines is gone.

The Coyote's firing order is different from the 4.6L and 5.4L V-8's at 1-5-4-8-6-3-7-2. The compression ratio reminds me of the 1960s at 11.0:1, making the most of its lower displacement and carefully executed valve timing, despite having port fuel injection instead of direct injection. Imagine being able to do this with 87-octane fuel, although 91-octane is preferable. This innovation comes of Ti-VCT, which enables each cam to adjust valve timing based on input from the powertrain control module (PCM).

What makes the Coyote Ti-VCT different from the 4.6L and 5.4L engines are great innovations that make it a user-friendly engine. And if you're considering a Modular engine swap, the 5.0L Ti-VCT double overhead "cammer" is the best way to go if you're going to go to all that trouble and expense.

Coyote Block

Retooling the Essex, Ontario, engine plant for the 5.0L Ti-VCT was simple because it remained within

The Coyote Ti-VCT engine's great architecture is on display in this long-block in Modular Motorsports' clean room. Although the Ti-VCT Coyote V-8 is considered a clean-sheet-of-paper engine with a lot of fresh and exciting engineering, it remains a close cousin of the popular Modular engine family that entered the marketplace in the 1991 Lincoln Town Car. With Coyote comes the strongest block in Modular history along with completely new downsized cylinder heads that reduce this engine's overall size. You can actually fit this thing into a Fox body Mustang without extensive modifications.

Ford's Team Coyote wanted the 5.0L Ti-VCT engine to be more compact in size than the 4.6L engine it was replacing. This engine is simply a smarter, well-thought-out performance engine born to perform. It was not borrowed from another car line or amassed from off-the-shelf parts. It was conceived first for the Mustang, ultimately finding its way into the F-150.

the parameters of the Modular engine family. The Coyote block shares the same bore spacing (3.937 inches or 100 mm), deck height (8.937 inches), bellhousing bolt pattern, and external dimensions as the 4.6L SOHC and DOHC engines. Bore size increased to 3.629 inches (92.2 mm) along with an increased stroke of 3.649 inches (92.8 mm), which is still a "square" engine design with identical bore and stroke. It differs in block design, which is entirely new, with heavier webbing and other internal improvements intended to support greater power output from modest displacement.

The Coyote engine has a rugged aluminum block with paper-thin ductile iron cylinder liners. Because the Coyote's iron cylinder liners are quite thin, this block must be sleeved with thicker liners for all-out racing in the 1,000 to 1,500-hp range. Modular Motorsports, as one example, offers racers the Pro Mod Coyote block with extra thick ductile iron cylinder liners that ensure block integrity. You can build one of these Pro Mod engines for the street if you're an avid weekend racer. Bores can be taken as high as 3.700 inches to achieve 5.2L.

Improved block architecture holds this engine together. The main bearing webs are thicker and heavier, which allows for performance extremes from enthusiasts and Ford product planners. This means the Coyote block can stand up to naturally aspirated performance demands, supercharging, nitrous, and direct injection. It can be said with great confidence that this block will withstand more than 1,500 hp sleeved with the thicker ductile iron cylinder liners mentioned earlier.

The Coyote block brings advances in crankcase ventilation known as "bay-to-bay" breathing. Ford engineers located venting in the main webs designed to allow the freedom of air scavenging without hurting power. These vents are known as chimneys. The result is a more positive piston ring seal, which helps efficiency and power.

The Modular V-8's cooling tube down the middle of the valley is not present on the Coyote. Instead, coolant is routed through the front of the block, leaving plenty of room for exotic induction systems and superchargers. Any way you view the Coyote block, it is a vast improvement over the Modular.

It is challenging to differentiate the Coyote block from a 4.6L block because the deck height and bore spacing are the same. However, basic dimensions are where the similarity ends between these engines. The Ti-VCT block is fresh thinking around basic Modular architecture with a much stouter block and common-sense racing cylinder head mindset. The cooling system has been redesigned to route coolant around exhaust valveseats and through the block instead of the valley, freeing up space for induction and supercharging.

The Coyote's bottom end employs indestructible skirted six-bolt main cap construction using larger bolts than the 4.6L engine. These main caps are a perfect fit without jackscrews and wedges. They don't move, even under extreme duty, enabling this engine to achieve a 7,000-rpm redline from the factory. The message here is that it was built with structural integrity like never before: heavier main webs, pan rails, and block walls.

Here's a closer look at the Coyote's main-cap–to–block-skirt relationship. Gone are the 4.6L/5.4L jackscrews and wedges because Coyote technology is zero adjust, meaning these six-bolt main caps are a perfect fit along with larger fasteners. With a sleeved Pro Mod Coyote block from Modular Motorsports, you can hammer this bottom end with more than 1,500 hp. There has never been a stronger Ford new-generation block.

Head on, it's challenging to differentiate the Coyote from a 4.6L block. However, closer inspection demonstrates revised cooling and oil passages. You no longer have to sweat out the valley cooling tube as you did with the 4.6L because cooling passages are now in the block.

The Coyote shares the same bellhousing bolt pattern with the 4.6L and 5.4L engines, making swaps simple and easy. This block bolts right up to a 4R70W/4R75W or any TREMEC/Getrag manual transmission.

Bore spacing is the same as the 4.6L and 5.4L blocks. However, bore size is larger via iron sleeves pressed into the aluminum block. In addition, the 5.0L embraces vastly improved cooling to handle higher compression and extreme performance duty. Note the generous cooling passages. This is a block engineered for the toughest racing conditions because Team Coyote didn't want to have to come back years later and do it again.

You've been told about the Pro Mod block in this chapter. Modular Motorsports offers racers the Coyote Pro Mod block, which is fitted with extra thick ductile iron cylinder liners that are siamesed as shown for unprecedented strength. Modular Motorsports says that the Pro Mod block can take more than 1,500 hp. These sleeves can be bored to 3.700 inches to get 5.2L displacement.

The Ti-VCT's forged steel crankshaft has the same dimensions as the 4.6L with 2.652-inch main journals and 2.086-inch rod journals along with a complete counterweight package. Ford stayed with this package because it is race proven. And, the Coyote's crank has withstood extremes of dyno testing without failure.

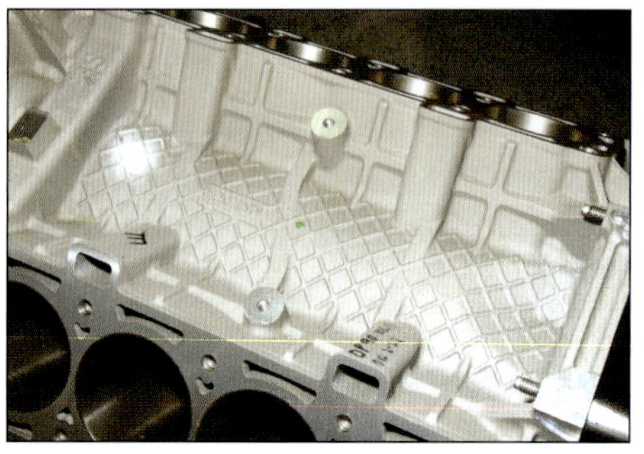

One of the quickest ways to identify the Coyote block is by this webbed crosshatch valley with a slight rise in the middle. None of the 4.6L block castings look this way. The nice thing about the Coyote block is plenty of valley space for superchargers and exotic induction systems. Gone is the 4.6L's cooling tube. The Coyote block routes coolant through the block instead of the valley.

The Coyote's forged steel crank has an eight-bolt flange and is an extreme-duty part. The 4.6L Romeo engines were six- and eight-bolt flanges depending upon application. All Windsor/Essex engines have been essentially truck engines and eight-bolt. Ford is extremely committed to eight-bolt in the interest of safety and durability.

Like the Modular engines, the Coyote has a powdered-metal connecting rod measuring 5.933 inches center to center and has proven quite durable in applications up to 500 hp. In fact, we've seen the stock rod pushed to 600 hp without consequence. However, would you want to take that chance? Anything beyond 600 hp calls for the brute Manley H-beam rod if your goal is true durability.

Bottom End

Because this is a 7,000-rpm engine, the Coyote is fitted with an induction-hardened, fully counterweighted crankshaft that's virtually indestructible, featuring an eight-hole flange. Team Coyote elected to stay with the 4.6L engine's main and rod journal dimensions because they have been a proven success in nearly two decades of production in every application imaginable. In addition, aluminum bearings were borrowed directly from the 4.6L engine instead of tri-metal bearings because they have worked successfully.

Ford learned a lot about durability with the Modular engines. It found you don't always need a forged piston; a well-thought-out hypereutectic piston works just as well. Hypereutectic offers strength without the challenges of forged. Forged pistons yield greater expansion properties and can be noisy when cold.

The Coyote engine shares the same connecting rod dimensions with the 4.6L engine at 5.933 inches center to center; yet it is not the same rod. It is a stronger rod with 12-point bolt heads. Rod ratio is 1.62:1 for excellent dwell time at each end of the bore. The Coyote's 5.933-inch cracked rod is a sintered metal I-beam piece engineered for extreme street

The Coyote piston, shown from another angle, demonstrates how different this slug is from those in the 4.6L/5.4L Modular. It is a lighter piston sporting a protective coating, enabling it to survive higher-combustion temperatures.

and weekend race duty. However, it is not a rod that stands up to the severe punishment of supercharging and nitrous. If you're planning a supercharger or nitrous induction, Manley H-beam rods are mandatory over the stock 5.933-inch rod. The stock rod takes a lot of punishment. However, you're pushing your luck if you use anything less than a heavy-duty forged-steel I-beam or H-beam rod if you plan to push it above 600 hp.

The Coyote is fitted with lightweight hypereutectic pistons with coated skirts for reduced friction and wear. Ford engineers weighed the benefits of forged versus hypereutectic and hypereutectic won for its weight and expansion properties. Forged pistons are noisy when they are cold due to excessive piston to cylinder wall clearances, which generate plenty of complaints with 4.6L and 5.4L engines. Hypereutectic pistons run quieter because you can run tighter tolerances without noise when they are cold. The Coyote piston tolerates the extremes of street and weekend race duty and offers durability. However, if you intend to supercharge or use nitrous you're better off with a forged and coated piston for best results.

Another reason Ford opted for a hypereutectic piston is the oil cooling jets that keep the pistons cooler, which improves piston life. This approach also allows for faster warm up because oil is in direct contact with one of the hottest parts of the engine right from the start. Ford engineers proved that the crankshaft runs roughly 25 degrees F cooler with the oil jets, which enables this engine to operate on 87-octane fuel and survive (although 91-octane is optimum).

Most important to remember is clearance issues. Heavy-duty I-beam and H-beam connecting rods don't always clear the tight confines of the Coyote block. You must first do a mock-up and make sure everything clears by at least .060 to .100 inch throughout 360 degrees of crank rotation with all rods and pistons (without rings) installed. Pay close attention to piston skirt to crank counterweight clearances, which can become very tight and prohibit the Coyote from accepting any more than a 3.649-inch (92.5-mm) stroke. Another area of consideration should be connecting rod interference issues with the piston cooling jets, which has happened in some builds.

Cylinder Heads

Ford's Ti-VCT Coyote has a new cylinder head design that makes the engine less bulky while providing extraordinary high-RPM breathing. The Ti-VCT's intake ports are free from restrictive tendencies, outflowing even some of the most legendary racing cylinder heads in the industry. Intake flow numbers are in excess of 300 cfm. Because the Coyote's top end was designed more as a package than just individual heads, cams,

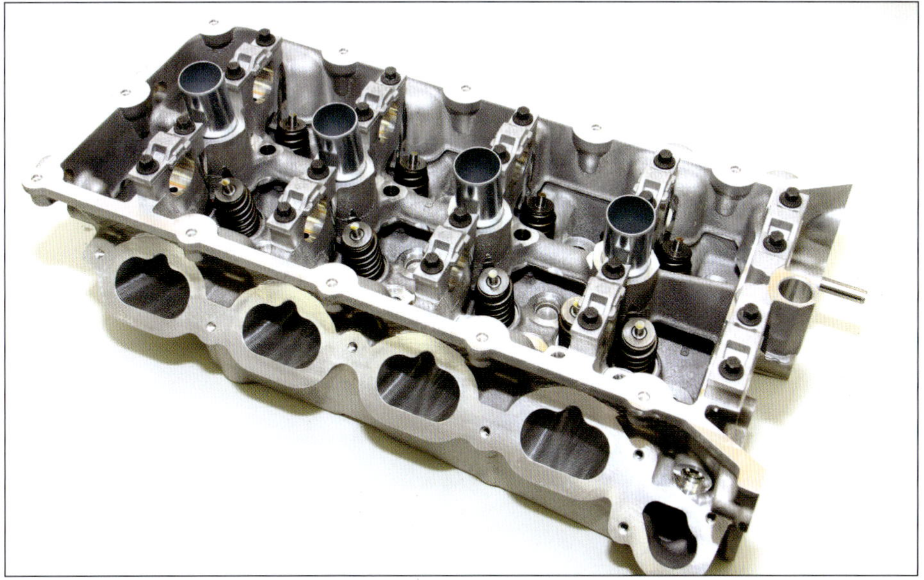

Coyote four-valve cylinder heads are left and right specific as well as being a fresh design from Ford. These DOHC heads are downsized for a more compact Modular design with less restriction and improved flow. Cam journal support is more "Windsor" in nature: void of girdles with the simplicity of standalone cam journals. This is a CNC-ported 2011–2014 cylinder head. The stock ports are roughcast.

The Coyote head is clearly different from the 4.6L/5.4L 4V and is not interchangeable. In front are provisions for the chain tensioner and Ti-VCT feature, which are oil-pressure controlled. As you can see, the cam journals are generously lubricated and the oil galleys are easily accessed. It also has a water jacket freeze plug.

Closer inspection shows the great advances of the Coyote's valvetrain system. The valve angle has been modified for improved flow, and valvesprings and retainers are smaller and lighter. In fact, you may opt for lightweight springs and titanium retainers for even greater freedom. The oil drainback is greatly improved.

With the left-hand cylinder head in place, identified with an "L," it's challenging to see where the head ends and the block begins. The Coyote is a well-thought-out package, where block and head become one. The objective was to come up with a lighter, smaller cylinder head to get unnecessary weight out of the Mustang while conceiving a more swappable engine that can fit more applications. This is how you design and produce a factory high-performance engine.

This is the right-hand (passenger) head, with an "R" (for "right") and the Ford casting number. Ford Motorsports offers a variety of 5.0L and 5.2L Gen II and Gen III castings in its latest catalog.

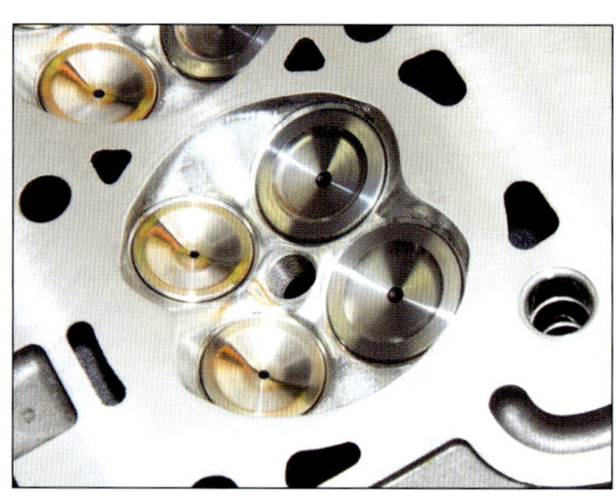

The Coyote's 57-cc four-valve hemispherical chambers demonstrate how different these heads are from previous Modular castings. Four valves per cylinder were surely a given with a performance engine such as this. However, in order to move the intake ports away from the crankshaft centerline and decrease cylinder head width, the valve angle and distance between valves were revised significantly. This revised geometry allows for more valve lift without the risk of valve to piston contact. The intake valves are 1.460 inches in size; exhaust valves are 1.220 inches. The spark plug firing tip is in the middle of the chamber.

and induction, it produces numbers never seen before in a factory Mustang engine. These heads flow very well without specialized port work, which leaves the door wide open for even more power if you decide to do port work.

Ford's Ti-VCT design team, specifically Todd Brewer and John Reigger, understood it would have to spend a lot of time to come up with a cylinder head that could do everything. First, they had to perform basic hotrodding tricks to achieve greater flow; then, these seasoned engineers had to jump into areas that they had never ventured into before. Although the Coyote cylinder head appears to be a derivative of the GT500 head, it isn't. A lot was learned from the GT500 head, yet none of it was carried over.

Engineers had to focus on aspects of port design that had never been considered, such as the distance between the four valves, valve angle, valveseat revisions, and more. Valve angle had to change to improve valve to piston clearances and air flow. Thanks to advanced computer technology, engineers were able to come up with a new cylinder head quickly. It took extensive development work for six months at seven days a week to create a new, more innovative head.

Cams and Valvetrain

When Team Coyote was finished with basic cylinder head casting development, it had to go back and look at cam profile along with valvetrain size and weight. Think of high-revving motorcycle engines; this is what Ford was faced with in developing the Coyote. Rocker arms and valvesprings had to be much smaller to improve both efficiency and performance. There had to be less reciprocating weight to enable these high revs. Put the 4.6L/5.4L and 5.0L rocker arms side by side and you see the difference in size. The 5.0L engine does it with less mass and weight. In addition, it enabled Ford to reduce cylinder head size and width, which reduced overall engine width.

The Coyote's valvetrain system is the most complex cam and valvetrain package ever installed in a Mustang, and it is designed to optimize all driving conditions. This task went to Kevin Shinners and Adam Christian, engineers who developed the camshafts and valvetrain. "Ti-VCT" means "Twin Independent Variable Cam Timing," which in turn means that the intake and exhaust cams work independent of each other based on driving demands. Each camshaft is indexed or phased around its centerline by oil pressure. Oil pressure is metered electronically via solenoids and phasers to control cam indexing as required.

Each camshaft reluctor works hand in hand with a cam sensor tied to the PCM (Powertrain Control Module). Pulses from each reluctor tip signal the PCM, which helps calculate engine speed, injector pulse width, spark timing, and more, which makes the Coyote the most precision-controlled Ford engine ever.

Ti-VCT enables the Coyote to deliver an incredibly wide power band across RPM ranges while giving you the bonus of high-end horsepower, which was not previously easy to achieve. What makes the Coyote's Ti-VCT different from the rest of the Ford line is cam torque actuation, which uses valvespring energy to advance and retard timing more quickly depending on engine RPM and driving demands. Instead of a complex electronically controlled shuttle valve and oiling system routing, the Coyote's

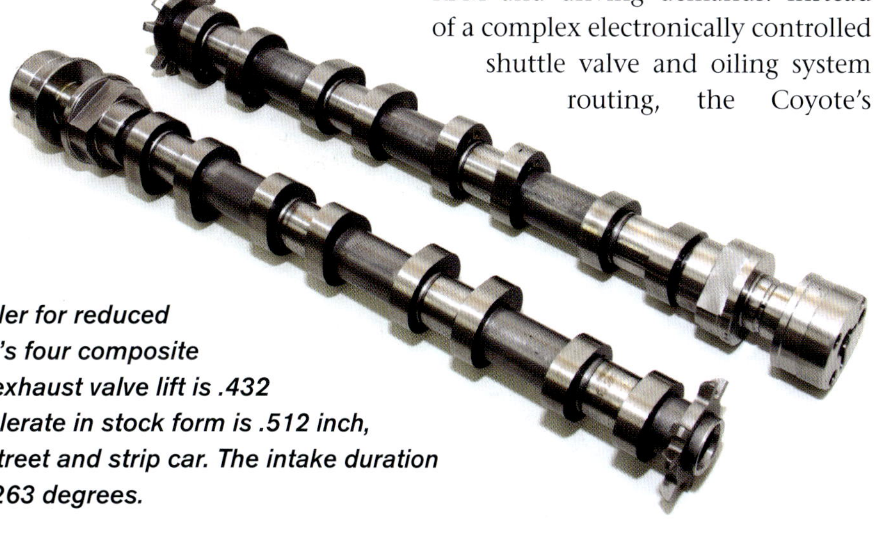

The Coyote's valvetrain has been made smaller for reduced weight and size. These are two of the Coyote's four composite camshafts. The intake valve lift is .472 inch; exhaust valve lift is .432 inch. The greatest lift these cylinder heads tolerate in stock form is .512 inch, which is more than enough for the average street and strip car. The intake duration is 260 degrees, and the exhaust duration is 263 degrees.

Ti-VCT is a simple on/off solenoid; cam torque does the rest.

Ti-VCT can advance/retard valve timing by as much as 50 degrees, and do it in .2 second. This approach offers you modest valve timing on the way to work and more aggressive valve timing when it's time to get the heat on. For the environmentally conscious, the Coyote doesn't need EGR (exhaust gas recirculation) because valve overlap is increased in certain types of driving, especially deceleration, which reduces hydrocarbon emissions.

In order to do the complex work of Ti-VCT and other critical functions, Ford's EEC (Electronic Engine Control) was asked to do more than it ever had in its history. This system is known as "Copperhead." It is a new multi-channel system designed to control every aspect of engine and driveline including Ti-VCT. Instead

Ford's goal was to downsize the Coyote's valvetrain in every respect: smaller valves and springs along with smaller roller rockers and hydraulic followers. The result is a higher-revving engine with less valvetrain weight to sling around.

These are the Ti-VCT adjustable cam sprockets/phasers, which advance valve timing as necessary. Cam momentum and valvespring pressure help these phasers, which in turn enables the cams to return to the normal position when the PCM signal terminates oil pressure.

This is the back side of the cam phasers, which faces the camshafts. This is a great example of engineering because it works very well to enable this engine to do what has never been done before. By controlling valve timing, you can run this engine hard even with 87-octane fuel without concern for detonation (although it is not suggested). These sprockets are cam specific and easy to identify. If it has one sprocket, it is intake; two sprockets is exhaust.

At the front of each cam is this journal, which carries the Ti-VCT articulating cam sprocket, or phaser, which advances valve timing as necessary based on driving conditions and demands. Oil pressure is routed through the number-1 cam journal and each solenoid. Four solenoids are present: one for each camshaft. Each solenoid controls oil flow to each cam timing phaser, which moves each camshaft around its axis.

Here is another look at the Ti-VCT variable cam timing sprockets/phasers. These solenoids activate cam-timing phasers at the end of each camshaft. Valvespring inertia (energy) counters the actuators for snappy valve timing changes. Each cylinder head has a chain tensioner for the dual-cam secondary chain drive.

Cutaways of the Ti-VCT oil-pressure-operated cam actuator sprockets show a pin at the center of each sprocket/actuator, which is operated by the Ti-VCT solenoid (electromagnet) and PCM.

of a simple on/off system of cam modulation, Ti-VCT advances and retards valve timing on each cam. Electronic control monitors and controls oil pressure to the cam phasers.

Ti-VCT isn't something you need to worry about maintaining or tuning. It is a life-of-the-engine system. If the cam phasers fail, all you have to do is remove the cam cover, align the timing marks, and replace the phasers. The Coyote's cam position sensor is located at the opposite end of the cam than on the 3V Modular, and this accounts for the difference in phaser function between the Coyote and 3V Modular.

The 5.0L Ti-VCT induction system is easily the most advanced from Ford to date. Because it is a composite design, it is lightweight and runs cooler than cast aluminum. Moreover, longer 16.5-inch intake runners give the 5.0L Ti-VCT a broader torque curve. And because it runs cooler, it keeps the intake charge cooler, therefore making more power. The good news for those who want more power is that Ford Performance offers a variety of induction packages that kick power up a notch.

Induction

The Coyote's induction system is a composite design, which is mainstream today because it is both lighter and a great heat insulator. It stays cool and keeps the intake charge cooler. It is also easier and cheaper to manufacture.

Induction design and tuning has changed considerably thanks to computer-aided design (CAD) and a lot of engineering time. The Coyote's intake manifold, also known as a plenum, is single plane with long intake runners for a broad torque curve. These are long 16.9-inch (430 mm) runners with gentle turns for improved flow. They are carved deep into the valley to allow for a lower vehicle hoodline. Because Ford has eliminated the coolant tube in the valley, there's more room for induction. The 80-mm throttle body is centered at the front of the engine on top. Another great evolution is a digital mass air sensor for extremes of fine-tuning as you drive.

Here's the Coyote's standard 80-mm throttle body, which is located at the front of this state-of-the-art intake manifold. The throttle body is modulated by a geared motor drive that is controlled by the PCM.

The 5.0L Ti-VCT's induction system for 2015–up also includes Charge Motion Control Valve (CMCV) assemblies. The CMCVs (which are actually flaps on the Coyote) close upon start-up; they give this engine a smoother idle and better low- to mid-range torque. When it's time to get it on, these vacuum-controlled charge motion control flaps move out of the way to improve high-RPM induction flow.

The Coyote continues with traditional port injection because Ford engineers felt it didn't need direct injection at this time. A lot of development work is yet to be done if you're considering direct injection. The Coyote's cylinder head castings have a provision for direct injection. The block is strong enough to support direct injection. Ford just isn't there yet.

In back are these CMCV actuators for 2015–up, one for each cylinder bank. Instead of the charge motion control valves being plates, as they were on the 4.6L engines, they are flaps that change intake air flow to improve idle quality and low- to mid-range torque. When you mash the throttle, they move out of the way to improve high-RPM performance. CMCVs can change intake runner length depending on driver demand.

Exhaust

The Coyote's exhaust system is just as critical to power and efficiency as the rest of the package. Headers might not seem important in the big picture, but they are important and were a great area of focus for Team Coyote. The Coyote has short tri-Y headers that were thought out painstakingly and well executed. Engineering had to fight for them. Bean counters didn't want them because they cost twice as much to produce as cast-iron exhaust manifolds, yet they were crucial to emissions, power, and fuel economy.

Because the Coyote's factory shorty header is extremely unique in its approach, it has enabled the Ti-VCT to produce more than 400 ft-lbs of torque. Try that with your 5.0L pushrod small-block. You can get horsepower all day long. Torque is another story and a huge challenge.

Lubrication

The Ti-VCT Coyote was conceived for high revs, and with that dynamic comes huge oiling system demands. The Coyote must sustain sufficient lubrication to 7,000 rpm and beyond and under extreme driving conditions. Ford opted for an 8-quart oil pan and a suitable windage tray/pan gasket combination. This is all good for keeping oil pressure and volume on target. It also created the huge challenge of oil drainback because oil arrives at moving parts in abundance. Ford solved this problem, and others, with crankcase breathing chimneys. These PCV chimneys improve both drainback and crankcase ventilation.

Cooling System

Close attention was paid to the Coyote's cooling system, which focuses on exhaust valve cooling along with other extremely hot areas of the engine. Ford calls this cross-flow cooling, which is different from the conventional cooling that the 4.6L and 5.4L Modulars employ. Cross-flow cooling routes coolant upward through the block where it enters cylinder heads at the exhaust valves for excellent heat transfer and reduced operating temperatures. Coolant runs through a long manifold cast into the cylinder head at the exhaust valveseats. This keeps detonation issues to a minimum and durability high.

The 5.2L Voodoo

Ford's 5.2L DOHC flat-plane crank V-8 is billed as the highest-revving factory V-8 in American automotive history, with 526 hp and 429 ft-lbs of torque on tap. It spins to 8,250 rpm but shuts off at 8,000 rpm. The sound of the 5.2L Voodoo is clearly different from the sound of the Coyote Ti-VCT V-8 it is spawned from. With flat-plane crank technology the Voodoo makes a snarly, raspy bark from its tailpipes. At high RPM it emits a goose bump–inspiring scream unlike any American V-8. On the surface, the 5.2L Voodoo looks like its smaller sibling, the 5.0L Coyote. Beneath the aesthetics it is a different animal entirely.

The 5.2L Voodoo has been conceived for the Shelby GT350 to make it a breed apart from anything else on the road. Jamal Hameedi, chief engineer at Ford Performance, describes the 5.2L flat-plane V-8 as a product for which every single performance target has been met, including a broad torque curve, crisp throttle response, and no weight increase.

The flat-plane crankshaft approach is nothing new, especially when it comes to exotic high-end European sports cars. However, it is surely a fresh idea for Detroit. When you look at more traditional cross-plane–crank American V-8s with 90-degree reciprocating intervals opposite the counterweights, the flat-plane approach puts pistons and rods exactly 180 degrees opposite the counterweights instead of the traditional 90 degrees. The result is a completely different sound from the traditional V-8 roar that you are used to hearing. The difference in sound comes from exhaust pulses, which happen at different intervals than with a cross-plane–crank V-8. Cylinder

This is the 5.2L Voodoo engine in a 2015 Shelby GT350. Although the 5.2L engine is based on the 5.0L Ti-VCT Coyote, it is not the same engine by any means. Its flat-plane crank design is only the beginning of what makes this engine different from any other American V-8. Traditional V-8s have a cross-plane crank with huge counterweights surrounding rod journals at a 90-degree angle. This makes for smoother operation, but a heavier crankshaft. The 5.2L's flat-plane crank weighs less and gives this engine a snarly buzz at high RPM, like European exotics. This comes from rod journals being 180 degrees opposite of where the crank looks flat, hence the term "flat-plane" crank.

Here's the 5.2L Voodoo head on. Although, at a glance, the Voodoo resembles the Coyote, there are many differences, including a more advanced induction system, GT350-specific cylinder heads, a Voodoo specific block, and more. (Photo Courtesy Ford Performance Parts)

banks fire alternately creating a buzzy exhaust harmony on a par with European exotics. At wide-open throttle at high RPM, it sounds like a Ferrari.

What flat-plane technology means for you at your backside is better exhaust scavenging and a notable increase in power. Even more, it enables Ford to produce a lighter crankshaft with a crisp, snappy throttle response that allows a 7,500-rpm top out, with peak torque coming in at 4,750 rpm. Redline (fuel shutoff) comes at 8,000 rpm.

The flat-plane 5.2L engine really is a racing mill that you can enjoy on the street because it delivers excellent fuel economy on the open road with a 3,000-rpm torque curve. Yet it makes 526 hp at wide-open throttle. What this means for you on the track is brute torque coming out of turns with an incredible blast of power coming down the straights. This is an engine that loves to rev.

Ford says torque begins to come on strong at 3,750 rpm with peak at 4,750. To achieve 5.2L, Ford infused a slightly oversquare bore and stroke ratio at 94.0 x 92.7 mm. This author wound up behind one of the 5.2L Voodoo Mustang engineering prototypes at a traffic light in suburban Phoenix, Arizona, for an intimate experience with the 5.2L Voodoo's exhaust tips.

The Voodoo is clearly a different experience because it is buzzy like a European exotic at high RPM. However, through the revs it resembles an American V-8. It is very Jekyll and Hyde as it makes its way to 8,000 rpm. At peak horsepower, it makes a European V-6/V-12 buzz like you've never heard in a Mustang. Compression ratio is an astonishing 12.0:1.

Even though there are positives to flat-plane technology, there are also negatives. If you're married to the traditional sound of a cross-plane–crank V-8 engine, the flat-plane–crank pulse will seem foreign to you. Harmonics issues also exist to some degree with flat-plane–crank engines when displacement rises above 4.5L. Low-end torque also suffers with flat-plane–crank engines. The 5.2L Voodoo isn't big on low-end torque. However, this isn't an engine designed or engineered for low-end torque. It is a race-bred high-end street/track engine that does its best work at mid- to high RPM.

The 5.2L "flat-plane" V-8's induction system is completely different from its 5.0L sibling's. This is an engine designed for high-RPM operation, which makes low- to mid-range torque rather lackluster. But who cares? This is an ultra-high-performance V-8 developed for the racetrack and canyon cutting, not grocery getting. However, if your plan is to buy groceries, this guy does it quickly.

Gen III Coyote: 2018–2023

Ford's Coyote message has always been improvement coupled with answering the call for increased performance and efficiency. The Gen III is easily the most improved Coyote to date, beginning with a dual-injection system consisting of high-pressure direct injection and low-pressure port "shower" injection. What that has meant for enthusiasts is a whopping 460 hp and 420 ft-lbs of torque along with improved durability. It is an engine that you can punish without fear of a catastrophic failure. The Gen III Coyote easily surpasses these factory numbers without breaking a sweat. The Gen III Coyote is good to 7,500 rpm. It loves to rev.

The Gen III doesn't call for high-octane fuel. Although, it's a good idea to run the Gen III on 91- to 93-octane fuel, budget permitting. However, you can get away with 87 octane because electronic engine control allows for it in terms of ignition timing and fuel curve. The Gen III sports an eye-opening 12.0:1 compression ratio, which is stunning, considering the more conservative compression ratios in modern times.

The Gen III block is similar to the Gen I and Gen II, but the Gen III block is clearly a different and much stronger block. The water jackets are different, and the bore size increased to 3.660 inches (93 mm), which is up from 92.3 mm, to accommodate larger valves. On top is a revised valvetrain geometry with a more aggressive rocker-arm ratio (more valve lift). The cam profile is more aggressive with greater lift. Stiffer valve springs allow the 7,500-rpm rev limit that was previously mentioned. Ford returned to the Coyote's original 12-mm head bolt size, which seemed to work best despite changes that came in 2012.

In back, the 5.2L Voodoo has a dual-mass flywheel, charge motion actuators, and a more advanced induction system. This is easily the most advanced intake manifold in Ford history, with the focus being high-RPM operation. Low-end torque isn't what this engine is about. It is race bred and born for Mustang. (Photo Courtesy Ford Performance Parts)

The Voodoo's side profile reveals a block that's a cut above the Coyote. This is the block you want if your goal is increased displacement and strength. Its cylinder heads are also more advanced than the Coyote's; they simply flow better. Note the high-capacity oil pan designed specifically for racing. (Photo Courtesy Ford Performance Parts)

Down below, the Sinter Forged connecting rods are borrowed from the 2012–2013 Boss 302 parts shelf for incredible strength. The Coyote's forged steel crank gets a more finite balancing process to rid the Gen III of destructive vibration, which has long been a Modular/Coyote dynamic. A viscous harmonic damper assists vibration tuning, which enables the Gen III to spin to 7,500 rpm. The Gen III employs a plastic 10-quart oil pan with improved windage and an integral pickup for a new high-capacity Gen II Voodoo oil pump.

What makes the Gen III block even more unique is "plasma transfer wire arc" cylinder walls like the 5.2L Voodoo block with 93-mm cylinder bores to accommodate larger intake and exhaust valves. This is a vastly improved block for your Coyote project. It employs improved strength over previous versions of the Coyote block.

The Gen III Coyote engine appears much the same as the Gen II on the surface. However, it is an improved block with better cooling, stronger rods, hypereutectic pistons, vastly different and improved cylinder heads, and dual fuel injection.

The Gen III block is the best the Coyote has ever been with GT350-style plasma transfer wire arc cylinder walls (instead of sleeved) with larger 93-mm bores to make way for larger valves, beefier webbing, and improved cooling.

Gen III Cylinder Heads and Valvetrain

The Gen III Coyote cylinder head casting is much stronger than its predecessors to accommodate high-pressure direct fuel injection and greater compression. High-silicon cast pistons (hypereutectic) with 8.411-cc domes have deeper valve reliefs to clear larger valves (37.7 mm intake and 32 mm exhaust). Induction is refined for improved flow along with Charge Motion (CMCV), which was introduced on Gen II Coyotes in 2015. Charge Motion varies induction dynamics depending upon RPM and load. Short runners are for high-RPM operation. Long runners are for good low-end torque.

On the intake side, variable valve timing with mid-lock phasers is carried over from the Gen II Coyote

Immediately apparent when the intake manifold is removed is the hidden high-pressure direct-injection manifold and injectors. This is the Gen III's most remarkable change.

The right-hand cam cover sports the direct-injection pump, which is positioned amid the cover. Beneath this pump is a cam lobe that works the pump along with an electronic trigger connector signaled by the PCM, which is working both port and direct injection.

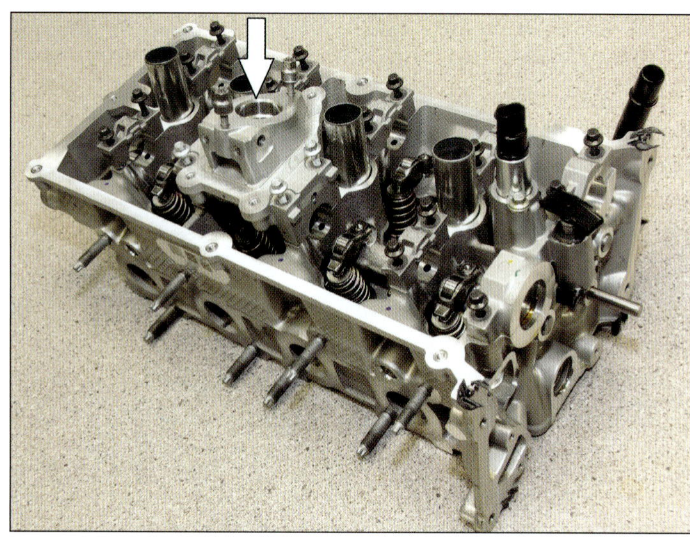

The right-hand cylinder head uncovered shows the direct-injection pump pedestal, which sits atop a single cam lobe that works the pump in time with the exhaust cam.

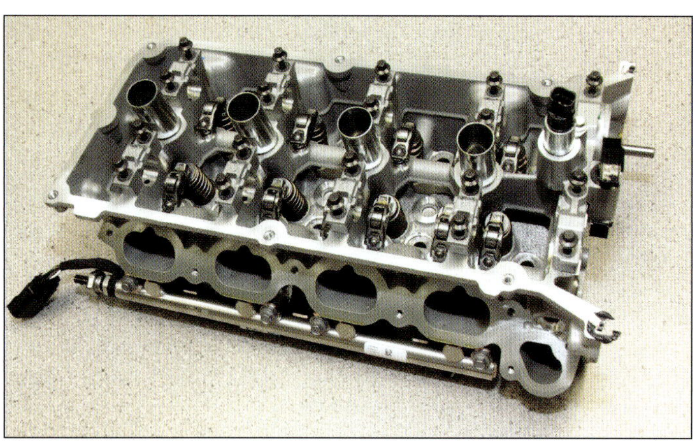

The left-hand Gen III cylinder head is Gen III specific due to direct injection, yet it is remarkably similar to the Gen II head. Both Gen III heads are designed specifically for direct injection.

engines. Exhaust cam phasers are oil-pressure controlled via an in-head oil-control valve for improved control at all speeds yet modulated by a watch-spring-style return spring like Ford used in the three-valve 4.6L and 5.4L Modular engines. Valve lift is increased to 14 mm for intake and exhaust. Compression is a whopping 12.0:1, which is the quickest path to power. Gen I and Gen II are 11.0:1.

The Gen III Coyote heads are vastly different than Gen I and Gen II. Gen III ports have better flow numbers that are more in line with Gen II 5.2L Voodoo heads. Gen III camshafts must be used with Gen III timing components and phasers. Exhaust cam journals are larger to accommodate oil seals, which prevent leakage from the exhaust phasers.

It gets a little confusing with timing components. Gen III engines use Gen II intake phasers and primary timing chains. Exhaust phasers are Gen III only and are attached with a single bolt. The Gen III timing system is Ford part number M-6004-A501B.

These heads have many other differences in alloys that are covered in Chapter 5.

Dual Fuel Technology

What makes the Gen III Coyote different is "dual fuel" technology—with both port injection and high-pressure direct injection straight into the cylinders like a diesel engine. You get high-pressure direct injection along with low-pressure port injection, which is known as port fuel and direct injection (PFDI). It is true that direct injection and port injection each have advantages and disadvantages. Port injection costs less to develop and refine. Port injection also keeps valve faces clean from crankcase fumes, which causes the valve faces to coke up. With tougher emissions standards, port injection loses the battle with direct injection. Ford admitted that fuel economy and emissions suffer with port injection versus the direct-injection counterpart.

The beauty of direct injection is that it allows fuel to be injected into

As you may expect, the Gen III's domed pistons are designed for direct injection and 12.0:1 compression. Sintered metal rods are also stronger than their Gen I and Gen II predecessors.

A closer look at the cam phasers shows the oil-pressure-modulated intake phaser and the oil pressure and spring modulated exhaust phaser.

The Gen III's cam timing system is different than the Gen I and Gen II due to valve timing considerations. Intake cams are oil pressure are modulated both ways. Exhaust cams are modulated by oil pressure yet returned to center via the watch spring, as was done on the 3V Modular engines with variable cam timing.

Charge Motion induction first used on the Gen II Coyote continues on the Gen III.

the combustion chamber (like a diesel) under very high pressure. This approach allows more precise control of the air/fuel volume and timing. It also helps to combine the air-fuel mixture in the combustion chamber instead of the intake port.

Direct injection is not without its issues. It costs more to engineer and produce, which calls for more expensive parts, such as high-pressure direct injectors and a high-pressure fuel pump, which is actuated by the camshaft and controlled by a solenoid/valve combination. It is

The Gen III Coyote from Ford Performance is shipped to your door in a protective crate ready for action. Make sure you add the appropriate synthetic engine oil before firing.

remarkable how quiet Ford managed to engineer direct injection.

Ford elected to combine these systems to achieve the best of both worlds: a dual-fuel system with both port and direct injection. The flexibility of this system allows both systems to function in unison. What's more is that the two systems blend on demand as you drive for reduced emissions, better fuel economy, and greater sums of power at the same time.

Ford 2011–Present Coyote Evolution at a Glance			
	Gen I 5.0L Coyote (2011–2014)	Gen II 5.0L Coyote (2015–2017)	Gen III 5.0L Coyote (2018-Present)
Fuel Injection	Port fuel injection	Port fuel injection	Direct/port injection
Bore Diameter	92.2 mm	92.2 mm	93.0 mm (larger to accommodate larger valves)
Stroke	92.7 mm	92.7 mm	92.7 mm
Firing Order	1-5-4-8-6-3-7-2	1-5-4-8-6-3-7-2	1-5-4-8-6-3-7-2
Compression	11.0:1	11.0:1	12.0:1
Peak Torque	390 ft-lbs at 4,250 rpm	400 ft-lbs at 4,250 rpm	420 ft-lbs at 4,250 rpm
Peak Power	420 hp at 6,500 rpm	435 hp at 6,500 rpm	460 hp at 7,500 rpm
Maximum RPM	7,000	7,000	7,500
Engine Weight	431	431	425
Crankshaft	Forged cross-plane	Forged cross-plane	Forged cross-plane
Pistons	Hypereutectic (cast)	Hypereutectic (cast)	Hypereutectic (cast)
Piston Dome (cc volume)	3,472 cc	4,451 cc (Deeper valve reliefs)	8,411 cc (Raised dome)
Connecting Rod Weight	582 g	618 g	618 g
Connecting Rod Length	150.7 mm	150.7 mm	150.7 mm
Cylinder Heads	AL319	AL319	AS7GU
Valve Material	Hollow chrome (sodium filled)	Hollow chrome (sodium filled)	Hollow chrome (sodium filled)
Valve Diameter	Intake: 37.0 mm, Exhaust: 31.0 mm	Intake: 37.3 mm, Exhaust 31.8 mm	Intake: 37.7 mm, Exhaust: 32.0 mm
Valve Lift	Intake: 12.0 mm, Exhaust: 12.0 mm	Intake: 13.0 mm, Exhaust: 13.0 mm	Intake: 14.0 mm, Exhaust: 14.0 mm
Valve Spring Load (closed/ open N)	265/650	300/760	293/813
Variable Cam Timing Phaser	N/A	Mid-lock intake	Mid-lock intake via oil control/ actuated exhaust
Intake Manifold Type	Non-Charge Motion	Charge Motion	Charge Motion
Throttle Body Diameter (mm)	80	80	80
Oil Pan Type	Steel 8-quart with filter	Steel 8-quart with filter	Composite 10-quart with filter

Cylinder Block

The 5.0L Ti-VCT Coyote block is a durable machined casting right out of the box. It can easily withstand outrageous amounts of power courting the 600- to 800-hp mark. The 5.0L Ti-VCT block shares the same bore spacing (3.937 inches or 100 mm), deck height (8.937 inches), bellhousing bolt pattern, and external dimensions as the 4.6L SOHC and DOHC engines. Bore size was increased to 3.629 inches (92.2 mm) along with an increased stroke of 3.649 inches (92.8 mm), which was still a "square" engine design with identical bore and stroke. Where the Ti-VCT 5.0L block differs is in an entirely new design with heavier webbing and other internal improvements intended to support greater power output from modest displacement.

When the Coyote was introduced for 2011, Ford said, "This aluminum block was developed for optimized windage and oil drainback under lateral conditions and high-RPM use, such as a track-day outing," meaning this was an engine designed specifically for performance. Ford added, "Increased main bearing bulkhead widths and nodular iron cross-bolted main bearing caps with upsized bolts were also employed to accommodate the significant performance increase."

The Ti-VCT engine employs a rugged aluminum block with paper-thin iron cylinder liners. Because the Coyote's iron cylinder liners are quite thin, this block must be sleeved with thicker cylinder liners for all-out racing in the 800- to 1,500-hp range. Modular Motorsports, as one example, offers racers the Pro Mod Coyote block with extra-thick ductile iron cylinder liners that stay put, ensuring block integrity. You can build one of these thick-cylinder bore blocks for the street if you're an avid weekend racer. Thick cylinder liners are a good life insurance policy for a block already able to take extreme punishment. Cylinders can be bored as high as 3.700 inches to achieve 5.2L.

Holbrook Racing Engines offers its own thick-cylinder-liner Coyote block as well. Holbrook can take your block or an existing block from stock and set you up with an improved thick cylinder block, which can also be bored to 3.700 inches.

Rugged block architecture is what holds this engine together. Main bearing webs are thicker and heavier,

The basic 5.0L Ti-VCT block is the most rugged Modular-based casting to date, but it has nothing in common with the 4.6L Modular except bore spacing and deck height. This block can withstand 800 to 1,000 hp, although it is suggested that you opt for the Pro Mod or Holbrook block with thicker cylinder liners if you plan on pushing power beyond 800 hp.

Performance enthusiasts like the Coyote block with its extensive network of ribs and beefcake support, which means strength and durability. These left-side (driver) block casting ribs and gussets provide unprecedented strength across block decks and pan rails. Cross-bolted main caps with interference fit provide the security of Fort Knox. One weakness has been among 4- and 8-cylinder bores, which have experienced cooling problems and blown cylinder walls. Improved coolant flow at the back of the block and heads can solve this problem.

Skirted blocks, an old-school design approach that went away with the 90-degree Fairlane V-8 (221/260/289/302/351W) and 385-series big-blocks (429/460) designed in the 1960s, is back because it provides the greatest strength around a high-revving bottom end. The 5.0L Ti-VCT is a "square" engine (identical bore and stroke) that likes to rev. This engine makes its greatest power at high RPM. The downside to this design is limited potential for growth. You can't make this engine any larger than 5.0L unless you go with thicker cylinder liners. And with that, the most you can go is 5.2L.

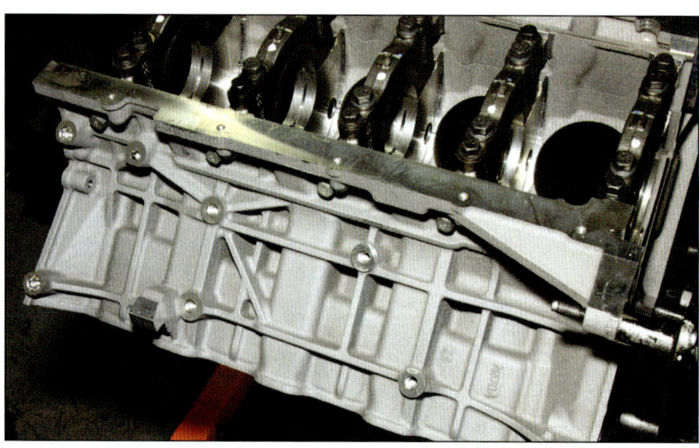

The right side (passenger) yields the same story of crossed, vertical, and horizontal ribs providing extraordinary strength. What this means for you is a bulletproof block for street and weekend strip activity.

It used to be that rear main seals were integral with the five-main-bearing cap; not anymore. The rear main seal is fitted into a bolt-on cast-aluminum aft block cover, which is separate from the five-main-bearing cap, which makes rear main seal replacement easier and ensures a more leak-proof seal.

allowing for performance extremes from enthusiasts and Ford product planners. This means the basic Coyote block can stand up to naturally aspirated performance demands, supercharging, nitrous, direct injection, and more. It can be said with confidence that this block will withstand more than 1,500 hp when sleeved with the thicker ductile iron cylinder liners mentioned earlier.

With this new block come advances in crankcase ventilation known as "bay-to-bay" breathing. Ford engineers located venting in the main webs designed to allow the freedom of air scavenging without robbing power. The result is a more positive ring seal, which helps efficiency and power. Gone is the Modular's coolant tube down the middle of the valley. Instead, coolant is routed through the front of the block, leaving plenty of room for exotic induction systems and superchargers.

In the spirit of classic Ford 406 and 427 FE-Series big-blocks, the Coyote has cross-bolted main caps. The Modular 4.6L/5.4L engines had jackscrews (Romeo) or dowel pins (Windsor) to shim up main caps. The Ti-VCT Coyote does the Modular engine one better with perfect-fit main caps machined exactly to the proper size so that jackscrews and dowels are unnecessary.

The Coyote's bottom end from another angle demonstrates how rugged this engine is. Whether you are towing, hauling, or racing, the Coyote is up to the task. Properly torqued to Ford's critical specifications, this is a virtually bulletproof bottom end that can take anywhere from 600 to 1,000 hp. With thick-wall cylinder liners and a studded ARP fastener bottom end, your Coyote will stay together beyond 1,000 hp.

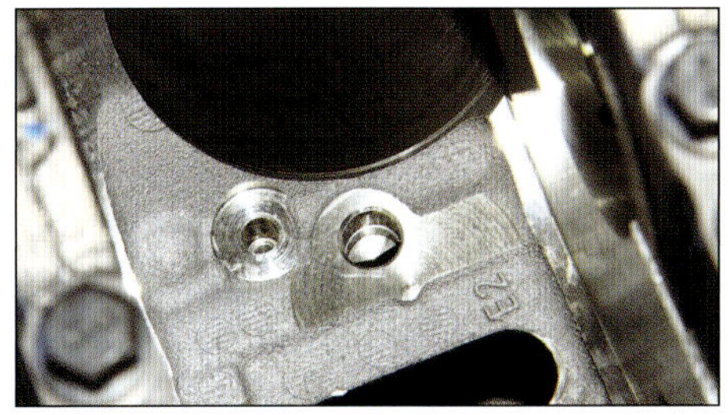

These piston-cooling oil jets provide good heat transfer to the oil, which carries excessive heat away, especially in boosted applications. Some confusion surrounds them because the 2011–2013 Coyote blocks had them and then Ford dropped them. In the course of 2015–2016 production, piston-cooling jets returned. Expect to see some blocks with this provision and some without.

A close-up look illustrates the Coyote's paper-thin iron cylinder walls. Believe it or not, these cylinder sleeves can withstand 600 to 800 hp. Although some have gone to 1,000 hp without consequence, it is strongly suggested that you opt for thicker cylinder sleeves if you're going beyond 800 hp. Note the abundance of cooling passages between block and heads. In addition, 11-mm head bolts reach deep into the bottom of this block, which prevents deck distortion. Some engine builders have concluded that you don't need torque plates for honing with this block. It is still suggested, however, that you use a torque plate for cylinder honing.

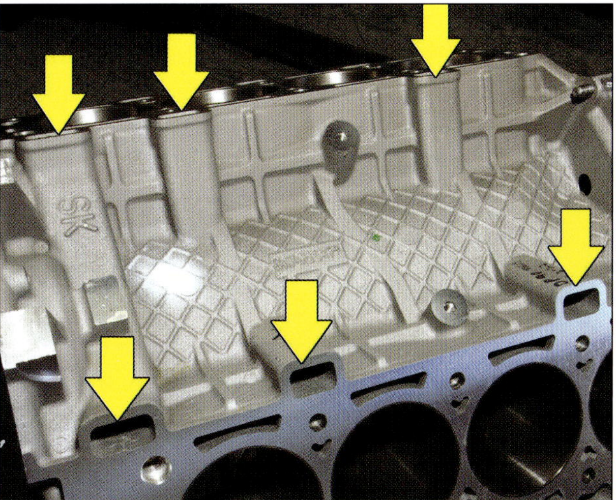

The Coyote block is easily identified by its deeply webbed valley, which is designed to clear almost any induction system. It has two knock sensor bungs, one for each bank. Also note the crankcase ventilation "chimneys" (arrows) known as "bay-to-bay" breathing. These chimneys also provide excellent oil scavenging.

Here's a Coyote block without the piston-cooling jet provision. Unless you're opting for supercharging, turbocharging, or nitrous, you probably don't need them. Forged and coated pistons probably don't need them either. The logic is better to have and not need them than need them and not have them.

Here's another look at the "bay-to-bay" ventilation chimneys, which improve crankcase breathing and oil drainback at high RPM. This ensures oil reaches all the right places at high RPM, when an engine is most vulnerable.

Here's a closer look at the Holbrook thick-sleeve Coyote block. In the background is a stock bored block. Closer is the Holbrook sleeved block. Because Chris Holbrook is himself a long-time avid drag racer, he understands what works with the Coyote and what doesn't. The Holbrook block isn't purchased from a supplier. It is bored, sleeved and finish-honed in the Holbrook shop where everything is closely monitored and inspected.

Block Modifications and Improvements

Although Ford has come up with a virtually bulletproof engine block capable of withstanding outrageous amounts of power, it does have its weak spots. Coyote blocks suffer from cylinder wall failures due to excessive heat issues, primarily in high-boost situations. Modular Motorsports offers a Head Cooling Mod Kit (455478), an easy bolt-on that improves coolant flow where it is needed most at the back of the engine.

If you're planning more than 800 hp you should opt for a sleeved block from Modular Motorsports or Holbrook Racing, which are purpose-built blocks for racers. These blocks are machined for the thicker cylinder liners, and they can be bored to a displacement as high as 5.2L. Thanks to the way these sleeves are configured in the block, they're virtually indestructible, which means they can withstand 1,000 to 2,000 hp. This is a remarkable statement for a lightweight aluminum block. Ford has never produced a stronger block; you can build your Coyote with confidence knowing it will stay together.

Traditional engine building technique applies to the Coyote block. As with any other production casting, you can expect to find flaws that can lead to engine failure. Deburr the block and remove any casting flash in your block preparation. Remove stress risers than can lead to cracking

Holbrook Racing Engines re-sleeves Coyote blocks with thicker cylinder liners for those of you seeking in excess of 800 to 1,000 hp. Holbrook can take your stock Coyote block and re-sleeve or can take a block from its inventory.

This close-up of the Holbrook block demonstrates what you're getting for your money. Cylinder bores are bored and step cut to the point at which there's no chance of cylinder movement. Cylinder bores in the Holbrook block are siamesed for security.

and failure. Thoroughly examine oil and cooling passages and chase them to remove debris that can do engine damage. Oil galley passages should be massaged to eliminate turbulence. All bolt holes should be chased for more accurate torque readings during assembly.

The Ford Performance M-6010-M50R Coyote race block enables you to take peak horsepower well into four-digit territory for just under $3,000. What makes this block stronger isn't so much the bottom end, which is the same as the stock block, according to Jesse Kershaw, former drag racing parts and competition manager at Ford Performance. It is the block deck and thicker material around the thin-wall cylinder liners that give this race block extraordinary strength. Cast-in cylinder supports on the intake side help hold things together. (Photo Courtesy Ford Performance Parts)

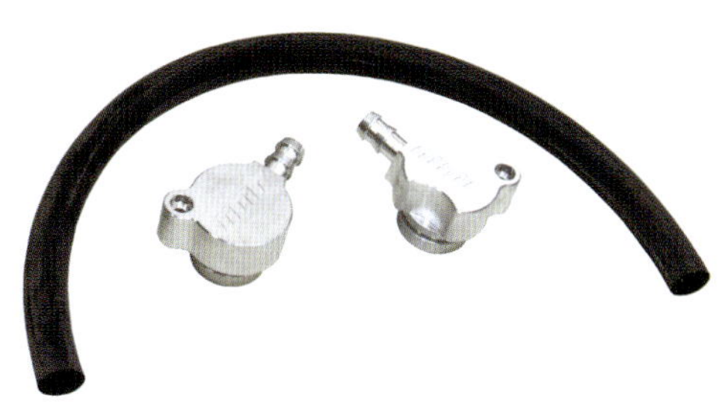

This Modular Motorsports' Head Cooling Mod Kit was developed to solve cooling problems at the rear of Coyote engines. It installs where the rear cylinder head freeze plugs are located, which allows improved coolant flow. The weakness is excessive heat around the number-4 and -8 cylinders, primarily in boosted applications.

This 2011–2014 oil filter mount with filter and dyno cell connections is different from the 2015–2016 version because it does not have the oil drainback provision.

The arrow indicates the additional block oil return passage along with a revised oil filter adaptor (not pictured) for 2015–2016. This change was adopted to improve fuel economy. The block and oil filter adaptor must match.

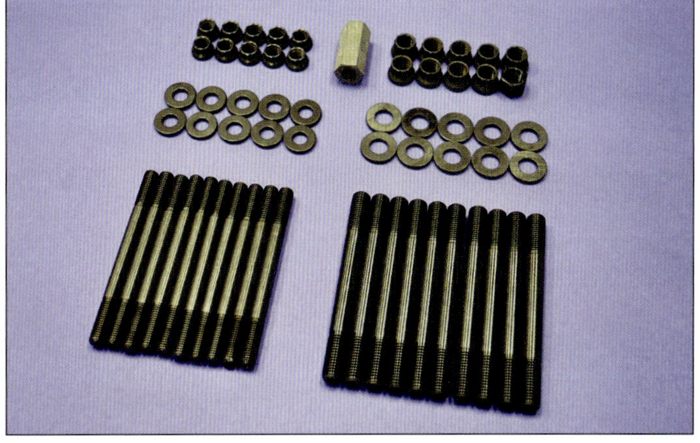

A nice option is to stud your Coyote block's main caps for improved durability. ARP and/or Ford Performance can help with main stud packages engineered to hold things together under extreme conditions. These engines are already rugged and use factory torque-to-yield fasteners. Studding the block makes them virtually indestructible.

5.2L Coyote/Voodoo Block

The 5.2L Voodoo block looks like the Coyote block at first glance. It is, in fact, a different block with larger 3.700-inch (94-mm) sleeveless cylinder bores. When you think of sleeveless cylinders in an aluminum block, it sparks memories of Chevrolet's sleeveless Vega 4-cylinder engine, which suffered from grave durability issues. Such is not the case with Ford's state-of-the-art DOHC V-8. Cylinder walls are finished using the Plasma Transferred Wire Arc (PTWA) coating process developed in a cooperative effort between Ford and Flame-Spray Industries. The result is a super tough, lightweight, low-friction surface also used on the 5.4L DOHC engine in the Shelby GT500. This process sheds 8.5 pounds from the 5.2L Voodoo block.

PTWA is nothing new in the aerospace and heavy-equipment industries. However, it is surely new for Ford Motor Company. PTWA uses compressed air along with high-intensity electricity to create an extremely hot, 35,000-degree F plasma jet that coats the aluminum cylinder wall. This, of course, is an oversimplification of the PTWA process. Suffice it to say, PTWA gets the weight out and durability up by spraying on the sleeve as a coating instead of inserting an iron sleeve. Where this process gets challenging for Ford is the amount of time spent per cylinder. PTWA is a very time-consuming process and is therefore costly. The PTWA process takes more time than just inserting an iron sleeve. This is something Ford and Spray-Flame are working on at press time.

This is the 5.2L Shelby GT350 block during manufacture. What makes the 5.2L block innovative is Ford's patented Plasma Transferred Wire Arc (PTWA) cylinder-liner technology. This process eliminates typical heavy iron cylinder liners with a deposition process. This is the 5.2L block in manufacture prior to the PTWA cylinder-liner process. (Photo Courtesy Ford Performance Parts)

Here's the PTWA cylinder-liner process being applied to the 5.2L block during manufacture. Ford has brought this technology in-house, which reduces production time and expense, to result in a lighter-weight block. (Photo Courtesy Ford Performance Parts)

Ford recommends a 500-mile break-in period with the new 5.2L engine to achieve good ring and bearing seating. Break-in with the PTWA cylinder bores is the same as with traditional ductile iron bores. Periodic hard acceleration in third or fourth gear at speed helps seat the rings. Keep revs conservative (under 6,000 rpm) when you're wearing in the rings. Change the break-in oil at 1,000 to 1,500 miles. Then, opt for a good synthetic 5W50 engine oil. Keep in mind the 5.2L Voodoo engine calls for 5W50. However, the 5.0L Coyote uses 5W20.

If you're impressed with the 5.0L Coyote block, the 5.2L Voodoo block is even more impressive, with thicker main webs within an even stronger casting. Ford Performance Parts will have a 5.2L Coyote block available by the time this book comes off the press, which means the sky is the limit for your S197, S-550, or F-150 engine project. It means greater displacement, thanks to a larger bore size. In fact, the new 5.2L Coyote block from Ford Performance makes it possible to get more displacement from the 5.0L's stroke without the thicker sleeves, which cost, on average, $1,000 if you're doing a 5.0L block. This is a nice alternative to a bored thick-sleeve 5.0L block because you get more displacement without having to sleeve.

This is the 5.2L GT350 block now available from Ford Performance Racing Parts. It is the same production block used in the Shelby GT350 and GT350R. You can get it now for your 5.2L big-bore Coyote build project. (Photo Courtesy Ford Performance Parts)

Gen III (2018–2023) Cylinder Block

The big news for the Gen III block is the use of plasma transfer wire arc cylinder walls instead of sleeved bores. This technology, borrowed from the Shelby GT350's 5.2L Voodoo block, became necessary to accommodate the Gen III engine's larger valves. This weaves high-end technology into the Mustang GT block. Aside from thicker block decks and improved cooling, the block has very little changed from the Gen II.

The Gen III Coyote block has little changed from the Gen II with the exception being improved cooling between the heads and block as well as a revised head gasket. The Gen III uses the same head bolts as the Gen II.

Head on, the Gen III block is virtually unchanged from the Gen II.

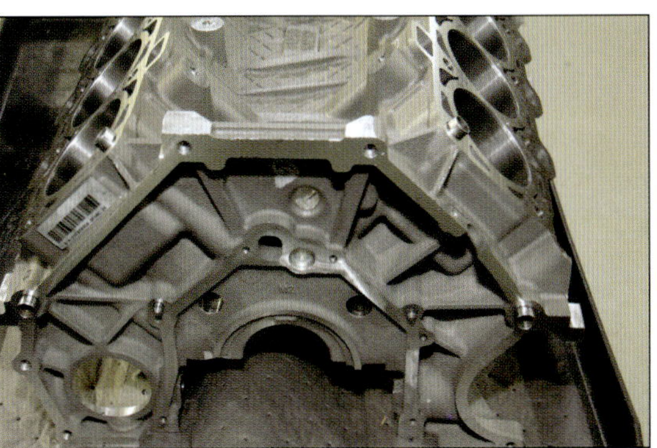

The back of the block is unchanged. Most of what's improved in the Gen III cannot be seen, which translates to greater strength. It is simply a better block.

The Gen III block, like the Gen I and Gen II, possesses thick webbing that provides unequalled strength over and above the earlier Modular engines.

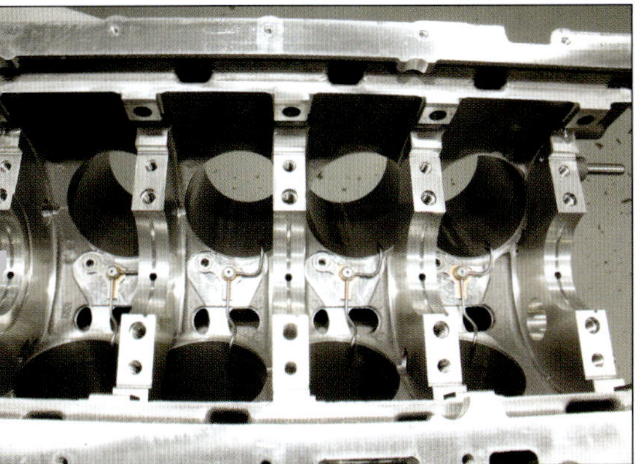

What makes the Coyote bottom end strong is its block skirting, which wraps around the rotating assembly. The Gen III is virtually unchanged from Gen I and Gen II.

The oil filter adaptor hole pattern is the same as Gen II with the drain hole.

The Gen III has a thicker block deck to handle increased cylinder pressures.

CHAPTER 3

ROTATING ASSEMBLY

The Coyote is fitted with an induction-hardened, fully counterweighted, forged-steel crankshaft that's virtually indestructible, featuring an eight-hole flange. Team Coyote decided to stay with the 4.6L engine's main and rod journal dimensions because they have been a proven success in nearly two decades of service in every application imaginable. Moreover, aluminum bearings were borrowed directly from the 4.6L engine instead of opting for tri-metal bearings. Aluminum main and rod bearings work just as well as tri-metal bearings and without the excessive cost and weight involved.

The Coyote engine shares the same connecting rod dimensions with the 4.6L engine at 5.933 inches center to center, yet it is not the same rod according to Ford. It is a much stronger rod with 12-point bolt heads. The rod ratio is 1.62:1, allowing for generous dwell time at each end of the bore. The Coyote's cracked rod is a sintered-metal I-beam forging engineered for extreme street and weekend race duty. Although "powdered metal" sounds lackluster compared to the word "forged," it is a high-tech form of alloy metal forging that produces a stronger connecting rod than a traditional forged piece. However, the cracked powdered-metal rod isn't up to the severe hammering of supercharging and nitrous oxide. If your goal is 600 to 1,000 hp, you need to consider a good aftermarket Manley or Oliver rod.

If you're planning a supercharger or nitrous induction, Manley or Eagle H-beams or Oliver I-beams are a must rather than using the stock rod. The stock rod takes a lot of punishment and does it to 7,000 rpm. However, it is pushing your luck to go with anything less than a heavy-duty forged-steel I-beam or H-beam connecting rod if you're going to push it above 600 to 800 hp.

The Coyote is fitted with lightweight hypereutectic pistons with coated skirts for reduced friction and wear. There's also less piston noise on cold start. Ford engineers weighed the benefits of forged versus hypereutectic and hypereutectic won for its weight and expansion properties. Forged pistons are loose and noisy when they are cold, which generated plenty of complaints with 4.6L and 5.4L engines. In fact, 4.6L/5.4L enthusiasts became extremely concerned about cold-piston noise in Modulars

The Coyote's induction-hardened forged steel eight-bolt crankshaft is fully counterweighted and up to the task from 400 to 1,500 hp. It has the same dimensions as the 4.6L with 2.652-inch main journals and 2.086-inch rod journals. Ford stayed with this crank because it is time and race proven. It just doesn't break.

Although a lot of different markings have shown up on Coyote cranks, such as this DW, there appears to be little or no difference in these eight-bolt flange crankshafts. All are eight-bolt flange in forged steel with the same nuances. Even the Boss crank isn't much different from the standard crank. If you're going to thrust horsepower above the 800 mark, consider the Boss crank. Closely inspect any crank and have it tested by a trusted machine shop.

The Coyote's steel crank is a class act with highly polished journals and chamfered oil holes. It is a remarkable piece, considering it is a production part and not a high-end racing part. There's very little you have to do to this crank whether you're building a stocker, weekend racer, or all-out full-time racer. Dimensions must be examined and documented along with a mock-up before the final build. Dynamic balancing is a must.

All Coyote cranks have this eight-hole flange, which is on a par with the 4.6L truck crank. This crank can withstand 400 to 1,500 hp. Some racers have pushed it close to 2,000 hp without failure.

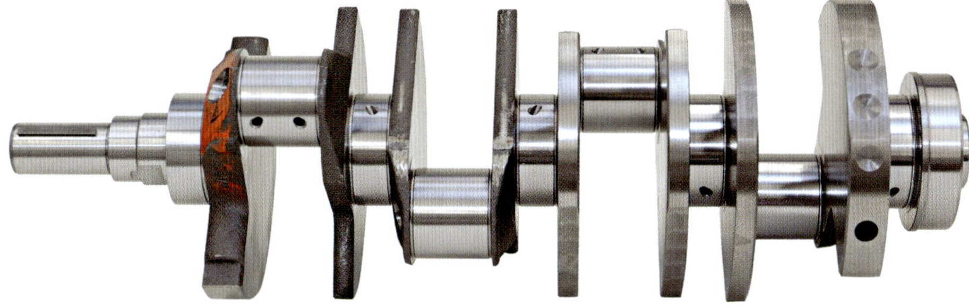

Here's the M-6303-M50B 2012–2013 Boss 302 crankshaft. This is a Boss 302–specific forged steel crankshaft, which is a cut above the Coyote's steel crank. What makes this racing specific is race-ready machining and balancing with chamfered oil holes and polished journals.

This is the high-compression 11.0:1 flattop hypereutectic piston for naturally aspirated Coyotes. With this much compression, you are limited in terms of boost and nitrous. You want to be careful about how much boost and nitrous you apply to prevent engine damage.

This is a stock 5.0L Coyote short-block with hypereutectic 11.0:1 pistons and powdered-metal rods. It is remarkable how well this engine endures in stock form under extreme abuse in the 400- to 600-hp range.

even though it really is nothing to worry about.

"Hypereutectic" piston is just a fancy name for "high-silicon-cast" piston. It takes more abuse than a cast piston and doesn't have the drawbacks and weight penalty of a forged piston. Hypereutectic pistons run quieter because you can run tighter tolerances without consequence. They tolerate the extremes of street and weekend race duty while offering durability. However, if you

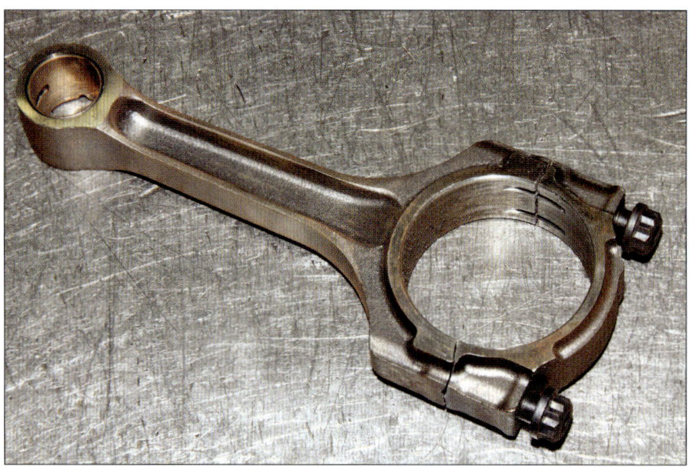

Although the Coyote's sintered-metal stock rod shares the 4.6L's rod dimensions, it is not the same rod and cannot be interchanged. Although enthusiasts are spooked by the "powdered metal" nomenclature, in truth "powdered metal" is a high-tech forging process that's actually stronger than classic I-beam connecting rods used in older pushrod engines.

intend to supercharge or go nitrous, you're better off with a forged and coated piston for best results.

Another reason Ford opted for a hypereutectic piston is oil cooling jets that keep the pistons considerably cooler, which improves piston life. This approach also allows for faster warm up because oil is in direct contact with one of the hottest parts of the engine right from the start. Ford engineers have proved that crankshaft journals run roughly 25 degrees F cooler with the oil jets, which enables this engine to operate on 87 octane fuel and survive (though 91 octane is optimum).

Most important to remember is clearance issues. Heavy-duty I-beam and H-beam connecting rods may or may not clear the tight confines of the Coyote block. You must first do a mock-up and rollover to make sure everything clears by at least .060 to .100 inch throughout 360 degrees of crank rotation with all rods and pistons (but without rings) installed. Pay close attention to piston skirt to crank counterweight clearances, which can get very tight and are the reason the Coyote doesn't accept any more than a 3.649-inch (92.5 mm) stroke.

Room for Improvement?

So what can you do with a Coyote bottom end to make it even more durable than it already is? Ford's factory steel-forged induction-hardened eight-bolt crankshaft is a masterpiece of engineering. It is virtually indestructible and can take upwards of 1,500 to 2,000 hp. All the Coyote crank really needs is dynamic balancing when you fit it with aftermarket connecting rods and forged pistons. Chamfering oil holes at the journals improves lubrication, and micropolishing journals improves oil control, but you don't even need that. Ford produces an outstanding piece right out of the box.

You have the option of going to the Boss 302 crank (M-6303-M50B), rods, and forged pistons (M-6100-M50BR as piston/rod assembly) if you're lacking confidence in the factory steel crank. These items are available off the shelf from Ford Performance Racing Parts. Suffice it to say the Eagle, Manley, or Oliver rod coupled with a Manley, Mahle, or Diamond forged piston will get the job done.

Manley's Platinum Series forged pistons are a good choice thanks to 2618 aluminum alloy, 9310 steel alloy wrist pins, and coated skirts that offer stability and a more user-friendly skirt to cylinder wall relationship. Total Seal piston rings are a Manley exclusive and an industry standard. And when the need warrants, Manley will make you a custom piston. Manley offers at least 16 off-the-shelf pistons in 9.0, 10.0, and 11.0:1 compression ratios. Bore sizes are 3.630, 3.635, 3.640, and 3.700 inches for the 5.933-inch connecting rod and 3.650-inch stroke. Compression height on all is 1.165 inches. Standard and Extreme Duty versions are available.

The most common aftermarket performance connecting rods come from Manley and Eagle Specialties, 5.933 inches center to center. The 4340 steel H-beam rod is available in most kits and the Ford Performance and Roush Aluminator crate engines. These rods are shot-peened, stress relieved, Magnafluxed, heat

Do You Have Oil Cooling Jets?

It gets confusing because Ford eliminated oil cooling jets in production for a short time, and then brought them back into production for 2015–2017. Not all Coyote blocks have the oil cooling jet provision. And if you're going to stuff H-beam rods into your Coyote, keep oil cooling jet clearances in mind. Not all rods and pistons clear. It is unknown why Ford dropped the oil cooling jets in production, aside from perhaps cost. As Ford stepped up the power for 2015, it became apparent that oil cooling jets needed to return, especially with high-boost turbo and supercharged applications.

Reciprocating Mass from Ford Performance		
Part Number	**Nomenclature**	**Details**
M-6303-M50B	Boss 302 crankshaft	Forged steel
M-6100-M50BR	Boss 302 piston/rod	Forged/coated piston, heavy-duty powdered metal cracked rod; no longer available from Ford

Stock hypereutectic pistons and rods can withstand 600 to 700 hp without breaking a sweat. However, if you're going to push it higher, opt for a good set of Manley I- or H-beam race rods and coated forged pistons that can take the heat. Ford Performance forged and coated pistons are engineered for reduced friction, which keeps heat down and power up. This is the reciprocating mass package Ford Performance and Roush Performance put into their Aluminator crate engines.

Manley forged pistons, available from Modular Motorsports, are available in a variety of positive and negative dish configurations to suit your performance agenda. This is a positive dish (domed) Manley piston. If you're going to boost or opt for nitrous, consult with your engine builder to determine the safest compression ratio best for your application. Expect to see 9.0:1, 9.5:1, 10.0:1, 10.5:1, 11.0:1, 11.5:1, and higher if needed. Custom configurations are available that fit your budget.

Here's a closer look at the Ford Performance forged, dished piston for 9.5:1 compression applications. This is what you can expect to see inside the Ford Performance and Roush crate engines for boosted and nitrous applications.

Here are two views of the Manley/Modular Motorsports forged high-compression. These are low-friction pieces; the ring pack contains 1.2-, 1.2-, 3.0-mm rings. Basically, three Manley forged pistons are available for the Coyote in 9.5:1, 10.0:1, and 11.0:1 dishes/compression ratios. You always have the option of ordering a custom piston.

Performance Assembly Solutions (PAS) builds all of the Ford Performance and Roush Performance Aluminator crate engines. This is the forged, low-compression 9.5:1 dished piston, which was what PAS was building in production in mid-August 2015 when this image was taken.

treated, and weight matched to +/–1.5 grams. And finally, they are fitted with 3/8-inch ARP cap screws. They are rated at more than 700 hp with the standard ARP 8740 cap screws and more than 750 hp with ARP 2000 bolts.

The 4340/330M aircraft-grade steel Pro Series I-beam rod from Manley is machined to yield the lightest-weight rod possible from the forging. When machining is complete, Manley shot-peens these guys, Magnafluxes them, and fits them with 7/16-inch ARP 2000 cap screws. This process makes these rods good to more than 900 hp for road racing and more than 1,200 hp for drag racing.

Oliver Racing Products has two 5.933-inch rods for the Coyote, the Standard Light and the Ultra Light. The Standard Light connecting rod is a heavy-duty rod designed for weekday driving and weekend racing. The Oliver Ultra Light is an extreme high-performance connecting rod for high RPM use in the 8,500-rpm range. This is the rod you go racing with. It is lighter and stronger than the Standard Light.

Aftermarket Connecting Rods

Manufacturer	Part Number	Nomenclature	Details
Eagle	16420	H-beam	5.933 inches
Manley	14042-8	H-beam rod	ARP 8740
Manley	14042R-8	H-beam rod	ARP 2000
Manley	14318-8	Pro Series I-beam lightweight	5.933 inches with 22-mm pin
Manley	14518-8	Pro Series I-beam standard weight	5.933 inches with 22-mm pin heavier beam
Manley	15318-8	Pro Series I-beam 300M alloy	5.933 inches with 22-mm pn
Oliver Racing Parts	F5933MDUL8	Ultra Light I-beam	5.933 inches
Oliver Racing Parts	F5933MDLT8	Standard Light I-beam	5.933 inches
Scat Enterprises	2-46L-5933	H-beam	5.933 inches ARP-8740
Scat Enterprises	2-46L-5933A	H-beam	ARP-2000

Coated Manley/Modular Motorsports pistons can withstand the extremes of heat and pressure. These colorful red coatings protect the piston from the extreme temperatures associated with boost and nitrous.

The Coyote's bottom end can withstand 600 to 700 hp safely with the stock powdered-metal connecting rods, which have the same 5.933-inch center-to-center dimensions as the 4.6L SOHC/DOHC engines. However, these engines do not share the same stock rod. These Manley H-beam forgings go 800 to more than 1,500 hp and 8,000 to 9,000 rpm. The beauty of the Coyote is how much abuse this engine can take with stock rods. When you add Manley forged slugs and rods, the sky is the limit.

This is the double-rung Coyote balancer, which is standard original equipment on these engines. All have the double rung dampener.

The aftermarket offers a variety of harmonic dampeners for the Coyote engine. This is the ATI Super Damper for Coyote applications. The Super Damper is engineered to dampen crank twist and it exceeds SFI 18.1 specifications. Although the stock Coyote harmonic dampener does an excellent job, it is suggested you opt for an SFI-rated dampener if you're going to push power above 800 hp. This particular Super Damper is for a supercharged application at Holbrook Racing Engines.

This is the Ford Performance Racing Parts M-6375-M50 164-tooth lightweight billet steel flywheel with 0.0-ounce balance for 2011–present 5.0L Mustangs. It meets SFI 1.1 safety standards. If you're going racing, this is what you want for your Coyote project for safety and durability.

Here's the Coyote's cast-aluminum rear main seal cover, which makes rear main seal replacement easier than ever. It is suggested you use Permatex's The Right Stuff in an extremely thin film around the perimeter during installation. Use a generous amount of engine assembly lube or SAE 30–weight engine oil around the inside lip. The inside lip is pointed toward the crankshaft, never away.

This is the crankshaft reluctor wheel, which is installed between the flywheel/flexplate and crankshaft. The shutter wheel for the pick-up sensor for the PCM is positioned at the back of the engine block. Both are accessible with the transmission removed.

Make Mine a Flat-Plane

It's hard to find anyone in the performance industry who isn't talking about the 5.2L flat-plane crank Voodoo Coyote cousin in the Shelby GT350. The Voodoo is a rapid departure from the conventional V-8 mindset thanks to its flat-plane crank where rod journals are spaced 180 degrees apart instead of the more routine 90 degrees. The flat-plane crank is what gives the 5.2L engine a more buzzy European sound.

The downside to a flat-plane crank is the absence of the counterweight balancing that you see with a 90-degree cross-plane crankshaft; this creates potential vibration issues not seen with a 90-degree. Ford has managed to tune vibration out with a crankshaft-mounted dampener system. The flat-plane crank 5.2L engine nearly didn't make production due to these vibration issues.

It doesn't take a long look at the 5.2L crank to see what's missing: counterweights that add weight and mass to a crankshaft. A lighter crank spins quickly and with more

fury because it enables you to get into the power band right away. The upside to counterweights is smoothness; the downside is weight. This is why Ford decided to take a crack at the flat-plane crank. Flat-plane

The timing chain drive gear on the right is a stock drive gear; on the left is Modular Motorsports' heavy-duty high-performance sprocket. Opt for the high-performance sprocket if you're going above 600 to 800 hp.

Whenever you're building a fresh Coyote from scratch, dynamic balance your crank, rods, and pistons for best results, even if you've purchased a pre-balanced assembly. Trust, but verify you have a balanced assembly. It is worth the expense to know rather than to guess. The Coyote is an internally balanced engine, which means you don't have to sweat out the flywheel and dampener. However, check dynamic balance on both.

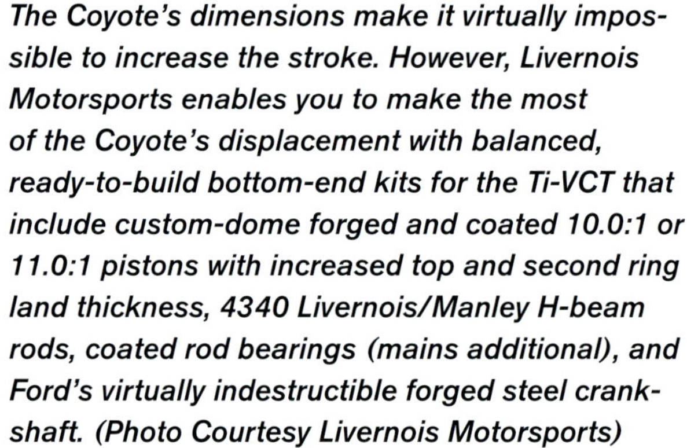

The Coyote's dimensions make it virtually impossible to increase the stroke. However, Livernois Motorsports enables you to make the most of the Coyote's displacement with balanced, ready-to-build bottom-end kits for the Ti-VCT that include custom-dome forged and coated 10.0:1 or 11.0:1 pistons with increased top and second ring land thickness, 4340 Livernois/Manley H-beam rods, coated rod bearings (mains additional), and Ford's virtually indestructible forged steel crankshaft. (Photo Courtesy Livernois Motorsports)

This is the 5.2L flat-plane Voodoo forged steel crankshaft. The flat-plane crank is a first for an American automaker because it employs an approach more common with Ferraris and other exotic European engines. Instead of 90-degree angle rod journal throws as you see in conventional American V-8s, the 5.2L flat-plane crank positions throws at 180 degrees, which makes the most of each power stroke. (Photo Courtesy Ford Performance Racing Parts)

From overhead, the 5.2L crank yields its true personality as a flat-plane piece. The penalty is vibration, which Ford engineers have managed to massage out. It has taken a tremendous amount of time to work through these issues. Because the flat-plane Voodoo is a true high-performance racing engine, noise, vibration, and harshness are less of a priority. (Photo Courtesy Ford Performance Racing Parts)

Here's the flat-plane 5.2L crank side profile. What you see here is a flat line of counterweights, which is a completely different approach to a crankshaft than you see in the Coyote crank with its 90-degree throws. (Photo Courtesy Ford Performance Racing Parts)

Domed hypereutectic pistons are designed specifically for direct-injection operation and higher temperatures. Coated skirts reduce internal friction and heat. Sintered-metal-forged connecting rods are borrowed from the 2012–2013 Boss 302 parts shelf. The base Coyote has never been better for Mustang GT buyers.

The Gen III's forged steel crank is virtually the same as Gen I and Gen II with improved dynamic balancing that is good well beyond 7,500 rpm. I like the factory-chamfered oil holes for improved flow.

Crankshaft identification is easy with Ford numbers cast into the journals. This helps when building a Coyote from scratch.

technology puts the 5.2L heads and shoulders above anything else from Detroit. As with the steel Coyote crank, the Voodoo crank doesn't have an aftermarket replacement because it isn't necessary. The factory crank is as good as it gets. Ford Performance Racing Parts will have a Voodoo flat-plane crankshaft available by the time this book hits the shelves.

Gen III (2018–2023) Rotating Assembly

Down under, the Gen III had little changed except for improvements in durability. Sinter-forged connecting rods borrowed from the Boss 302 parts shelf make the base Coyote brute tested tough. The forged steel crankshaft is a rebalanced piece engineered to support much higher-rpm operation.

Hypereutectic domed pistons are designed for direct injection and a whopping compression ratio of 12.0:1. I theorize hypereutectic instead of forged are used due to the expansion properties of forged pistons. Hypereutectic pistons (high silicon cast) employ lower expansion rates, which means quieter operation when cold.

LUBRICATION

The Ti-VCT Coyote was born to rev high, a dynamic that carries with it huge oiling system demands. The Coyote's oiling system must sustain lubrication to 7,000 rpm and beyond and under extreme driving conditions, which is why Ford designed a fiercely capable system from the start. Ford opted for an 8-quart oil pan and a windage tray/pan gasket combination for easy installation and leak-resistant performance. A one-piece rear main seal, which has been commonplace on Ford engines since 1982, keeps oil where it belongs, inside the engine and off your garage floor. This is all good for keeping oil pressure and volume on target.

The challenge that Ford's great new lubrication system created was oil drainback from the abundance of oil that arrives at the top of the system. Ford solved this problem, and others, with crankcase ventilation chimneys. These PCV chimneys improve both drainback and crankcase ventilation. They allow for a pressure balance between both cylinder banks.

The standard 5.0L Coyote oil pump requires no modifications for street and weekend racing duty. It is a durable pump with tried and proven technology borrowed from the 4.6L/5.4L Modular program. There is no standard or high-volume Coyote oil pump. This is a high-volume pump from the get-go. One pump. Lots of volume. What you want to remember most is to mount this pump properly during installation. You want it centered on the crankshaft with no side loading. The pump hub should turn freely and smoothly.

Pump Pointers

The Coyote does not offer a choice between a standard or high-volume oil pump. There is but one basic pump. You can improve the durability of this pump with a hardened-steel rotor package available from Ford Performance Parts or Modular Motorsports Racing. Check the clearances before putting the pump back together. You may also purchase a heavy-duty pump from Ford Performance Parts and not have to sweat out clearance issues. It is extremely important to center the oil pump properly on the crankshaft to avoid sideloading on the pump rotor. Side stresses on the pump can cause failure. Install it and get it properly centered on the crankshaft and you're good to go.

Improvements

You may wonder what can be done to improve your Coyote's lubrication system. In truth, very little,

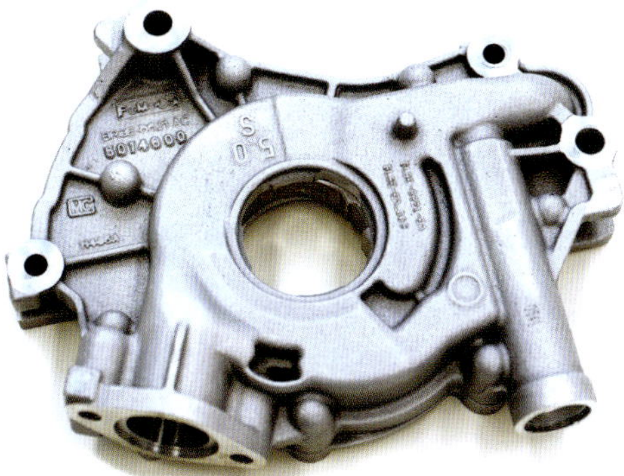

This is Ford Performance Racing Parts' Steel Billet G-rotor pump, M-6600-50CJ. It doesn't deliver greater volume because it doesn't have to. What it does offer is durability thanks to its steel billet rotor construction and close attention to detail in manufacture. The M-6600-50CJ pump has the Coyote's standard pump housing, just tougher guts inside.

Coyote's oil pick-up is routed from the front crank-driven pump to a deep 8-quart oil sump in back. This pick-up can handle the volume. Check out the factory windage tray and pan gasket combination.

The O-ring seal is installed and lubricated where the pick-up joins the oil pump. When you install this pick-up make sure you have the O-ring seal installed and that it is generously lubricated.

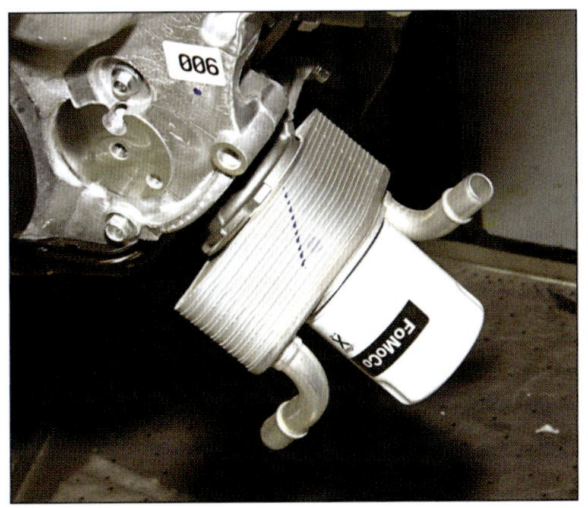

The 2015–2022 oil-to-water cooler installed on all factory Coyote 5.0L Ti-VCT engines (including the Ford Performance Aluminator and Roush Aluminator crate engines) improves overall engine cooling. The oil filter mount/adaptor is different (oil drainback hole in the block) and cannot be interchanged with 2011–2014 Gen I engines. However, it does fit all Gen II and Gen III 2015–2022 engines.

because Ford has it covered. Extensive thought and engineering went into this engine's oiling system. A crank-driven positive displacement oil pump keeps the system well fed from an 8-quart pan from the factory. The Coyote has virtually no issues with oil starvation. In many respects, it has exactly the opposite problem: too much oil at times during high-RPM operation, hence the need for improved oil scavenging.

You can improve the Coyote lubrication system's durability with a billet steel pump G-rotor. Traditional engine building logic is to adjust the pressure relief valve to increase pressure. However, this is unnecessary with the Coyote because Ford has thought of that for you. It has plenty of pressure as is. All you have to do if you're opting for hardened internals is to check rotor-to-pump clearances during assembly and perform generous pump priming during installation. Fill the cavity with engine assembly lube to ensure a good oil wedge on start-up.

Because the Coyote comes with only one standard pump, unlike the Modular 4.6L/5.4L engines, the only modification available is the steel billet rotor inserts in the premium performance pump. Pump housings are the same.

The Ford Performance Racing Parts' M-6600-50CJ oil pump is an easy bolt-on with factory calibration already done for you. Here's what you get:

- Fits all 5.0L Ti-VCT Coyote engine applications

The high-performance steel billet oil pump from Modular Motorsports Racing improves durability. It is red for identification and employs the factory pump housing. What makes it different are billet steel internals for durability.

Ford offers two indication elements to help keep you out of trouble. This is the oil pressure sender for instrumentation. This sender controls continuity to ground.

The second line of lubrication protection is the low-oil-level sending unit, which indicates low oil in the pan. As with the oil pressure sender, this sender controls continuity to ground.

You may modify your existing Coyote oil pump with these billet steel pump inserts from Modular Motorsports Racing. You want to check pump clearances. Apart from that this is an easy modification to make.

- Oil pump assembly with billet steel G-rotor set
- Produced by OEM manufacturer to minimum allowable tolerances
- Pump assembly is pressure and flow tested with OEM procedure
- Recommended for race and power adder applications requiring improved durability under extreme conditions
- Used on 2013–2014 Cobra Jet engines and Ford Racing Aluminator crate engines

When you're preparing the block, it is always a good idea to detail all parts of the block to ensure durability. Ragged casting and machining edges cause turbulence and foaming, which can harm the oil wedge between moving parts. The oil wedge is that protective cushion of oil under pressure between moving parts that prevents metal-to-metal contact. Any time you lose that oil wedge, you have a high risk of severe engine damage.

Examine crankshaft journals and shoulders for any irregularities. Seal contact surfaces should be

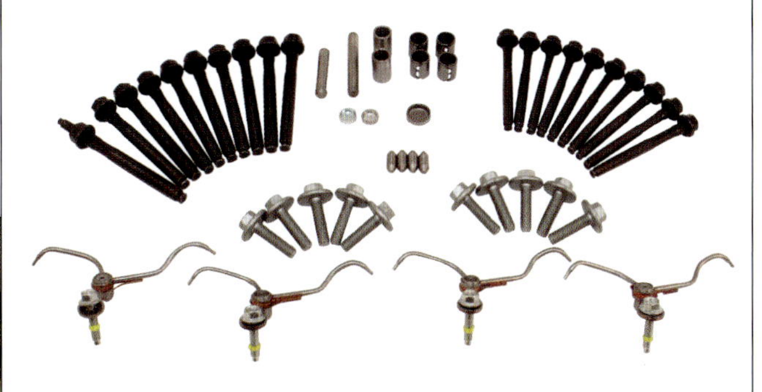

This is Ford Performance racing parts block hardware kit M-6026-A50A, which includes main-cap hardware and piston-cooling jets for your Coyote build project. (Photo Courtesy Ford Performance Parts)

From 2011 to 2013, Ford employed these piston cooling jets in the block to help carry away piston heat. Somewhere in production, these jets were dropped and the block provision eliminated. Piston cooling jets have returned for 2015–2023, adding to the confusion.

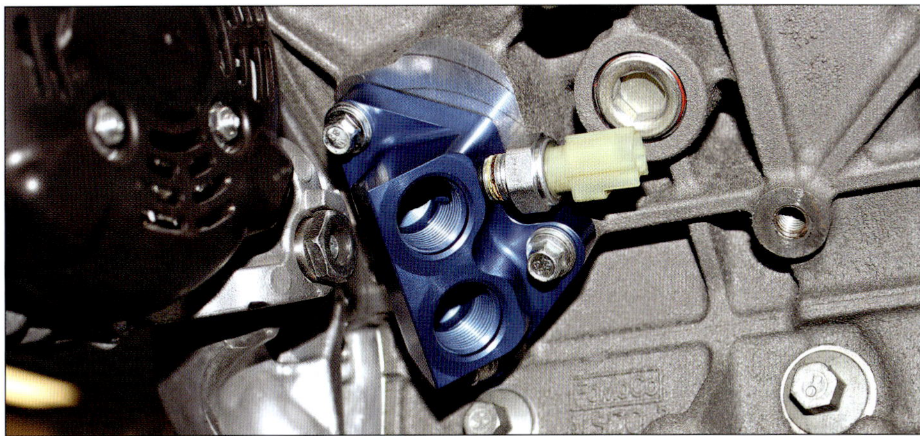

Ford Performance offers this external oil cooler adaptor kit, M-6881-M50, which is a great asset for almost any Coyote build. Any time you take heat away you are gaining engine life. Not shown here is an external oil cooler kit, which is available through the aftermarket.

This is the Boss 302 oil cooler (part number M-6642-MB) from Ford Performance Parts. It is a self-contained oil-to-water heat exchanger used on the 2012–2013 Boss 302 Mustang, which uses the Boss 302's special lower radiator hose with its two quick-disconnect fittings to tie into the engine's cooling system. The Boss 302 oil-to-water cooler is an easy bolt-on that can be adapted to your Coyote-equipped Mustang GT. (Photo Courtesy Ford Performance Parts)

buttery smooth. Oil galleys in the crank must be inspected for obstructions of any kind. Although this is a world-class forged steel crankshaft, mistakes do happen in production and you are ultimately the final phase of inspection. Micropolishing the crankshaft journals improves oil flow and wedge. Always do an assembly mock-up and examine oil passages at the main and rod bearing journals.

Ford has provided a factory oil cooler on 2015–up Coyote engines to help further carry heat away from the oil. Ford Performance Parts offers you the option of an external oil-to-air cooler/filter adaptor, which is installed instead of the factory oil filter/cooler mount. There's also the oil-to-water cooler, which is easy to install and provides extraordinary cooling capacity. Even if you do a little weekend canyon cutting, an external oil cooler is always a nice option because they don't cost much and can prevent a lot of engine wear.

A Smooth Journey

Your Coyote build should include cleanup work in the oiling system. All galleys and passages should be chamfered to the point where there is no oil turbulence under pressure or during drainback. All oil contact surfaces should be smooth. Remove all ragged surfaces and stress risers.

Here's the B&M Supercooler from Summit Racing Equipment, BM 70270, which is easily applied to your Coyote-powered Ford Mustang or F150. Installation takes a couple of hours. The result is less engine heat and extended longevity. Mount the cooler in front of the air conditioning condenser or in the slipstream. (Photo Courtesy B&M Racing & Performance)

The Coyote's excellent lubrication system provides a solid oil wedge at the aluminum main bearings. Although some believe that the Coyote needs tri-metal bearings, it has been proven that this engine makes 1,500 to 2,000 hp with aluminum bearings.

The 2011–2014 Coyote block sports this oil filter mounting location void of the drainback cavity (arrow) that you see on the 2015–2016 block.

This oil galley passage (arrow) uses a restricted head gasket passage for 2011–2014. For 2015–2022, it is unrestricted as shown here on a production 2015 Coyote engine.

Gen III (2018–2023) Oiling System

The Gen III engine sports a new plastic oil pan with improved baffling and windage that's a simple bolt-on installation because the pickup is an integral part of the oil pan. It is a push-on affair with an O-ring installed with the oil pan. The checkerboard oil pump is that way for strength and rigidity. If you're performing a Coyote swap in a classic Ford with a front sump, Moroso makes a front sump pan (part number 20573) and pickup (part number 24573) for the Gen III.

Here's the 2015–2022 Coyote block with the oil drainback feature (arrow), which means that any remote oil filter adaptor or cooler must be compatible with the 2015–2016 block. You cannot use 2011–2014 oil filter adaptors on a newer block and vice versa.

Here's a closer look at the Coyote's cam journals (arrows), which won't require any modification besides minor chamfering if that is important to you. These journals have proven to be successful even under extreme conditions.

The Coyote's camshafts ride directly on cylinder head journals. There are no cam bearings, just the oil wedge that the Coyote's lubrication system provides. This design nuance was carried over from the 4.6L and 5.4L Modular engines. Here, Performance Assembly Solutions, which builds Ford Performance's crate Coyotes, applies engine assembly lube to cam journals during assembly. When you're building your Coyote, always be generous with engine assembly lube for safe start-up.

The Coyote's cam phasers are activated by oil pressure applied via solenoid-operated valves that direct oil pressure to the phasers. The phasers index camshafts to affect valve timing events. Signals come from the powertrain control module per driving demands. What makes 2011–2014 different from 2015–2022 is how the phasers operate. For 2015–2022 the phasers operate in a finite manner to fine-tune cam timing based on real-time driving demands.

The 2012–2013 Boss 302/Cobra Jet oil pan and pick-up (M-6675-M50BR) can be installed on any Coyote engine. The Boss pan is engineered for road racing and hard cornering by keeping sump oil around the pick-up. (Photo Courtesy Ford Performance Racing Parts)

The Gen III oil pump is as good as it gets with its 5.2L GT350 hardened gears.

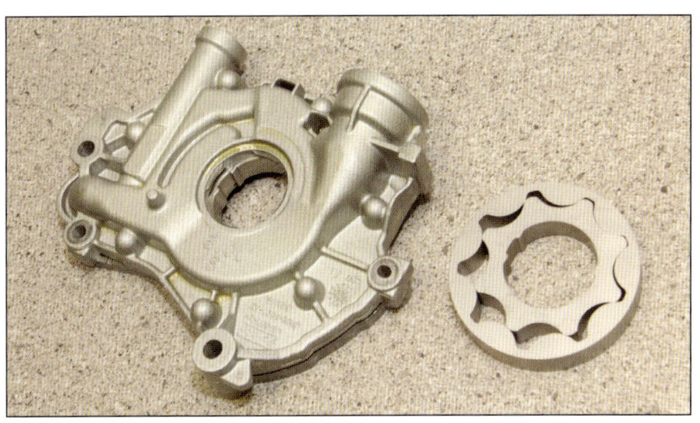

Here are the hardened gears that give the Gen III Coyote improved durability.

Here's a broader look at the Gen III's oil-cooling jets.

This is the Gen III's plastic oil pan, which has its pickup integrated into the pan assembly. The pickup is a press-on affair that is installed with the oil pan. There is no fastener.

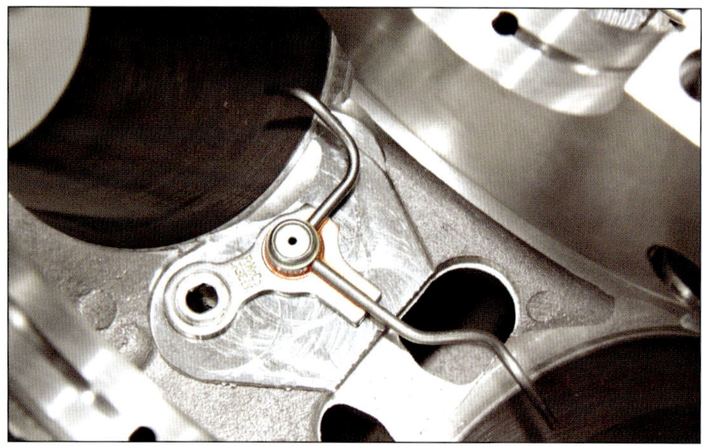

The Gen III employs piston oil-cooling jets (a continuation from the Gen II) for improved cooling.

Externally, this plastic pan is clearly different. The checkboard pattern is there for rigidity and strength. Plastic is lighter than steel too.

Moroso Coyote Pan

- Details: steel, wet sump, 7-quart capacity, 6-1/4-inches deep
- Engine application: Ford 5.0 Modular "Coyote" engines
- Fits: early Ford chassis requiring a front sump oil pan (check measurements)
- For Ford 5.0L and 5.2L Coyote engine blocks
- Designed to install on Ford 5.0L and 5.2L Coyote engines into early Ford chassis that calls for a front-sump oil pan
- The oil pan has a thick steel rail with a front sump that is 6-1/4-inches deep and 12-inches wide x 8-inches long and has a 2-3/8-inches-deep rear section
- Designed to be used with the 5.0L and 5.2L Coyote factory windage tray and dipstick
- Features a race-proven trap door assembly and anti-slosh baffle that keeps oil contained in oil-pump-pickup area during road racing and drag racing

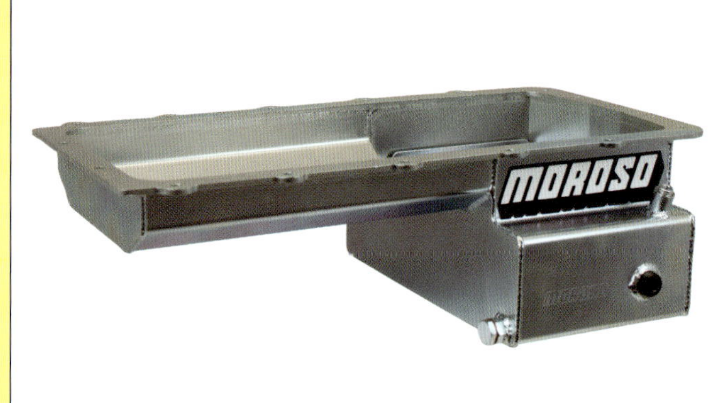

The Moroso Coyote pan (part number 20573) fits all of the Coyote engines and has a separate pickup specific to the Gen III Coyote. If you're not using the in-pan oil sensor, order the screw-in plug.

Moroso Coyote Pan *continued*

- A 1/2-inch NPT fitting for oil temperature sender and dipstick provision
- A 20-mm fitting for the factory oil-level sensor
- Requires the use of oil pump pickup No. 24573
- Note that if the factory low-oil-warning sensor is not going to be used, part number 22738 (20-mm plug with copper washer) is available

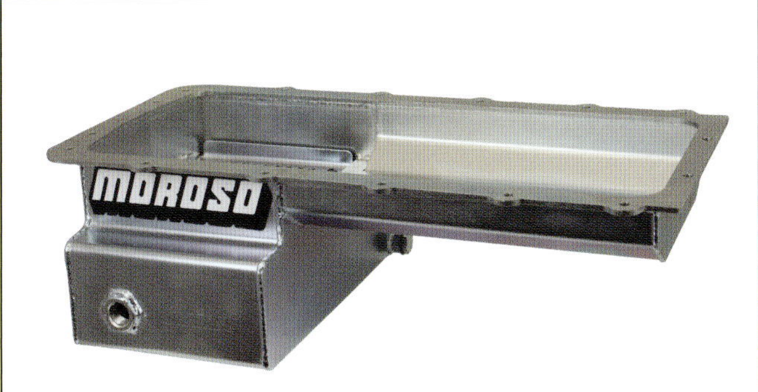

Here's another look at the front sump Coyote pan for front sump installations.

The Moroso part number 20573 pan sports baffling that keeps oil around the pickup under extreme conditions. I like the thick pan rails that provide stiffening where it counts.

This is Moroso's remote oil filter adaptor (part number 23689) for 2015–2022 Coyote blocks with the oil drain-back hole. This will not work with the Gen I 2011–14 Coyote block.

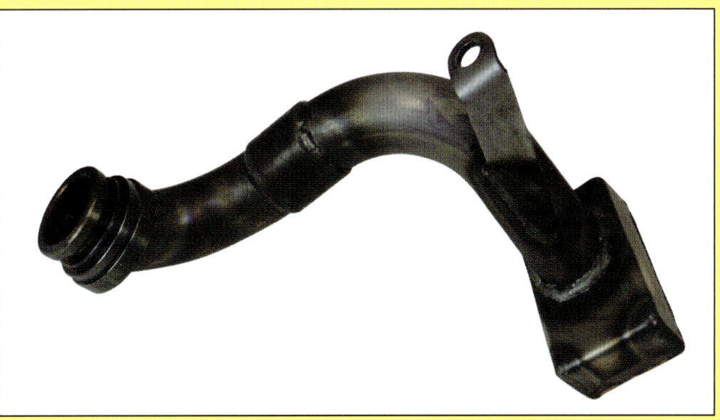

Moroso's press-on pickup (part number 24573) is a Gen III–specific part.

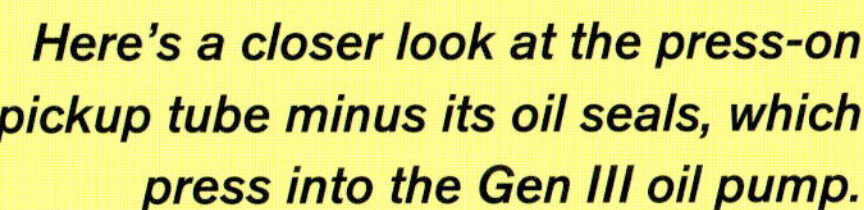

Here's a closer look at the press-on pickup tube minus its oil seals, which press into the Gen III oil pump.

Cylinder Heads

Ford's 5.0L Ti-VCT Coyote employs a revolutionary new cylinder head design that makes the latest member of the Modular engine less bulky while providing extraordinary breathing. The Coyote's intake ports utilize true drive-through service because they outflow even some of the most legendary race heads in history, including the Yates D3 casting for the small-block Ford. Perhaps this is an unfair comparison when you consider a two-valve versus a four-valve. But airflow is airflow and power is power. What counts is what you get at the crank and rear wheels.

Known stock Coyote intake port head flow numbers are 289.4-cfm intake and 201.4-cfm exhaust at .500 inch, which is remarkable, but there's more. Because the Coyote's top end was designed more as a package than just cylinder heads, cam, and induction, it produces impressive airflow numbers rarely seen from a factory Ford engine. Call it the team approach to induction, cams, and heads. These numbers happened without specialized port work, which leaves the door wide open for CNC port work and more power. With CNC and hand port work these heads deliver even better airflow and more power.

Ford's Coyote design team understood at the outset it would have to burn a lot of midnight oil to come up with a cylinder head that could do everything. Ford engineers looked first to basic hotrodding tricks to achieve their goals and then went to work conceiving a better cylinder head. Although the Coyote cylinder head appears to be a derivative of the Shelby GT500 head, it isn't. If you study this head closely it is a completely different casting. A lot was learned from the GT500 head, yet none of it was carried directly over to the Coyote, according to Ford.

Ford engineers also took what they learned from the 3.5L and 3.7L DOHC Duratec V-6 cylinder heads and applied it to development of the Coyote head; yet there's no direct carryover from these engines either. However, the 3.5L/3.7L four-valve combustion chamber technique was applied to the Coyote to some degree in terms of shape and valve placement. Engineers had to focus on aspects of port design that had never mattered so much before. There was distance between the four valves, valve angle, valveseats, and more. Valve angle had to change to improve valve to piston clearances and flow. It

The incredible Coyote four-valve cylinder head is the most advanced production Ford cylinder head ever produced. Ford has actually designed a production cylinder head that cannot be beaten. These intake ports flow in the neighborhood of 300 cfm. When the Coyote was introduced for 2011, it was said in the media these heads will actually outflow the Yates D3 small-block head casting, which is a race head.

The Coyote's cylinder heads are specific to the left (driver) side and right (passenger) side and are easily identified by "L" and "R" in addition to respective casting numbers. This is a left-hand 2015–2017 Gen II cylinder head as (indicated by the "L"). Visible are cam sensor ports and bolt holes.

This is a right-hand 2015–2017 Gen II Coyote cylinder head (as indicated by the "R"). As with the left-hand cylinder head, there are two cam sensor ports.

The lower oil gallery (orange arrow) provides tensioner oil pressure to the primary timing chain. The oil gallery on top (yellow arrow) provides tensioner oil pressure for the secondary timing chain connected to both camshafts.

A closer look at the Coyote cylinder head demonstrates the petite nature of this redesigned Modular head with its smaller valvetrain. It reminds me of a motorcycle valvetrain because it is so small. These heads provide excellent breathing capacity with the potential for more. Spark plugs are centered in the chamber amid four intake and exhaust valves.

Another angle shows the tighter valve angle of the Coyote cylinder head, which was exactly what Ford engineers were going for to conceive a more compact cylinder head.

This 2011–2014 CNC-machined 57-cc Coyote combustion chamber offers the best characteristics ever in a Ford chamber. The spark plugs are centered right in the middle of the action amid two 1.460-inch/37.0-mm intake and two 1.220-inch/31.0-mm exhaust valves.

also had to change in order to reduce the overall size of the Coyote head and ultimately engine size.

Everything in the Coyote's cylinder heads had to be downsized to achieve a more petite cylinder head casting size. This meant smaller lash adjusters, springs, and rocker arms. When you compare the Coyote's valves and valvetrain to the 4.6L and 5.4L Modular's, there's an obvious difference in size. The Coyote's valvetrain

Coyote Head Quick Facts

- DOHC casting produced from 316-grade cast aluminum
- Left- and right-hand–specific heads: 6049 right and 6050 left
- 2011–2014 head is most common
- 2015–2017 head is a new casting with extended intake port flange for CMCV system
- 2011–2014 has 37.0-mm intake valve and 31.0-mm exhaust valve
- 2015–2017 has 37.8-mm intake valve and 31.8-mm exhaust valve
- Finger-style stamped roller rockers and lash adjusters
- 2011–2014 valvespring pressure: 265 pounds closed; 650 pounds open
- 2015–2022 valvespring pressure: 300 pounds closed; 760 pounds open

This is the revised 2015–2017 Coyote cylinder head with revised high-flow intake ports, stiffer valvesprings, larger intake and exhaust valves, and a wider intake port flange for the CMCV induction system.

This is the revised 2015–2017 Gen II head from the exhaust-port side. If you have the budget, the 2015–2017 cylinder head is the best of the two Coyote head choices. Just remember the 2015–2017 head is considerably different than the 2011–2014 head, which means you must use the 2015–2017 head gasket with its larger unrestricted oil passage for VCT operation. You must also use the 2013–2014 intake manifold, which will clear the revised 2015–2017 head. The 2011–2012 intake manifold will not fit.

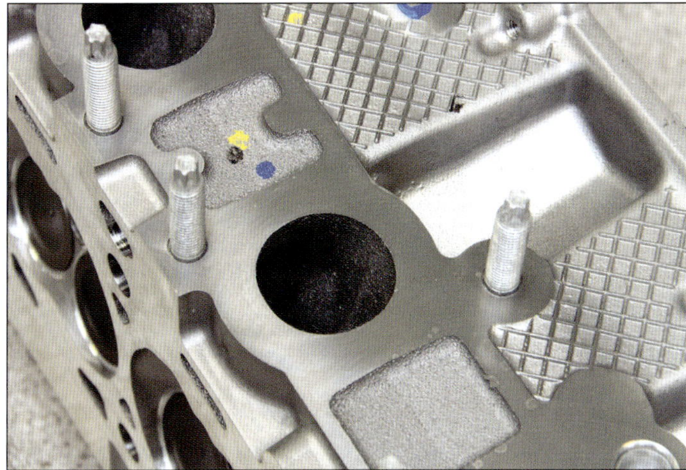

The Coyote's generous exhaust ports provide exceptional scavenging compared to their Modular 4.6L/5.4L siblings. Exhaust valve size for 2015–2017 grew from 31.0 mm/1.240 inches to 31.7 mm/1.248 inches.

Here's the revised 2015–2017 57-cc chamber with larger 37.3-mm (1.485-inch) intake valves and 31.8-mm (1.248-inch) exhaust valves. This is the as-cast factory chamber, which has not been CNC machined.

The revised 2015–2017 head has these extended intake port flanges, which accommodate the CMCV system. This creates interference issues with the 2011–2012 intake manifold because of its extensive ribbing.

The 2011–2014 head has a shorter intake port flange. This is also a CNC-machined intake port. The stock port is roughcast.

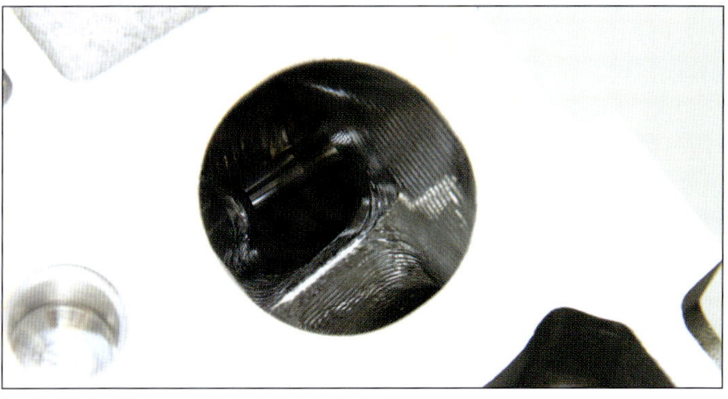

A CNC-machined Coyote exhaust port yields vastly improved flow over the roughcast stocker. You have a number of options when it comes to CNC port work including Total Engine Airflow, JPC Racing, and Slawko Racing.

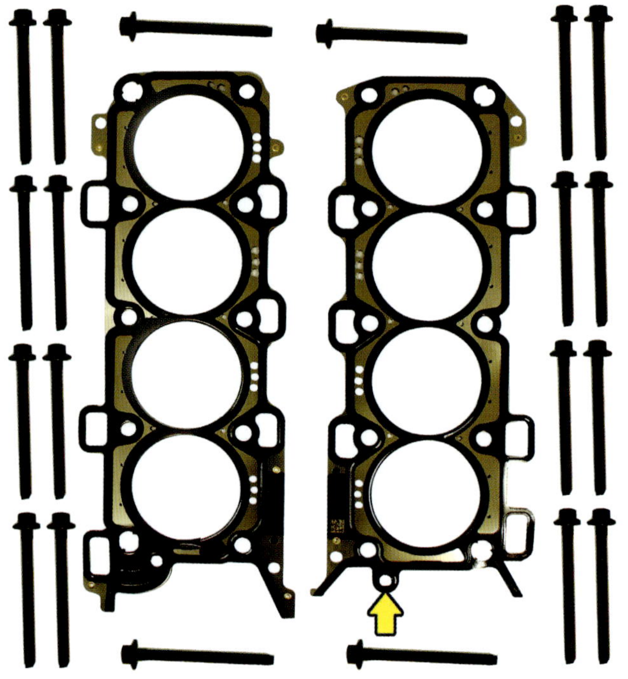

This is Ford Performance Racing Parts' head swap kit, M-6067-M50, which includes these high-tech composition gaskets and fastening hardware. Plan on fresh gaskets and bolts whenever you swap heads. This is the 2015–2017 head gasket with enlarged VCV provision (arrow). (Photo Courtesy Ford Performance Parts)

reminds me of motorcycle engine sizing, which means you can spin the Coyote higher and without consequence. Cams had to be brought 20 mm closer together to shrink the package. Romeo-style camshaft journal girdles were abandoned for Windsor-style camshaft journal towers. Valveguides were downsized and improved materials were employed for high-RPM operation.

Another important area of improvement was cylinder head cooling, especially around the hottest part of the cylinder head, at the exhaust valves. Ford calls the improved method "cross-flow cooling"; it eliminated the Modular's cooling tube in the valley. Coolant flows up through cylinder heads at the exhaust valves toward the front of this engine. Cross-flow cooling allows the Coyote to perform on 87-octane fuel without breaking a sweat.

Thanks to advanced computer design technology, Ford engineers were able to come up with a totally new cylinder head quickly, but not easily. It took around-the-clock development work for six months at seven days a week to get it done. The Coyote head's development and execution was a remarkable turn of events for Ford because it had never been done.

Boss 302 Head

When development began on the base Coyote head, Ford engineers were presented with another challenge: the 2012–2013 Boss 302 cylinder head, which was also known as the "Roadrunner" project inside Ford. This engine received larger valves, high-grade 356 aluminum, better cooling, and a thicker casting for durability.

Ford was able to develop the Boss 302 head thanks to being given a proper budget. What resulted were the left-hand M-6050-M50BR (driver) and right-hand M-6049-M50BR (passenger) heads. The engineers were able to take existing Coyote head tooling and produce the Boss head as

This is the 2012–2013 Boss 302 cylinder head casting, M-6050-M50 and M-6049-M50 (shown), which really is a different casting of an improved 356 aluminum alloy (versus 319 with base Coyote heads) with CNC-machined ports and chambers. According to Ford, there's a measure of copper in the 356 alloy, which improves heat transfer under extreme conditions. (Photo Courtesy Ford Performance Parts)

Here's the Boss 302 head's exhaust side, again the M-6049-M50 head casting. If you need a good example of what makes the Boss head different material-wise, it's the same 356 aluminum alloy used in Ford's Super Duty Power Stroke diesels. There's more mass in the Boss head around larger valves. In addition, cooling passages are improved for better heat transfer. (Photo Courtesy Ford Performance Parts)

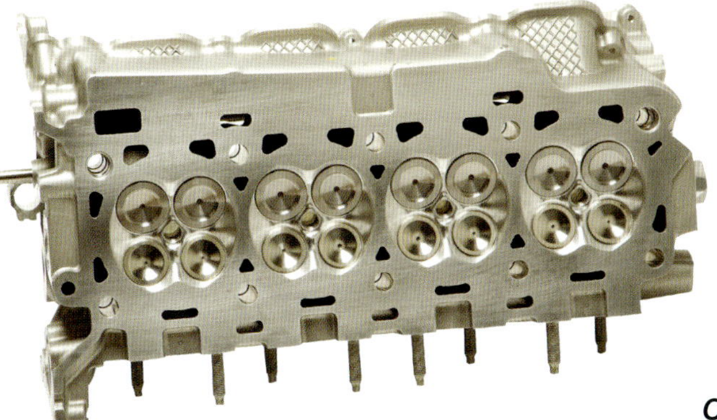
The Boss 302's chamber side employs a thicker deck for exceptional strength around the 57-cc four-valve chambers. Ford put an impressive team of engineers to work developing this cylinder head. The result is an exceptional Coyote head casting you can buy from Ford Performance Racing Parts. Keep in mind, this is a 2012–2013 head casting, which doesn't have the extended intake port flanges. (Photo Courtesy Ford Performance Parts)

This close-up of the Boss 302 head port configuration conveys what makes this head better: Better aluminum. As well as CNC port work going in and coming out. (Photo Courtesy Ford Performance Parts)

It is suggested that you head-stud your Coyote build unless you're planning in-vehicle head removal. Cylinder heads cannot be removed in the vehicle if you use head studs. Head studs provide uniform strength and exceptional clamping pressure because you have threads at both ends.

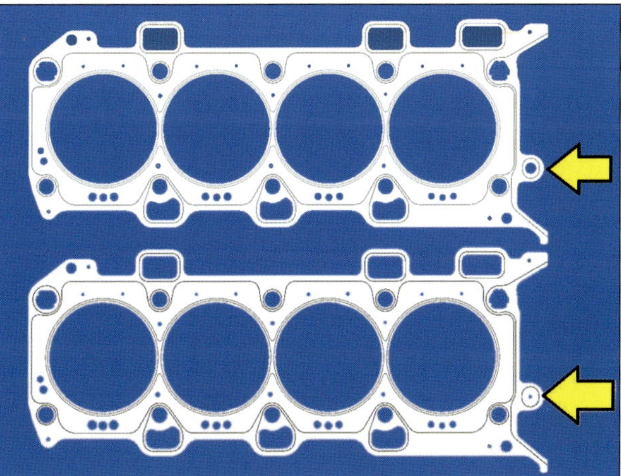
The difference between the 2011–2014 and 2015–2017 head gaskets is shown here. On top is the 2015–2016 head gasket with a revised VCV oil galley passage (arrow), which is larger. Bottom is the 2011–2014 gasket with a pinhole-sized galley passage (arrow). (Photo Courtesy Ford Performance Parts)

a unique Boss-specific casting. Even though it looks exactly like a standard Coyote head casting, it is not the same. The Boss head is cast of 356 aluminum alloy with a smattering of copper for both strength and good heat transfer. It sports plenty of thick aluminum stock where it counts, at the deck and around the valves.

When a casting emerged from the Windsor foundry, CNC machines went to work to massage the unique Boss casting which, to the naked eye, isn't much different from the standard Coyote head. In terms of power and function, however, it is surely a different head. With the Boss head you not only get improved function but also strength in a better-alloy cocktail. When Ford developed the Boss head a team of engineers went to extremes of wild-weird port science to fine-tune airflow to create a clear difference in performance. Ford engineers worked day and night on intake and exhaust port shape with grueling dyno tests to determine how much they had gained. It didn't happen all at once. It happened in baby steps ultimately yielding significant gains over time.

As engineers massaged intake ports they found that conventional port logic didn't always net them improvement. Improvement came with minute changes in port shape. Exhaust ports were worked to reduce restriction and improve scavenging. Ford engineers achieved improved flow by also lowering the port floor.

GT350 Voodoo Cylinder Head

Ford Performance is introducing the Shelby GT350 5.2L cylinder head at press time, along with the corresponding induction and cylinder block, making it possible to build a

Boss 302 Head Facts

A nice thing about the Boss 302 heads is that you don't have to buy a Boss 302 Mustang to get them. They're available from Ford Performance Racing Parts and Summit Racing Equipment, just to name two sources. Here's what you get:

- Fits 2011–2014 Mustang GT, 2012–2013 Boss 302, Boss 302S, and Boss 302R race cars
- Production DOHC cylinder head used on the Boss 302S and 302R race car
- Fully CNC-machined ports and chambers
- Loaded head assembly minus camshafts, rocker arms, and lash adjusters
- 37.0-mm (1.460-inch) hollow stem intake valve
- 31.8-mm (1.248-inch) sodium-filled exhaust valve (31-mm/1.220-inch) on base 5.0L Coyote
- Increased-rate valvesprings can support 12-mm (.476-inch) intake and 13-mm (.511-inch) exhaust max lift (base head is 12 mm/12 mm)
- Intake side flows approximately 4 percent more than the base 5.0L head
- 193-cc intake port volume (more than 300 cfm)
- Chamber volume 55.6 cm (smaller than the standard 57-cc chamber)
- Use head changing kit M-6067-M50BR from Ford Performance Racing Parts or Summit Racing Equipment.

Boss 302 DOHC cylinder head production has been discontinued and heads will no longer be available after the current supply is sold out. However, you can also find them on eBay and craigslist, just to name two options.

The new Shelby GT350 5.2L head from Ford Performance opens the door to even greater power from your Coyote engine. The GT350 head is a different casting entirely with its own valvetrain geometry, which does not interchange with other Coyote heads. (Photo Courtesy Ford Performance Parts)

5.2L Coyote with the cross-plane crank (more cubes for your Coyote project and the added benefit of these GT350 heads). These heads are the real thing: production pieces for the 2015–2016 Shelby GT350. Here's what you get:

- Production cylinder head for the 5.2L GT350
- Fully CNC-ported intake ports, exhaust ports, and combustion chamber
- Larger port sizing than the 2015 5.0L Coyote CMCV cylinder heads
- 38.3-mm intake valve and 32.5-mm exhaust valve; 2015 5.0L Coyote valve sizes are 37.3-mm intake, 31.8-mm exhaust
- New valvetrain geometry allows for greater valve lift
- Lightweight hollow-stem intake valves and sodium-filled exhaust valves
- Heads do not include camshafts, rocker arms, and lash adjusters
- Requires unique camshaft due to valvetrain geometry (M-6550-M52)
- Also requires 5.2L rocker arms and lash adjusters (M-6564-M52)

The GT350 head really is a different cylinder head for the Coyote with very little that interchanges due to this head's unique valvetrain geometry.

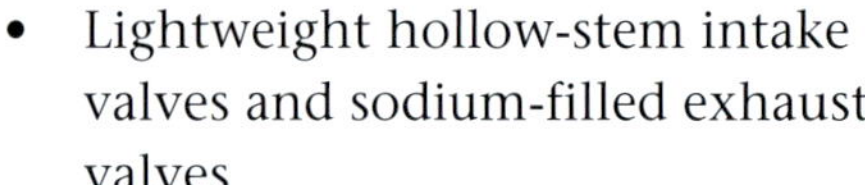

Ford Performance has recently added the production GT350 5.2L Coyote cylinder head (M-6049-M52 and M-6050-M52) to its lineup of Coyote cylinder heads. The M52 head has larger 38.3-mm intake and 32.5-mm exhaust valves. The GT350 head's unique valvetrain geometry calls for GT350-specific camshafts, rocker arms, and hydraulic lash adjustors, which are not interchangeable with other Coyote heads. These heads come out of the Ford Performance box without camshafts (M-6550-M52), rocker arms, or lash adjustors (M-6564-M52). (Photo Courtesy Ford Performance Parts)

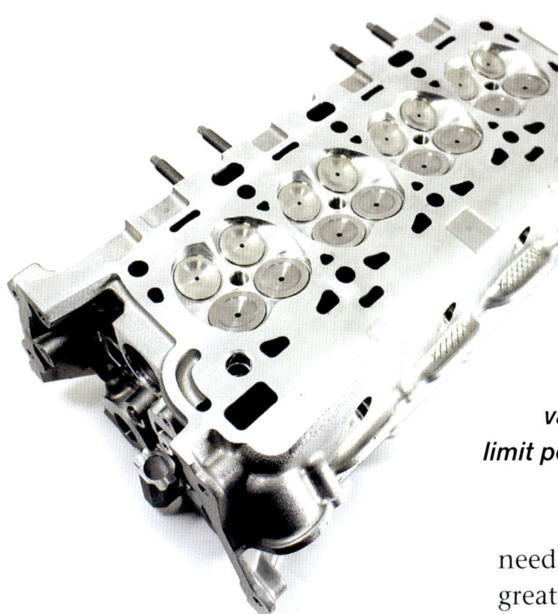

The GT350 5.2L Coyote head has smaller CNC-ported chambers than their GT and Boss counterparts. More generous valve sizing makes this head a terrific choice. However, if you're bolting these heads onto a 5.0L Coyote block, be advised that you will run into valve shrouding issues, which may limit power gains. (Photo Courtesy Ford Performance Parts)

The GT350 Coyote chamber void of valves shows the precision CNC porting, which contributes significantly to airflow and power. Expect to see in excess of 320 cfm intake and 220 cfm exhaust with these heads. Although you can bolt these heads onto the 5.0L block, consider building a 5.2L short-block to go with these heads due to valve shrouding issues with the 5.0L short-block. (Photo Courtesy Ford Performance Parts)

Budget permitting, you can build a complete Ford Performance 5.2L Coyote to create a completely compatible mill. Ford Performance expects to have a complete 5.2L Coyote crate available by fall of 2016 that you can order with the cross-plane crank. Sorry, flat-plane cranks are not expected from Ford Performance anytime soon. They are a GT350 exclusive; you have to buy a GT350 to get one. Complete 5.2L Voodoo flat-plane engines are not expected either from Ford Performance.

The GT350 cylinder head is a ready-to-race piece right out of the box with its larger valves, generous ports, and revised valvetrain dimensions. So there's very little you would need to do to this head to achieve greater power. Real power comes from engine tuning once you have the 5.2L together.

The GT350 head's exhaust ports are CNC precision machined, which offer excellent scavenging. They are factory production pieces for the flat-plane crank 5.2L 2015–2016 Shelby GT350. (Photo Courtesy Ford Performance Parts)

Improving the Coyote Head

How do you improve on such a perfect factory cylinder head? No one I have spoken with in the automotive aftermarket is planning a high-performance cylinder head for the 5.0L/5.2L Ti-VCT Coyote engine at press time because the factory castings are exceptional pieces to begin with. The best Coyote cylinder head in the marketplace is the factory casting with port work to improve flow numbers.

Regardless of what cylinder head you have planned for your Coyote project, the basics remain the same. Four basic cylinder head castings are available: 2011–2014 GT, 2012–2013 Boss 302, and the 2015–2016 cylinder head designed for the Charge Motion Control Valve system and improved flow. The new Shelby GT350 5.2L head can also be included.

If you're going to run the 2015–2016 cylinder head on your 2011–2014 block, use the 2015–2016 cylinder head gasket with the larger VCT oil feed hole in front. If you're going to run the more aggressive 2015–2017 camshafts on 2011–2014 cylinder heads, you must use the 2015–2017 timing chains, sprockets, and cam phasers. You cannot interchange 2011–2014 and 2015–2016 timing components. Variable cam timing (VCT) phaser bolts are new for 2015–2016 and must be matched to the 2015–2017 VCT solenoids. If you opt for 2015–2017 cylinder heads, be prepared to go the entire way with the complete timing chain and phaser package.

While I'm on the subject of cylinder head compatibility, also keep

Ford Coyote 5.0L/5.2L Gen I and Gen II Cylinder Head Specifications			
Type	*Part Number Details*	*Port Size*	*Valve Size (mm)*
2011–2014 base head, right-hand (passenger)	M-6049-M50	193-cc intake volume	37.0 intake, 31.0 exhaust
2011–2014 base head, left-hand (driver)	M-6050-M50	193-cc intake volume	37.0 intake, 31.0 exhaust
2012–2013 Boss 302, right-hand (passenger)	M-6049-M50BR; better alloy, CNC-ported, increased spring rates	4-percent flow increase over base Coyote head	37.0 intake, hollow stem, 31.8 exhaust, sodium filled
2012–2013 Boss 302, left-hand (driver)	M-6050-M50BR; better alloy, CNC ported, increased spring rates	4-percent flow increase over base Coyote head	37.0 intake, hollow stem; 31.8 exhaust, sodium filled
2015–2016 base head, right-hand (passenger)	M-6049-M50; wider intake port flange, larger valves, greater spring rates		37.3 intake, 31.8 exhaust
2015–2016 base head, left-hand (driver)	M-6050-M50; wider intake port flange, larger valves, greater spring rates		37.3 intake, 31.8 exhaust
2015–2016 5.2L GT350, right-hand (passenger)	M-6050-M52; fully CNC ported, requires unique GT350 camshaft and rocker arm due to valvetrain geometry	Greater port volume than GT head	38.3 intake, 32.5 exhaust
2015–2016 5.2L GT350, left-hand (driver)	M-6049-M52; fully CNC ported, requires unique GT350 camshaft and rocker arm due to valvetrain geometry	Greater port volume than GT head	38.3 intake, 32.5 exhaust

in mind that the 2015–2017 induction system is also different from 2011 to 2014 with ribbing that interferes with the 2011–2014 cylinder head's extended intake port flange. The 2015–2017 intake manifold has the Charge Motion Control Valve system, which the 2011–2014 did not have. Charge Motion changes intake manifold runner length via flapper valves in the intake manifold. Greater runner length gives you better low-end torque. Shorter runners make horsepower at high RPM.

So how do you improve an already great factory cylinder head? You can improve the Coyote head with precision CNC port work. Oh sure, you can spend a lot of time hand porting this head if you have a lot of time on your hands. However, you are money and time ahead buying the Ford Performance Racing Parts CNC-ported head or sending your heads to Total Engine Airflow for CNC port work. Total Engine Airflow CNC machines the intake and exhaust ports along with the combustion chambers. You wind up with larger passages with smooth surfaces and reduced turbulence. The result, regardless of how you look at it, is improved flow.

Ford Performance is no longer producing the Boss 302 cylinder head. However, these heads are still available from sources like Summit Racing Equipment, eBay, craigslist, and a host of others. Remaining inventories of new Boss heads as well as used show up at swap meets and parts houses. Because the Coyote V-8 in all its forms has been in production a short time, it's going to take time for used castings to become available. In the meantime, search for new castings for your Coyote project.

TEA CNC-Ported Coyote Heads

Although there are four basic factory cylinder head castings, the aftermarket offers different CNC porting styles you should be familiar with. Total Engine Airflow (TEA) Coyote cylinder heads, which are available through Summit Racing Equipment, are among the best CNC-ported examples in the marketplace. You need to send TEA your cylinder head cores to get started. Here's what you can expect:

Valve Jobs

TEA valve jobs optimize airflow to deliver power and durability. They are also blueprint, meaning all seat depths are equal from valve to valve and head to head. There are no variations.

Airflow

All TEA head ports and chambers are hand blended in critical areas, and then flow tested to ensure they perform as designed. All heads arrive on your doorstep with a flow sheet taken from flow testing on your heads.

Assembly

Every set of heads is ready to install directly out of the box. All are "blueprint assembled" to ensure all

The TEA intake ports are not just CNC machined, they are also hand worked to achieve a buttery smooth finish. There are no lines and ridges to cause turbulence.

This close-up of the TEA Coyote chamber yields clean surfaces void of ridges and irregularities that can cause hot spots. Rough surfaces are gone.

Exhaust ports on the TEA Coyote CNC-ported head are hand worked after all CNC machining has ended. The result is thorough scavenging.

Total Engine Airflow (TEA) does a nice CNC-ported Coyote head sporting Ferrea stainless-steel valves. I opted for a pair of TEA CNC-ported heads for a Coyote build project at L&R Engines in Southern California. These are nice, handcrafted pieces that you can bolt onto your Coyote. Airflow improvement is in the 4- to 5-percent range.

clearances are checked and all spring heights and pressures are equal. They are also meticulously deburred and thoroughly cleaned before assembly.

Custom Options

Many options can be performed on your Coyote cylinder heads. For example, chamber volume can be milled from any TEA cylinder heads to the customer's requested chamber volume; in some cases they can remove additional material to make the chambers larger if needed. TEA also stocks parts from all the leading valvetrain manufacturers and can supply countless variations of valvesprings, retainers, and valve materials.

Total Engine Airflow Numbers (94-mm Bore)

Valve Lift (inch)	*Intake (cfm)*	*Exhaust (cfm)*
0.100	91	82
0.200	165	160
0.300	228	206
0.400	283	219
0.500	305	228
0.550	318	231

Experience

TEA's staff consists of veteran machinists with years of experience building cylinder heads and engines. They understand what lives and what doesn't.

When your Coyote heads arrive at TEA, here's what happens:

- Disassemble and clean
- Fully CNC port intake and exhaust runners
- Competition multi-angle valve job
- Precision grind all 32 valves with backcut on intake valve
- Hand blend valve job into porting
- Flow test with sheet included
- Flat mill
- Custom assembly ensuring all tip heights are at stock height

- Trickflow/Pac racing 85-pound valvesprings
- OE valvestem seals

JPC Racing Coyote CNC-Ported Heads

JPC (Justin's Performance Center) Racing, located between Washington, D.C., and Baltimore, Maryland, delivers a great CNC-ported Coyote Stage 1 head for those of you looking for nice power gains from your naturally aspirated or forced-air Coyote. Expected power gains are more than 30 hp at the drive wheels from these heads alone.

These CNC-ported heads are actually a joint venture between JPC Racing and Rich Groh Racing (RGR) Engines. On its website JPC says, "The Stage 1 CNC-ported heads increase flow 9 to 14 percent (depends on lift) and utilize OEM valves, valvesprings, and retainers. A five-angle valve job is standard with all Stage 1 CNC-ported heads. JPC and RGR completely disassemble the heads, including the valveguides, for maximum porting during the CNC process." JPC adds that turnaround time is approximately one week because they keep CNC castings in stock. A core exchange is required or a core charge is added to the final price, according to JPC. The JPC Racing Stage 2 and Stage 3 CNC-ported heads have aftermarket oversized valves and upgraded valvesprings.

Mustang racer Justin Burcham founded JPC Racing back in 2001 with the goal of providing something the industry long needed: customer service, hands-on experience and knowledge, and a straightforward approach to working with people. Justin and his experienced staff bring many years of high-performance expertise to the table, along with several NMRA national championships.

Slawko Racing Heads

Slawko Racing Heads is another source for CNC-ported Coyote cylinder heads that contributes a strong racing background and a wealth of experience.

Slawko Racing Heads says these are the same CNC-ported Coyote heads used by Justin Cyrnek in his 2013 Mustang GT racecar. An Evolution Performance and L&M Engines–built GEN 1 5.0L Coyote engine powers Cyrnek's Mustang. Justin's best times in this Mustang have been as fast as 7.92 at 173.56 mph in the quarter-mile.

JPC Racing/RGR Coyote Heads: The Numbers (92.2-inch Bore)

JPC/RGR Stage 1 Heads		
Valve Lift (inch)	*Intake (cfm)*	*Exhaust (cfm)*
0.100	54	37
0.200	197	158
0.300	266	201
0.400	303	213
0.500	321	224
0.600	335	232
JPC/RGR Stage 2 Heads		
Valve Lift (inch)	*Intake (cfm)*	*Exhaust (cfm)*
0.100	100	87
0.200	197	158
0.300	266	201
0.400	303	213
0.500	325	224
0.600	331	232
0.650	337	235
JPC/RGR Stage 3 Heads		
Valve Lift (inch)	*Intake (cfm)*	*Exhaust (cfm)*
0.100	101	88
0.200	205	160
0.300	271	205
0.400	305	221
0.500	327	232
0.600	339	243
0.650	342	249

Slawko Racing Heads

Valve Lift (inch)	*Intake (cfm)*	*Exhaust (cfm)*
0.100	94	88
0.200	189	176
0.300	260	215
0.400	302	230
0.500	330	239
0.600	339	245
0.650	346	247

Gen III Cylinder Head Changes

Changes to the Gen III Coyote cylinder heads are significant. The Gen III Coyote cylinder head casting is much stronger than its predecessors to accommodate high-pressure direct fuel injection and a greater compression ratio.

These heads are vastly different than Gen I and II. Gen III heads sport better flow numbers more in line with Gen II 5.2L "Voodoo" heads. What's more, Gen III camshafts must be used with Gen III timing components and phasers. Exhaust cam #1 journals are larger to accommodate different oil seals. Gen III engines use Gen II intake phasers and primary timing chains. Exhaust phasers are Gen III only and are attached with a single bolt. The Gen III timing system is Ford part number M-6004-A501B.

The Gen III head gasket and cylinder heads employ "bridge" cooling holes for improved cooling. Gen I and Gen II heads do not. Gen III cylinder heads are made of a more advanced grade of aluminum (AS7GU) than Gen I and II (AL319). AL319, an alloy, is 6-percent silicon and 3.5-percent copper alloy with 1.0 iron maximum. AL319 has outstanding casting and machining characteristics. Corrosion resistance and weldability of this material are very good. The anodized color of AL319 is generally gray with a brown cast, depending on the amount and ratio of silicon and copper.

Newly developed alloys, such as AS7GU, are a variant of A356 strengthened with 0.5-percent copper. Like the A356 aluminum alloy, AS7GU alloy has excellent castability while the minute addition of copper to this alloy improves creep resistance and tensile strength at intermediate temperatures. AS7GU is more user friendly. This is what makes the Gen III Coyote head better and stronger.

Cast-aluminum alloys, such as AL319 and AS7GU, are being used more in applications, such as engine blocks and cylinder heads, to reduce mass and weight. Because fuel economy standards have gone higher along with high-temperature-property demands, the properties of cast-aluminum alloys have become more critical.

The maximum operating temperature of Coyote cylinder heads has increased from approximately 338°F to temperatures exceeding 392°F. These higher operating temperatures result in more severe high-cycle fatigue and more low-cycle fatigue and/or fatigue damage in regions of cylinder heads exposed to high thermal gradients.

The most common cast-aluminum alloys are A356, 319, and AS7GU (which is A356 plus 0.5 percent copper). A356 is a primary aluminum alloy with good ductility and fatigue properties at low-to-intermediate temperatures. Yet, above 392°F, creep resistance and tensile strength of this alloy are rapidly degraded. Something had to be done to improve these issues. AS7GU was the solution. This is what you get with the Gen III cylinder head casting.

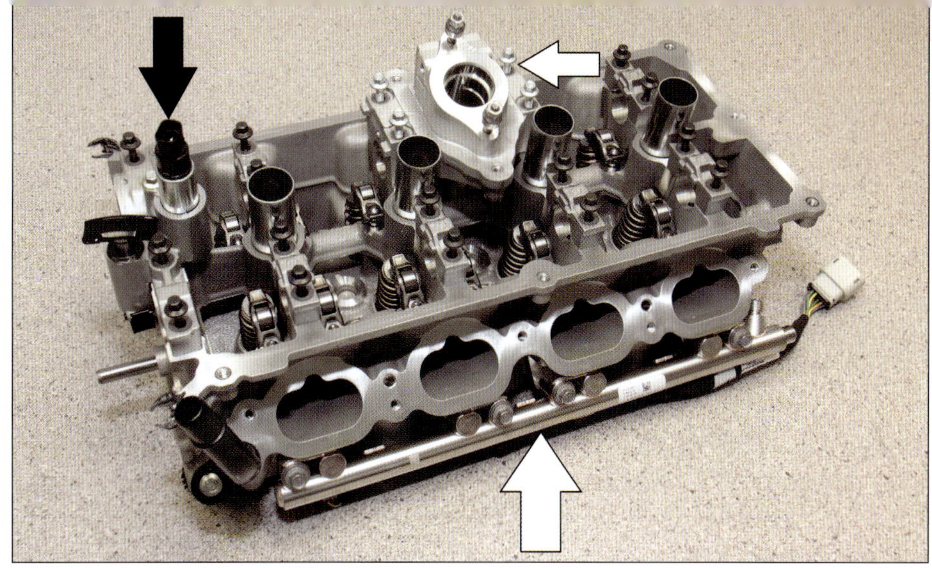

The Gen III Coyote head is a vastly improved casting designed for dual injection (two fuel-injection systems sharing the cylinder heads). That's the high-pressure direct-injection manifold across the bottom. There are ports (not visible) that accommodate the fuel manifold. Above is the direct-injection-pump pedestal that sits above a cam lobe that actuates the pump. Exhaust cam phaser modulation is activated by an in-head solenoid (black arrow) in each head and returned to center by a spring. The intake port volume is 205 cc.

On the performance side, the Gen III heads sport improved airflow characteristics along with larger valves that give these heads flow mighty close to that of the GT350 Voodoo 5.2L CNC-ported castings. Ford has also brought back the larger 12-mm head bolts for greater strength. The Gen III cylinder heads feature larger intake and exhaust valves (37.3 mm intake and 31.8 mm exhaust for Gen II, which was increased to 37.7 mm intake and 32 mm exhaust for the Gen III) along with increased lobe lift for both intake and exhaust camshafts (13 mm intake/exhaust in the Gen II with a change to 14 mm intake/exhaust for the Gen III). The Ti-VCT variable valve timing system witnesses a significant update. The exhaust cam phaser is all-new for the Gen III. Ford relocated the exhaust phaser to the cylinder head instead of where it was originally located ahead of the cam phaser. Both phasers are still computer actuated.

Here's a closer look at the direct-injection-pump pedestal, which is situated above an additional cam lobe that works the spring-loaded high-pressure pump.

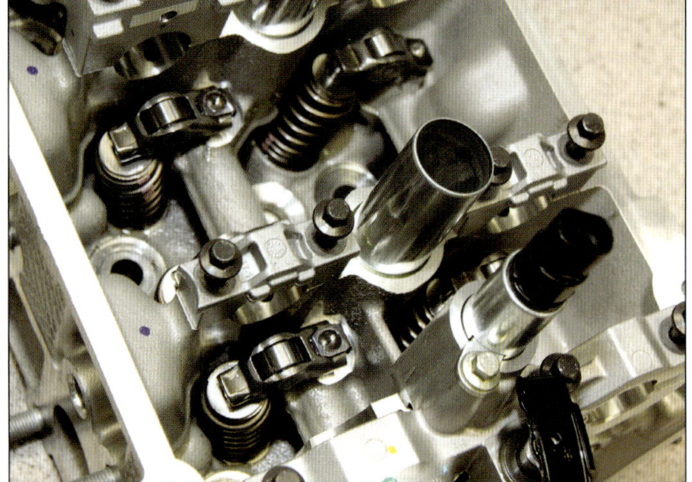
The Gen III Coyote's proven valvetrain remains much the same with stiffer springs for higher 7,500-rpm redline performance.

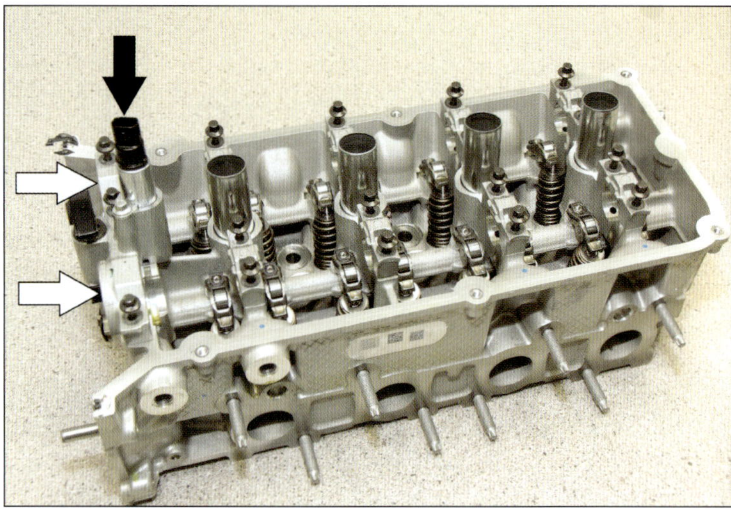
The left-hand Gen III head is a completely different casting compared with the Gen II. Exhaust cam #1 journals are larger. The exhaust cam phaser solenoid has been relocated to the cylinder head (black arrow).

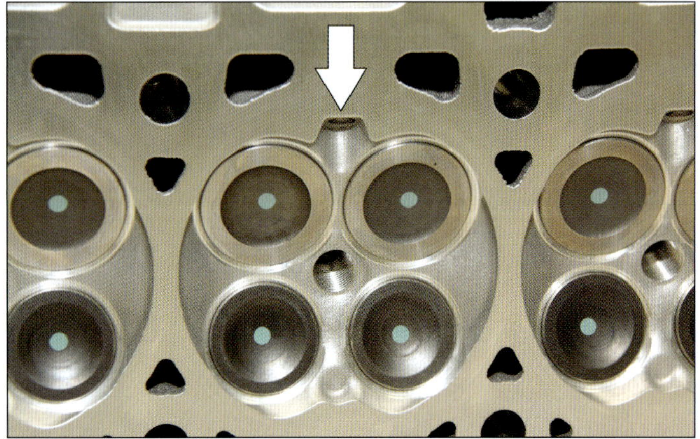
The Gen III combustion chamber has been revised to accommodate direct injection (arrow) along with larger valves and improved airflow on par with the GT350 CNC-ported Voodoo heads. Chamber volume is 55.9 cc, which is smaller than the Gen II's 57 cc to bump compression to 12.0:1. Intake valve sizing is 37.7 mm (1.484 inch), which makes it 0.4 mm larger than Gen II. Exhaust valves are 32 mm (1.259 inches), which is 0.22 mm larger than the Gen II. Not bad for a box stocker.

The Gen III head gaskets have been revised for improved cooling and cylinder sealing. They do not interchange with Gen II.

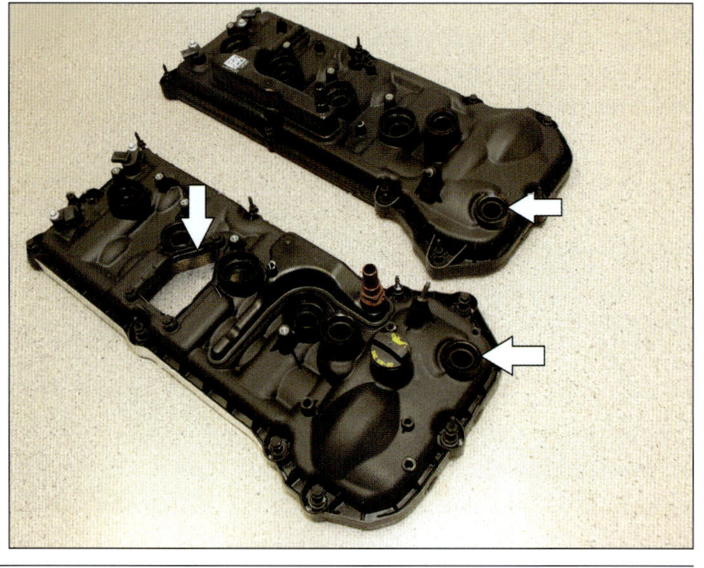
Valve covers are different than Gen I and Gen II due to the dual-injection fuel system. The greatest difference is the direct-injection-pump pedestal located midway on the right-hand valve cover. The exhaust cam-phaser solenoids protrude through each of the valve covers because these solenoids are now in the cylinder heads instead of ahead of the cam phasers in front.

Camshaft and Valvetrain

When Team Coyote was finished with cylinder head casting development, it had to go back and look at cam profile and the very size and weight of valvetrain components. Ford had to improve mechanical advantage between the camshaft and valvesprings by reducing load. Reduced load came from larger cam lobes, which was a nuance that began with the 4.6L SOHC engine a quarter-century ago.

A lot of research and development went into these heads to get them where Ford engineers wanted them in terms of size. Consider high-revving motorcycle engines: This is what Ford was faced with in developing the Coyote. Coyote heads and parts had to get smaller, as did valvetrain components. Rocker arms had to be smaller to improve both efficiency and performance. Less reciprocating weight on top meant freedom of speed at higher-RPM ranges.

Put the 4.6L DOHC and 5.0L Ti-VCT DOHC rocker arms side by side and you see the obvious difference in size. The Coyote's rocker arms are smaller. The 5.0L and 5.2L engines do it with less mass and weight. Furthermore, it enabled Ford to reduce cylinder head size and width, reducing overall engine width. The result has been a higher-revving engine with less mass from shoulder to shoulder. In fact, the Coyote is small enough to fit into a 1979–1993 Fox Mustang or the 1994–2004 SN-95 thanks to this overall reduction in size.

The Coyote's valvetrain system is the most complex ever installed in a Mustang or F-Series truck and it is designed to optimize all driving conditions. Remember that "Ti-VCT" stands for "Twin Independent Variable Cam Timing." This means intake and exhaust cams work independent of each other based on driving demands. The system advances cam timing on each side as necessary based on conditions and throttle position. Each camshaft is indexed, or phased, around its centerline by oil

The Coyote's overhead cam Variable Cam Timing (VCT) system is the most advanced in Ford history. It advances cam timing as required by the PCM. Oil pressure, which is applied to the cam phasers by electronic solenoids at each phaser, advances cam timing by turning the cam on its axis. For 2011–2014, this system isn't as advanced as it is for 2015–2017 where cam timing is more finite in scope.

These are the cam phasers, which advance cam timing based on PCM input via solenoids at each phaser. This is the right-hand-side (passenger) cylinder bank.

Here's the left-hand (driver) cylinder head with the same cam phasers and solenoids. The timing chain drives the exhaust cam. The exhaust cam sprocket (right) drives the intake cam sprocket (left). Oil pressurized chain tensioners maintain chain tension at the cam phasers and secondary timing chains.

In back of each cylinder head are trigger wheels at the end of each camshaft (top arrows). In the cylinder head is a Hall Effect sensor for each cam (bottom arrows). The sensors are missing here; arrows indicate the sensor bung holes in the head.

pressure. Oil pressure is metered electronically via solenoids and phasers to control cam indexing as required.

Ti-VCT enables the Coyote to deliver a wide power band across the RPM while giving you the bonus of high-end horsepower, which was never easy to achieve before with conventional methods. Cam torque actuation, which uses valvespring energy to retard timing more quickly depending on engine RPM and driving demands, is the feature that sets the Coyote's Ti-VCT apart from the rest of the Ford line. Instead of a complex electronically controlled shuttle valve and oiling system routing, the Coyote's Ti-VCT is a simple on/off

The Coyote V-8 employs a similar camshaft drive system to the 4.6L and 5.4L DOHC engines with a timing chain for each bank, which drives the exhaust cam. A smaller secondary chain between cams drives the intake cam.

solenoid to advance valve timing; cam torque from valvespring pressure does the retarding. Oil pressure advances cam timing and cam torque from spring pressure retards timing.

Ti-VCT can advance/retard valve timing by as much as 50 degrees and do it in .2 second. This approach offers you modest valve timing on the way to work and more aggressive valve timing when it's time to get it on. For the environmentally conscious, the Coyote doesn't need EGR (exhaust gas recirculation) because valve overlap is increased in certain types of driving, especially deceleration, which reduces hydrocarbon emissions.

In order to do the complex work of Ti-VCT and other critical functions, Ford's EEC (Electronic Engine Control) was asked to do more than it ever had in its history. It became known as the Copperhead system, a new multi-channel system designed to control every aspect of engine and driveline including Ti-VCT. Instead of a simple on/off system of cam modulation, Ti-VCT advances valve timing on each cam for fine-tuned operation. Electronic control monitors and controls oil pressure to the cam phasers. It isn't just advance/retard; it actually modulates

What makes the Coyote different is the VCT sprockets/phasers that index the cams based on PCM input and oil pressure modulation at the phasers. As with the 4.6L and 5.4L engines there are chain guides and tensioners that keep the chains tight. Tensioners are oil pressure modulated.

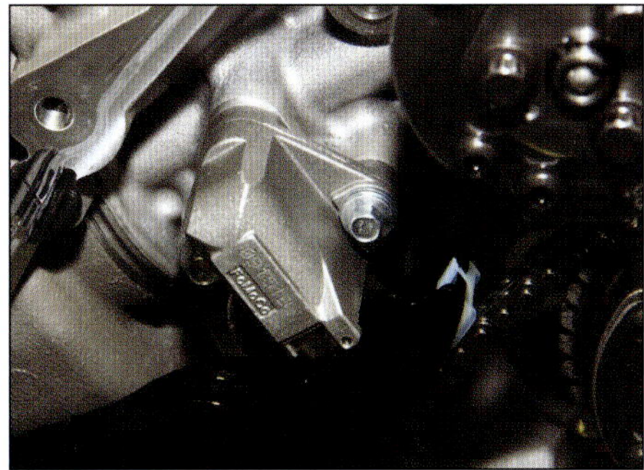

Here's a close-up look at the left-side oil pressure–actuated chain tensioner. These are no-adjust components. They apply pressure to the chain guide to maintain chain tension.

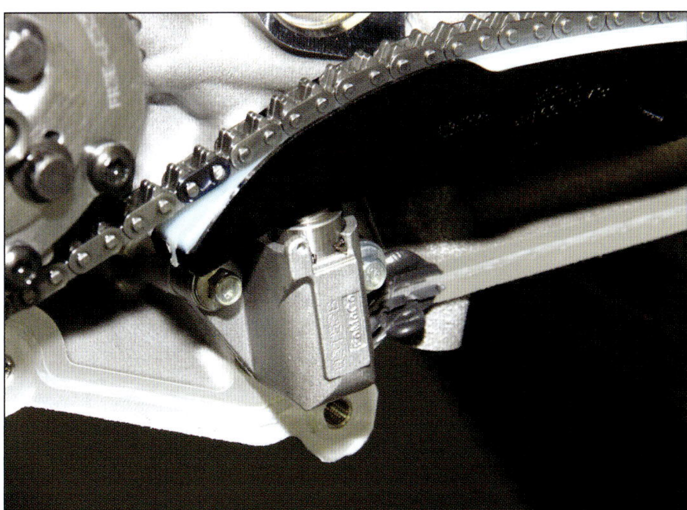

This is the right-hand (passenger) chain tensioner. It is, in principle, virtually the same as the 4.6L and 5.4L chain guide system.

Both timing chains meet at the crank sprocket as shown. The left-bank (driver) chain is installed first, then the right (passenger). Timing marks on the links and gears allow timing adjustment during chain installation.

both elements in degrees based on driving demands.

Ti-VCT isn't something you need to worry about maintaining or tuning. It is a "life of the engine" system. If the cam phasers fail, they're easily replaced by removing the cam and timing covers, aligning timing marks, and replacing the phasers. What makes the Coyote's phasers different from the 3V Modular's is cam position sensor location, which is at the opposite end of the cam on the Coyote.

On top is a look at the complete valvetrain system. Before you are the intake and exhaust cams, which ride in pressurized journals on an oil wedge. Beneath the cams are finger-style roller rocker arms, which are positioned on top of lash adjusters.

This chain tensioner is properly prepared for installation. The installation pin keeps the tensioner piston compressed. After you have the chains, guides, and tensioners installed, the pin is pulled, which applies chain tension.

These lightweight petite roller rocker arms are a no-adjust affair. Pressurized hydraulic lash adjusters or followers maintain valve lash. Moreover, these rockers can withstand the severe punishment of a radical cam and 1,500 to 2,000 hp.

Cam sprocket phasers advance cam timing as solenoids actuate a button in the middle of the phaser, which is valved to modulate cam movement. These phasers are interchangeable from side to side. These are 2011–2014 phasers. The 2015–2017 phasers are different in both appearance and function. The "R" and "L" timing marks are left- (driver) and right-bank (passenger) installation.

The back side of the phasers shows the modulation valve in the center.

These PCM-triggered solenoids meter oil pressure to the cam phasers to advance cam timing (VCT). There is a difference between 2011–2014 and 2015–2017 VCT systems. You must have complete compatibility, all 2011–2014 or all 2015–2017.

Here are the Coyote's twin cams: one intake and one exhaust. At one end of each cam are the triggers/reluctors. At the other end is the cam phaser (not pictured here) journal.

A close-up view of the cam phaser end with its oil passages for cam phaser function. This end goes toward the front of the engine. The "D"-shaped indent is also a timing mark for proper cam indexing during installation.

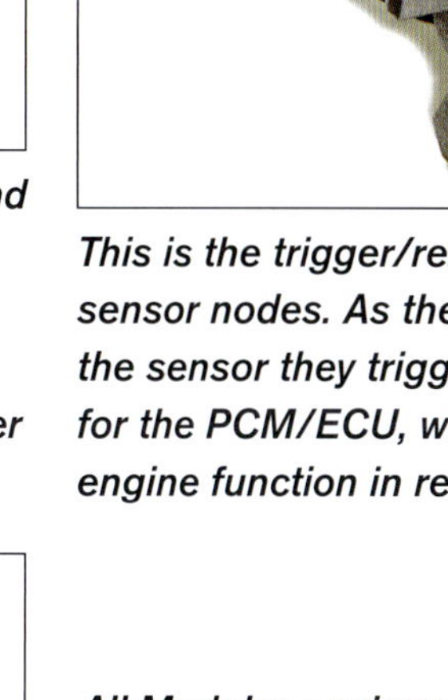

This is the trigger/reluctor end with its sensor nodes. As these nodes pass the sensor they trigger a pulse signal for the PCM/ECU, which controls engine function in real time.

All Modular engines, including the 4.6L, 5.4L, 6.2L, and the new 5.0L, are factory fitted with composite camshafts, which are a hollow tube with individual lobes that are positioned onto the shaft as shown. Note the deep peen marks in each lobe.

Improving the Coyote Valvetrain System

What can you do to improve the Coyote's valvetrain system? The Coyote's rocker arms are petite, stamped-steel, heavy-duty rollers that can stand up to the punishing abuse of the most aggressive cam profiles. At present, the aftermarket isn't producing a roller rocker for the Coyote. As cam profile aggressiveness increases, however, valvespring pressure must increase accordingly. The key to durability and performance is matched components from the aftermarket. Ideally, you buy camshafts and springs as a set. Your cam manufacturer can advise you on which spring, retainers, and keeper to choose.

Unless you are going racing or are on a steady diet of street/track it makes little sense to lock in cam timing. If you opt for a hotter cam you're going to need to install cam phaser limiters or adjustable sprockets for more controlled valve timing.

You may opt for a more aggressive cam profile from Comp Cams or Ford Performance Parts and wind up with a user-friendly valve action program that infuses more power into your Coyote. Cam swaps are easy on the Coyote. Even valvespring replacement is straightforward if you have the right tools. You can do a cam and/or valvespring swap without pulling the heads. And if you have to pull heads for something like CNC port work, cylinder head removal and replacement is straightforward whether you have a Mustang or F-Series truck.

When you are performing top-end work on your Ti-VCT Coyote, you're going to need the head swap kit (M-6067-M50) from Ford Performance Parts. Cometic and Fel-Pro cylinder head gaskets are another viable option available from your local auto parts store or Summit Racing Equipment. Always replace cylinder head and cam journal bolts, which are torque-to-yield and can only be used once. Once torque-to-yield bolts have stretched one time they're basically a throwaway and should not be used again.

Camming Up

Ford did a good job of camming the Ti-VCT Coyote from the factory, including the Boss 302 sticks. However, Comp Cams has undertaken a lot of research and development time with the Coyote and come up with aggressive cam profiles engineered to meet some of the toughest street and strip requirements.

Comp Cams claims that its billet hydraulic roller cams for the Coyote unlock a lot of hidden power, which I have proven via dyno testing at JGM Performance Engineering for this book. Cams are available for naturally aspirated and blown applications with three cam profiles each from Comp. Each is dynamic balanced for smooth operation in the Coyote. Comp Cams says the XFI NSR (191160) cam can produce as much as 417 hp and 382 ft-lbs of torque at the rear wheels with long-tube headers and a JLT induction system, based on in-house testing.

We have dyno tested a 2011–2014 crate Coyote from Ford Performance at JGM Performance Engineering and experienced in excess of 500 hp at the crank from both the Ford Performance Boss 302 cams and the Comp Cams 191160 with Boss 302 and Cobra Jet induction. With the Comp 191160 grind and Cobra Jet induction it came in just shy of 600 hp.

The Coyote's front timing cover has nothing in common with the 4.6L engine it replaces. It is not interchangeable.

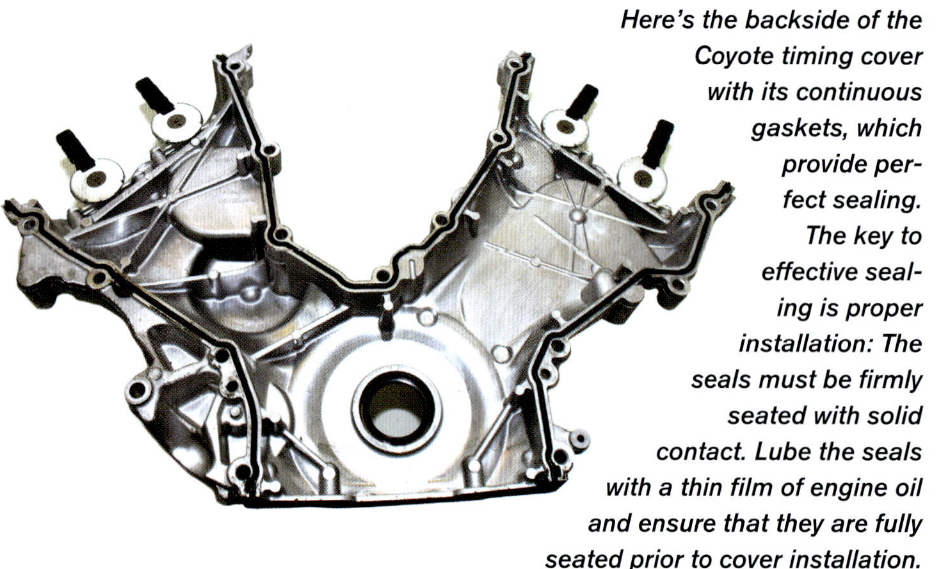

Here's the backside of the Coyote timing cover with its continuous gaskets, which provide perfect sealing. The key to effective sealing is proper installation: The seals must be firmly seated with solid contact. Lube the seals with a thin film of engine oil and ensure that they are fully seated prior to cover installation.

Ford Performance Boss Cam

The 2012–2013 Boss 302 camshaft set (M-6550-M50EXT and M-6550-M50BINT) offers more lift and duration for improved performance without having to use cam phaser locks. These cams were used in both the Boss 302 Coyote and the Cobra Jet. They are good cams for the money with few modifications required.

Boss 302 Cam Specifications

	Lift (mm)	Duration (degrees)
Intake	12 (.472 inch)	260
Exhaust	13 (.512 inch)	263

Chains and Guides

The 5.0L Ti-VCT Coyote has a series of timing chains and guides similar to the 4.6L DOHC engine. Chain tensioners are oil pressure modulated just like the 4.6L/5.4L engines. Chains travel through plastic

Although the Coyote's finger-style roller rocker arm and lash adjuster resemble those on the 4.6L/5.4L Modular family, these rockers are downsized from their Modular cousins and are not interchangeable. At press time the aftermarket hasn't produced a high-performance roller rocker arm for the 5.0L Coyote. The factory stamped-steel roller rocker can withstand 1,500 to 2,000 hp, which makes it suitable for any Coyote project.

Comp Cams Grinds

Part Number	*RPM Range*	*Advertised Intake Duration (degrees)*	*Advertised Exhaust Duration (degrees)*	*Intake Duration at .050 inch (degrees)*	*Exhaust Duration at .050 inch (degrees)*	*Intake Lift (inch)*	*Exhaust Lift (inch)*	*Lobe Separation Angle (degrees)*	*Details*
191060	1,500–6,800	260	267	220	223	0.492	0.453	126	Great stock upgrade with gains over 4,500 rpm; calls for phaser limiter kit and ECU programming
191100	1,700–7,000	268	275	228	231	0.492	0.453	126	Power gains in mid- to upper-RPM range; calls for phaser limiter kit and ECU programming
191160	1,900–7,200	276	283	236	239	0.492	0.453	126	Maximum effort street/strip; strong power gains above 5,500–7,200 rpm; calls for phaser limiter kit and ECU programming
191260	1,500–6,900	260	271	220	227	0.492	0.453	128	Blower cam; calls for phaser limiter kit and ECU programming.
191360	1,700–7,100	268	279	228	235	0.492	0.453	128	Blower cam; big power increases in mid- to high-RPM ranges; calls for phaser limiter kit and ECU programming
191460	2,000–7,300	276	287	236	243	0.492	0.453	128	Blower cam; maximum effort street/strip cam; high RPM use; calls for phaser limiter kit and ECU programming
243420	1,500–6,900	263	277	227	229	0.516	0.514	127	For 2015–up. Power upgrade for stock engine
243430	1,850–7,250	267	281	231	233	0.516	0.514	129	For 2015–up. Power gains in mid- to high-RPM ranges
243440	2,000–7,500	271	285	235	237	0.516	0.514	131	For 2015–up. Maximum effort street/strip cam
243460	1,900–7,300	267	285	231	237	0.516	0.514	130	2015–up. Blower Cam. Great power upgrade across the board
243480	2,100–7,600	275	293	239	245	.516	.514	134	2015–up. Blower cam; maximum effort street/strip cam
433420	1,900–7,600	276	286	228	230	0.550	0.550	123	Stage 1 grind for 2018–up Coyote; best for factory intake and stock gearing; great power and response
433430	2,100–7,900	280	290	232	234	0.550	0.550	125	Stage 2 grind for 2018–up Coyote. Best for increased gearing, headers, and intake, operating above the factory redline
433560	2,000–7,900	280	294	232	238	0.580	0.580	126	Stage 1 blower/turbo grind for 2018–up Coyote; optimized with higher lift for part number 26001 spring kits, allowing more RPM and added exhaust for forced induction; stiffer valve springs required
433580	2,500–8,400	288	302	240	246	0.590	0.580	130	Stage 2 blower/turbo grind for 2018–up Coyote; close to a competitive NHRA factory shootout or race turbo grind but mild enough for limited street use; Valve spring upgrade required.
433700	2,000–7,600	276	309	228	238	0.550	0.540	124	2018–2023 Gen III, maximum effort street/strip cam
433710	2,000–7,600	280	313	232	242	0.550	0.540	126	2018–2023 Gen III, maximum effort street/strip cam

Note: The 2015–2017 Coyote engines do not require modified cylinder heads or changes to cam phasers. The CR Series cams for 2015–2017 have revised lobe centers and more lift yet will work with stock valve springs and Ford mid-lock phasers. Two upgrade spring kits are available if you desire greater spring pressures. Gen III engines call for a different cam package entirely due to significant differences in cams and phasers. See manufacturer websites for more information.

guides between the crank and camshaft sprockets. The installation and proper timing of these chains and sprockets is simple if you take your time and pay close attention to what you're doing. It can be said with confidence that the stock Ford chain guides take tremendous amounts of abuse in excess of 1,000 hp. They are "life-of-the-engine" pieces engineered to last 100,000 to 200,000 miles in normal use.

If you're concerned about failure issues, you can step up to hardened crankshaft gears from Modular Motorsports Racing or Ford Performance Parts. Modular Motorsports Racing (MMR) has billet chain guides for your Coyote project if you're going racing. The MMR pieces can be found in a lot of racing Coyotes, be they drag or road race. For the street only you can get by with original Ford parts, the M-6004-A504 complete chain drive kit, which is available from Ford Performance Racing Parts or Summit Racing Equipment.

If you are opting for an aftermarket high-performance camshaft package, some kits call for the installation

Hydraulic lash adjusters make the Coyote's valvetrain system self-adjusting. All you have to do is install them and forget them. These Ford lash adjusters are available in complete sets with 32 in a set. These guys operate just like a hydraulic lifter/tappet. They maintain valve lash adjustment via engine oil pressure. (Photo Courtesy Ford Performance Parts)

The Coyote's timing chain drive system is easy to understand and simple to time. All you have to do is match marked chain links and phaser/sprocket timing marks. This is a Ford Performance Racing Parts Aluminator Coyote, 9.5:1 compression, for supercharged applications. Note the stock chain guides. Yeah, it's that good.

When you're planning your Coyote project there's comfort in knowing that this engine has few weak links. Valvetrains are traditionally the weakest element in any engine. Your valvetrain system can benefit from compatible spring pressures and cam profiles. You want the best retainers and keepers money can buy, even if you're building a stocker. If you're opting for an aggressive performance cam for your Coyote, buy a complete cam and valvetrain kit.

The Modular aftermarket offers high-performance billet timing chain guides such as these from Modular Motorsports Racing (MMR). They provide extraordinary durability under extreme conditions.

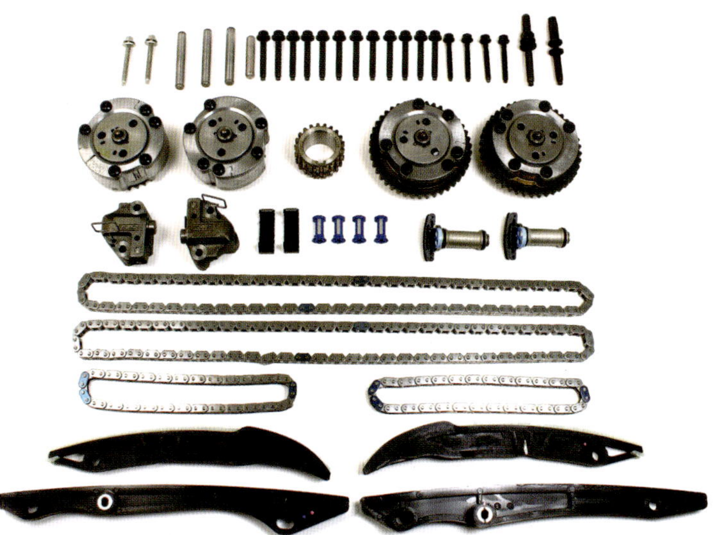

Ford Performance Racing Parts offers a complete timing system kit, M-6004-A504, for the Coyote, which makes your job as an engine builder easy. Everything you need to finish out a Coyote build is here, including timing chains, phasers/sprockets, chain guides, tensioners, crank sprocket, and all mounting hardware. (Photo Courtesy Ford Performance Parts)

Chain tensioners are available from Ford Performance Racing Parts, M-6266-M50B, if you're equipped with everything else you need to assemble the timing system package. These tensioners are powered by engine oil pressure (hydraulics) to do the grunt work of timing chain tension and security. (Photo Courtesy Ford Performance Parts)

Heavy-duty timing chain tensioners are available from Modular Motorsports Racing (MMR) for your Coyote build. These are a nice asset for a stock or modified engine build because they offer extreme durability.

If you're building a 2011–2014 Coyote, you can lock-in cam timing with these MMR cam phaser delete plates. These Ti-VCT phaser deletes eliminate 274 grams on each exhaust cam and 330 grams on each intake cam, which means 1,208 grams or 2.6 lbs of rotational weight lost, plus allowing full adjustability of your Coyote camshafts.

of cam phaser locks to keep timing consistent and eliminate the risk of valve to piston contact. Comp Cams has an adjustable cam phaser lock system that enables you to lock in cam timing. In addition, you can fine-tune the lock system for your individual requirements. MMR also manufactures an adjustable cam phaser lock kit for the Coyote.

Whenever you step up to a more aggressive camshaft, make sure that you confirm valvespring requirements from the manufacturer. If you're in doubt, go to a stiffer valvespring for better results at high RPM. Few things are more discouraging than a hot cam and valve float at high RPM. Always follow the cam manufacturer's instructions to the letter. If you get stumped, call the manufacturer's tech line. The one thing you do not want is bent valves or more serious engine damage because you didn't follow instructions.

The nice thing about the Coyote is the easy access to camshafts, valvetrain, and cam phasers. Remove

These are Comp Cams' fully adjustable cam phaser elimination plates, which enable you to lock in cam timing. These plates are easy to access on the Coyote, enabling you to fine-tune cam timing quickly.

the cam and timing covers and it is all right there for easy access. The key to success is getting the number-1 piston at true top dead center with all of the marked timing chain links at the marks before you start swapping cams. When you are there, never change either the cam or chain position. If you are performing a cam swap, take note of camshaft position and install new cams at the exact same indexing. If you are not focused, this is an easy mistake to make.

Based on dyno testing at JGM Performance Engineering and a series of cam and induction system swaps, we've learned that you can make at least 100 more hp with a box-stock Coyote. The key is to choose a camshaft carefully based on the kind of driving you will do most of the time. Cam tech help lines can be very helpful, helping you to choose the right cam and spring combo. If you're content with the factory's Ti-VCT system, stay with it; and use phaser limiters when required. If you prefer to lock in valve timing, degree in the cams carefully along with a professional performance tune while you're at it. In fact, a professional performance tune on a chassis dyno is something you must do any time you perform a cam and induction swap.

When you eliminate the cam timing phasers you no longer need the VCT solenoids, which protrude through the cam covers. Remove solenoids and plug cam cover holes.

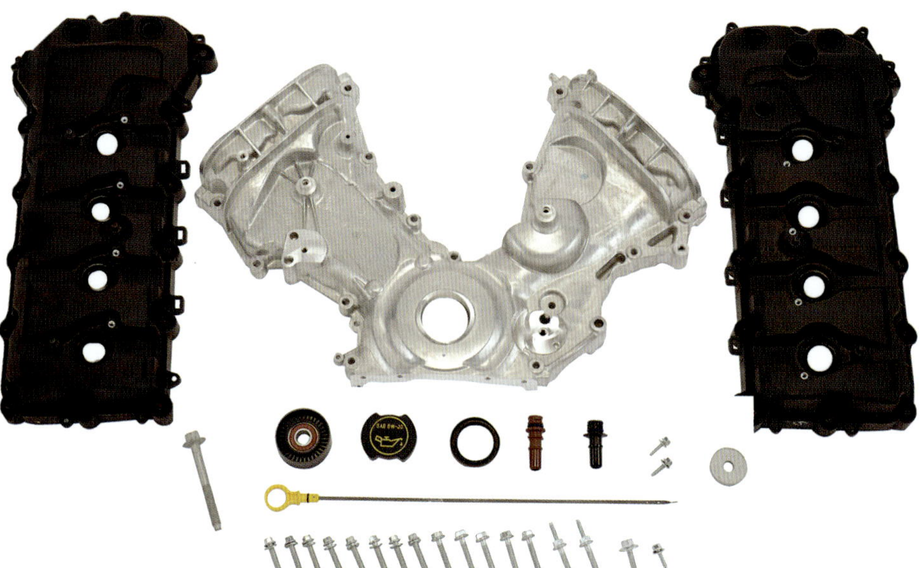

If you're building a Coyote from scratch and are beginning with a short-block and heads, it's nice to know that you can still buy everything new from Ford Performance Parts. This is the M-6580-M50-1 timing and cam cover kit, which includes everything, including idler pulleys and all hardware. Everything is here to button it up. (Photo Courtesy Ford Performance Parts)

Gen III Camshaft and Valvetrain

The Gen III Coyote heads are fitted with more-aggressive camshafts that provide greater lift with the same duration (14 mm/263 degrees on both intake and exhaust) as the Gen II engine. The Gen III cams still employ the same twin independent variable cam timing approach as the Gen II. However, instead of a separate solenoid in front of the exhaust cam phaser, phaser operation is modulated via a solenoid control valve in the cylinder head behind the phaser. When you inspect the exhaust cam phaser, you will see a return spring. The exhaust cam does not return to center with oil pressure. Instead, it uses a "watch spring" like the 3V 4.6 and 5.4L Modular engines.

Because the Gen III camshafts are different than Gen I and Gen II, you must opt for an aftermarket cam and phasers that are compatible with the Gen III head, cams and phasers. Because you are dealing with a different journal size and the addition of a direct-injection pump cam lobe, there's no interchangeability with Gen I and Gen II. Another notable change to the Gen III valvetrain system is a greater rocker-arm ratio, more lift, greater valve-spring installed height, and a longer valve stem. Finally, Ford went back to the 12-mm head bolt used on the Gen I engine in light of issues that needed attention.

The Gen III camshaft package is just different enough to be in a league of its own. There's a larger #1 exhaust cam journal (arrow) on both sides, which means these cams are not interchangeable with Gen I and Gen II. There's greater valve lift (14 mm) but the same duration. On the right-hand side (not pictured) is an additional direct injection pump lobe on the intake cam.

This overhead view of the left-hand cylinder doesn't yield much difference from Gen I and Gen II. However, changes are significant, including larger #1 exhaust cam journals and a corresponding difference in the head casting. The intake cam solenoid valve (black arrow) is at the front of the phaser. When actuated, it opens the cam phaser valve, advancing the cam. Oil pressure also returns the intake cam to center. The exhaust cam solenoid behind the exhaust phaser (yellow arrow) advances the exhaust cam. A watch-spring-style spring returns the exhaust cam to center.

The right-hand head is virtually a mirror image of the left-hand head with intake and exhaust cams modulated the same way. What makes it different is the pedestal for the direct-injection pump (arrow) and one additional cam lobe to actuate the pump.

On the right-hand side is this very different exhaust cam with a direct-injection pump lobe that actuates the pump, which is located beneath the follower shown here in the bore. This is the direct-injection pump pedestal and follower.

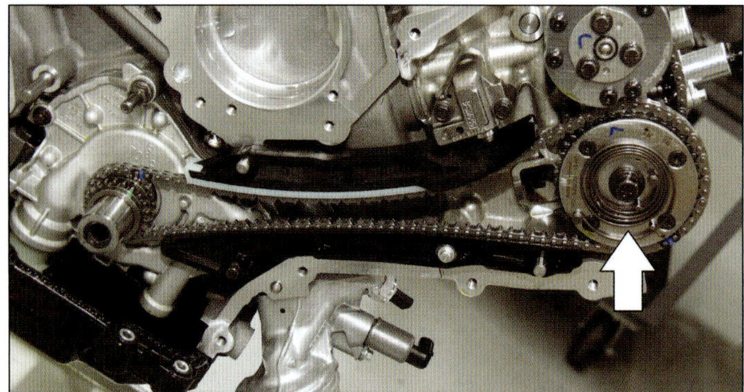

The primary timing chains are the same as the Gen II engine. However, the exhaust cam phasers are different. The intake phaser, which is oil-pressure modulated, remains the same as Gen II. The exhaust phaser is oil-pressure modulated internally via a solenoid in front, but the spring is returned like the 3V 4.6L and 5.4L Modular engines.

The Gen III cam phasers work differently than Gen I and Gen II and, therefore, are not interchangeable with Gen I and Gen II. The intake cam phaser works the same way as Gen I and Gen II, using signaled oil pressure. The exhaust cam advances via oil pressure and returns to center via spring pressure (spring shown here).

Gen III chain tensioners look like this. Set up the chains and sprockets and pull this pin on each to apply tension.

The right-hand side is a replay of the left with the same primary chain, guides, and tensioners as Gen I and II.

The backside of the Gen III's cam phasers show how different the exhaust cam phaser is and that it is not interchangeable with Gen I and Gen II.

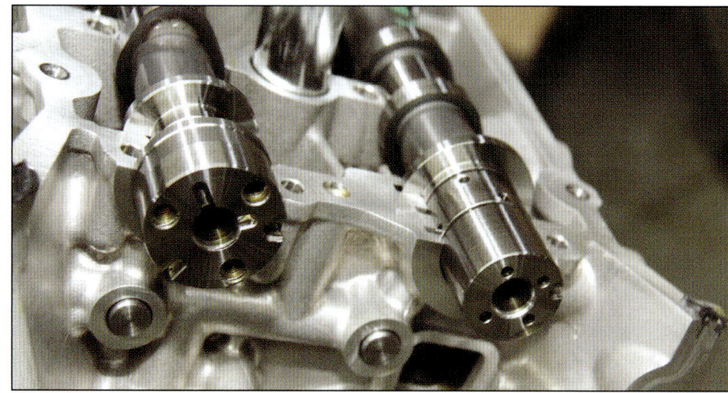

Check out the Gen III camshafts and how they differ from Gen I and Gen II Coyotes. On the left is the intake cam, which differs little in function from the Gen I and Gen II. Where the exhaust cam differs is #1 journal sizing, which is larger, and how the exhaust cam is modulated. Instead of a solenoid ahead of the exhaust cam, the solenoid is located in the head. Oil pressure is modulated via the in-head solenoid valve to the exhaust cam. The exhaust cam phaser is attached to the cam with a single bolt.

CHAPTER 7

INDUCTION

The Coyote's induction system is easily the most advanced in Ford history. It is a composite design that has become mainstream today because it is both lighter and a great heat insulator. It stays cool and keeps the intake charge cooler. It is also easier to manufacture.

Induction design and tuning has changed considerably thanks to computer-aided design and a lot of midnight oil at Ford. The Coyote's intake manifold, also known as a plenum, is single plane with long intake runners for a broad torque curve. These are long, 16.9-inch (430-mm), runners with gentle turns for improved flow. They are scrolled deep into the valley to allow for a lower hoodline. Because Ford has eliminated the coolant tube in the Modular engine's valley, there's more room for induction wizardry. The 80-mm throttle body is centered at the front of the engine on top. Another great evolution is a digital mass air sensor for extremes of fine-tuning as you drive.

The Coyote has traditional port injection because Ford engineers felt it didn't need direct injection at that time. A lot of development work is yet to be done before Coyote receives direct injection. The Coyote's cylinder head castings have a provision for direct injection, which tells you where Ford is headed with this engine. Ford just isn't there yet, but look for the Coyote to get direct injection and even Ecoboost in time, perhaps by 2018–2019. The ultimate factory Coyote could be considered one with Ecoboost.

The Coyote is available with two basic types of induction packages: conventional single-plane long runner (2011–2014) and Charge Motion Control Valve (2015–up) that allows you to change intake runner length via flapper valves, thereby improving idle and low-end performance quality. The factory Coyote induction system is an adequate

The Coyote's induction system is easy to understand. From 2011 to 2014 you have this simple long-runner, single-plane plastic intake manifold and an 80-mm throttle body. Function is very simple with little more than the throttle body, non-return fuel system, and the evaporative emissions canister purge control valve (arrow).

What makes the 2011–2014 intake manifold different from 2015–up is the absence of CMCV and vacuum actuators. This makes the 2011–2014 manifold simple in scope and function compared to 2015–up.

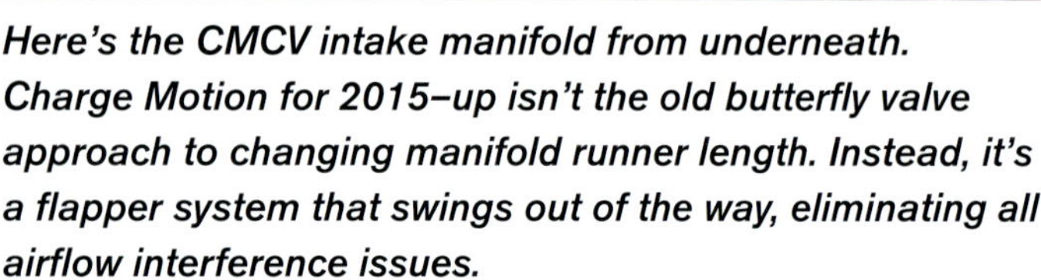

Here's the CMCV intake manifold from underneath. Charge Motion for 2015–up isn't the old butterfly valve approach to changing manifold runner length. Instead, it's a flapper system that swings out of the way, eliminating all airflow interference issues.

The Coyote has a "drive-by-wire" electronically controlled 80-mm throttle body. It is an electric-motor gear-drive throttle body, which is controlled by the PCM/ECU. Behind it is the evaporative emissions purge valve (arrow). The Coyote tends to respond differently to accelerator pedal movement because it is drive-by-wire and doesn't react in linear fashion when you romp on the gas. The key to success is smooth throttle tip-in.

Ford made significant changes to Coyote induction for 2015–up with CMCV, which varies the length of the intake runners to improve low-end performance and idle quality. CMCV and the 2015-2017 Coyote cylinder head are a married package, meaning that they were designed for each other. The 2015–2017 head has extended intake port flanges designed to accommodate the CMCV intake manifold.

These are the Charge Motion Control Valve actuators at the back of the manifold. Two actuators (left bank and right bank) control the Charge Motion flapper valves. They function primarily at low RPM ranges for improved torque and idle quality.

This is the evaporative emissions canister purge valve located in front above the throttle body, which is cycled by the PCM/ECU based on driver input and conditions. If you're doing a Coyote swap into an older vehicle, this valve gets capped off. However, it must be connected for proper PCM/ECU function.

Here's another look at the CMCV actuators, which are vacuum-controlled and sensed by the PCM/ECU sensors (arrows) at each actuator to indicate CMCV position.

The Coyote has a non-return electronic fuel injection system, which means no return line back to the fuel tank.

The Coyote's fuel rail system isn't just raw plumbing like we've long been used to. This is a really nice boxed stainless rail with Bosch EV14/US Car pencil-style 24 lb/hr fuel injectors.

This is the right-hand-side (passenger) fuel rail with four Bosch EV14/US Car injectors. The aftermarket, specifically BBK and Summit Racing Equipment, offers a wealth of billet aluminum fuel injector rails for the Coyote if you seek improved heat dissipation qualities and good looks.

This Ford Performance Racing Parts illustration shows the 2011–2014 intake manifold's right-hand side with its generous runners and rugged construction. (Photo Courtesy Ford Performance Parts)

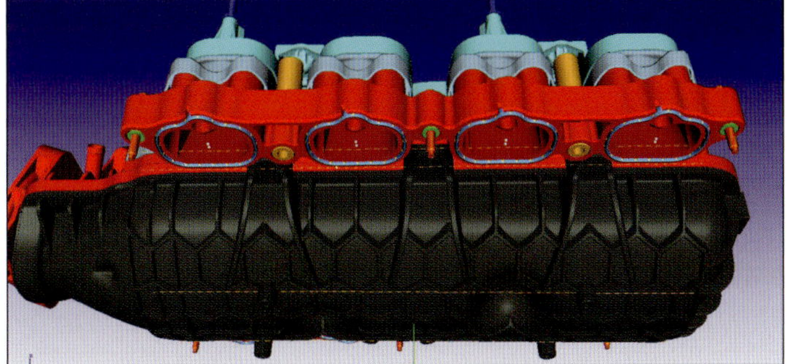

Here's the flip side of the 2011–2014 manifold's left-hand (driver) side. This may help you understand why the 2015-up cylinder head is a rough interchange. The 2015–up head's extended intake port flange presents clearance issues when mated to the 2011–2014 intake manifold. (Photo Courtesy Ford Performance Parts)

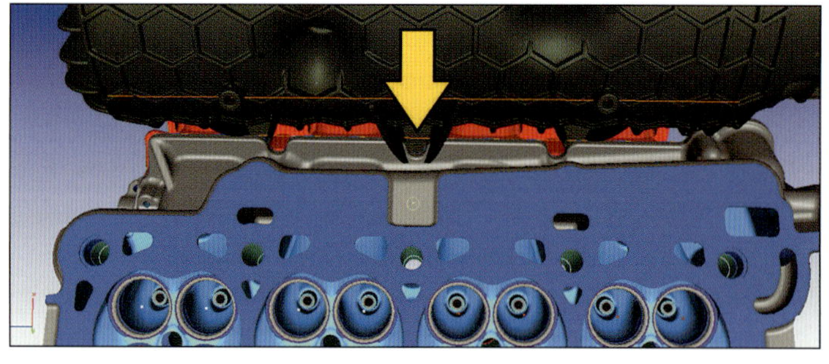

Here's an even better example of what you can expect to find with 2015–up cylinder heads on a 2011–2014 Coyote. You have to modify the manifold (arrow) to get the manifold to clear the extended lip. This is a trial-by-error approach to swapping. (Photo Courtesy Ford Performance Parts)

performance manifold, especially with CMCV. However, optional factory and aftermarket manifolds are engineered to make it better. Edelbrock appears to be the front-runner with a new aftermarket intake manifold for the Coyote; other aftermarket companies are following suit.

Because there are two types of Coyote engines (2011–2014 and 2015–up), there's not much interchangeability. You can run 2015–2017 heads on your 2011–2014, but you must be mindful of the broader intake port flange on the 2015–2017 cylinder head, which creates clearance issues with the 2011–2014 intake manifold. It does not fit out of the box. You can make minor modifications to the 2011–2014 to get this manifold to clear the flange.

The Ford Performance Racing Parts Boss 302 manifold, M-9424-M50B, is a simple swap for any 2011–2014 Coyote engine. It is your first step toward real power from a stock or Aluminator crate Coyote from Ford Performance Racing Parts. See the install of a Ford Performance Racing Parts Coyote stocker in Chapter 12. You need the M-9444-M50B Boss 302 manifold installation kit to get this guy onto your Coyote. (Photo Courtesy Ford Performance Parts)

Boss 302

The 2012–2013 Boss 302 intake manifold/plenum, M-9424-M50BR, is a high-performance single-plane piece that you can bolt onto your Coyote in a day to net a real increase in power. It is also priced to sell at just under $500 at press time. You also need the larger Ford Performance Parts 90-mm throttle body for best results. This manifold rocks for a factory induction system and it's a perfect fit because it was factory installed on the 2012–2013 Boss 302 Mustang. If you want to take this modification all the way, opt for the Boss 302 cylinder heads (no longer available from Ford Performance Parts, but still on the shelves elsewhere) or a CNC head-port job from Total Engine Airflow. Fit your CNC-ported heads with more aggressive cams with good streetability yet excellent road course manners. With the Ford

The Ford Performance Racing Parts Cobra Jet induction system, M-9424-M50CJ, serves a different purpose than the Boss 302 intake. Where the Boss 302 intake is more all-around mid- to high-range street and strip performance, the Cobra Jet intake is more wide-open throttle full-on racing because it loves high RPM. You're going to need the twin-bore GT500 throttle body, M-9926-SCJ. Like the Boss 302 intake, the Cobra Jet manifold is 2011–2014 only and does not fit the 2015–up due to CMCV. (Photo Courtesy Ford Performance Parts)

Here's the Ford Performance Racing Parts Cobra Jet manifold with cold-air induction, M-9603-M50CJ. (Photo Courtesy Ford Performance Parts)

Performance Parts Boss 302 intake manifold you can expect up to a 61-hp increase. A professional street/strip tune is also encouraged to make the most of these modifications.

What you get from the Boss 302 induction is a higher power band. Low- to mid-range torque moves the power band higher. At high RPM is where the Boss 302 intake manifold does its best work, pushing your Coyote into the 7,000- to 7,500-rpm range. This is easily the best all-around performance intake manifold for the Coyote. It provides excellent drivability for the daily commute and weekend getaway while providing outrageous performance when it's time to get it on.

Cobra Jet

Although it is easy to compare the Boss 302 manifold to the Cobra Jet, the two manifolds are not the same. Each manifold is engineered to perform differently. Your 5.0L Coyote's stock manifold, as well as the Boss 302 manifold, is designed to perform well at low- to mid-range RPM; however, the stock manifold chokes off airflow at high RPM, which limits power.

When you want peak power on the drag strip or even on a road race course at high RPM, the Ford Racing Cobra Jet intake manifold (M-9424-M50CJ) is designed to channel more air directly into your Coyote's chambers with runners tuned for high-RPM peak power with no loss of torque. The torque factor makes the Cobra Jet manifold productive for road racing as well as drag racing.

The Ford Racing Performance Parts Cobra Jet manifold is a lightweight composite all-out racing induction system with short runners engineered for high-RPM operation. The Cobra Jet is in no way a street plenum and should never be viewed as one. Peak power rolls in around 7,750 rpm at wide-open throttle on a racetrack. Total intake volume is 635 cfm. The Cobra Jet manifold is designed for the 2011–2014 GT and 2012–2013 Boss 302 engines.

Installation of the Ford Racing Cobra Jet Intake Manifold requires either the GT500 Throttle Body (M-9926-CJ65) or a Cobra Jet Throttle Body (M-9926-SCJ). You also want to use the Cobra Jet 5.0L Cold-air Intake Kit (M-9603-M50CJ), to work with the oval Cobra Jet/GT500 throttle body.

Intake manifold selection depends on how you intend to operate your Coyote most of the time. Choose the Boss 302 for street/strip and the Cobra Jet for racing. The aftermarket is faced with a huge challenge with the Ford 5.0L Ti-VCT engine: how to make it better than Ford has with better heads and induction. Thus far, Ford has come up with an engine that is virtually unbeatable in every respect. Some race shops have developed and are producing sheet-metal aluminum intake manifolds for the Coyote for professional drag racers. These tend to be custom-built pieces that have not made their way to mass production at this time.

Edelbrock Victor II

Edelbrock is the first aftermarket performance company to introduce a true high-performance intake manifold for the 5.0L Coyote. The all-new Victor II Series intake

Looking for quick bolt-on power? The M-9926-M5090 90-mm throttle body from Ford Performance Racing Parts is an improvement over the 80-mm stock piece, but honestly, you should invest wisely in not just a throttle body but also the entire induction package from Ford Racing Performance Parts. The 90-mm throttle body should be married to the Boss 302 intake plenum for best results, along with the appropriate injectors. (Photo Courtesy Ford Performance Parts)

manifold for the 2011–2014 and 2015–up Ford Ti-VCT Coyote 5.0L V-8 engine combines long-tapered crossover runners with a large plenum for incredible performance numbers. Its cast-aluminum construction (yes, cast aluminum) makes the Victor II ideal for nitrous, supercharged, and turbocharged applications. The Victor II is good for 1,500 to 7,500 rpm, making it one of the most versatile intake manifolds in history.

The Victor II manifold also includes provisions for all emissions equipment and reuses the stock fuel rail. Or, you can opt for an aftermarket billet fuel rail for an upgrade in appearance. The Victor II also features nitrous Bosses for adding a direct port system for competition applications. This slightly lower design allows it to fit all 2011–2014 and 2015–up Mustang stock hoods and strut tower braces. Edelbrock's engine dyno testing resulted in 27 more ft-lbs of torque over a common aftermarket plastic upgrade intake manifold and an additional 16 hp over a stock manifold.

You may opt for the base Coyote 80-mm throttle body from Ford or the optional 90-mm from Ford Performance Racing Parts. It is suggested you go with the larger 90-mm for best results. The Edelbrock Victor II is 50-state emissions legal.

GT350 5.2L Intake Manifold

Although this is the 5.2L GT350 intake manifold, you really need the cylinder heads that go along with it to get any real benefit. Moreover, you want to opt for the entire 5.2L engine package to get all of the benefits of Ford Performance Parts' new increased-displacement Coyote. Because this manifold is fitted with CMCV, it is really not designed for 2011–2014 Coyote engines. Here's what you get for your hard-earned money:

- GT350 intake manifold assembly with CMCV
- Requires GT350 87-mm throttle body
- Intake is tuned for 7,500-rpm peak power
- Fits 2015–up 5.0L Coyote engines

Edelbrock was the first outside of Ford Performance Racing Parts to put its toe in the water with a great high-performance intake manifold for the Coyote. As you might imagine, Edelbrock is calling this manifold the Victor II, which combines long-tapered crossover runners with a huge plenum for impressive performance numbers. This guy is cast-aluminum construction, which makes the Victor II ideal for nitrous, supercharged, and turbocharged applications. The Victor II is good for 1,500 to 7,500 rpm. (Photo Courtesy Edelbrock)

Here's the Shelby GT350 intake manifold for the 5.2L engine. What makes this manifold different from the standard Coyote intake is where it makes power. This is a high-RPM racing manifold with runners designed to come on strong at 7,500 rpm. You want the 87-mm throttle body, minimum, for this manifold, which is designed only for engines with Charge Motion Control. (Photo Courtesy Ford Performance Parts)

Here's a look at the 5.2L manifold in a 2015 GT350. The 2015–2016 Shelby GT350 is a factory racecar you can drive to work. This manifold is available as a bolt-on and with the 5.2L Coyote crate engine.

Nitrous Oxide = Cheap Power?

Nitrous oxide technology dates back to at least World War II when it was used in classic war birds to help make large amounts of power on demand and at high altitudes. The use of nitrous oxide in racing has been commonplace for decades. Much of it began with the Pro 5.0 movement in the 1990s and has spread across drag racing in the years since. Nitrous is quick and easy bolt-on horsepower; however, you must know what you're doing before making the investment. If you are careless or abusive with nitrous oxide it can cost you plenty, ranging from personal injury to complete and total engine destruction.

Summit Racing Equipment has available plenty of nitrous oxide systems for the 5.0L Ti-VCT Coyote. Should you opt for nitrous and, if so, why? Nitrous remains the easiest path to horsepower without having to knock an engine apart. You don't have to increase or decrease compression, or swap cams and valvetrain parts. All you have to do is install the system and properly tune both the fuel and the ignition systems. However, you should be educated on how to operate nitrous oxide before getting started.

David Fuller of Summit Racing Equipment explains how nitrous oxide makes power in an engine: "The principle of nitrous oxide is simple: air and fuel plus ignition equals horsepower; therefore, more air and more fuel equals more horsepower. It's the equation that nitrous systems manufacturers use to help produce incredible power gains (in some cases up to 400 extra ponies) in everything from sport compacts to dedicated race vehicles."

David goes on to say, "Still, many performance enthusiasts don't fully understand how nitrous systems make additional horsepower. More important, they don't understand how to tune their nitrous system for optimal performance. Summit Racing Equipment sells nitrous kits and accessories from top nitrous system manufacturers like NOS, Nitrous Express, Zex, Edelbrock, Trick Flow Specialties, and Venom. A nitrous oxide system enhances this combustion process (and the resulting horsepower output) by altering the air/fuel mixture three ways."

Dry Nitrous Systems

Summit Racing Equipment says that a dry nitrous system is generally the easiest way to add nitrous to a fuel-injected vehicle. Dry systems work with your existing fuel system to supply the needed fuel to make

Summit Racing Equipment offers a variety of nitrous-oxide systems for the Coyote engine. This is only one example from Nitrous Express. (Photo Courtesy Summit Racing Equipment and Nitrous Express)

ZEX from the Comp Performance Group is another popular choice from Summit Racing Equipment for the Coyote. Remember, when you opt for nitrous oxide, it is not free. You must dial in a tune that gets fuel and nitrous on the same page. If you don't have enough fuel or have too much timing, there will be serious engine damage. (Photo Courtesy ZEX)

Summit Racing Explains Nitrous Power Three Ways

1. Nitrous Changes the Oxygen Level

By injecting your engine with gaseous nitrous oxide, you're essentially adding concentrated oxygen to the intake charge. Nitrous oxide consists of two parts nitrogen and one part oxygen. When your engine receives a shot of nitrous, the heat of combustion breaks the nitrogen and oxygen apart and allows your engine to use the oxygen molecules to burn more fuel. A nitrous oxide system gives your engine the capacity to burn larger amounts of fuel by supplying the necessary oxygen to burn the greater quantity of fuel.

2. Nitrous Improves Fuel Atomization

Atomization of fuel, which is the process by which raw fuel is broken down into tiny droplets (a mist), helps the ignition spark burn fuel more quickly and efficiently. Atomization is necessary because fuel must be converted into a vapor before combustion can be achieved. Engine heat and fuel atomization are the key ingredients in accelerating this evaporation process.

Although the combustion process provides the heat, a properly designed nitrous system delivers proper fuel atomization by spraying the fuel supply in very small droplets. This promotes quicker evaporation and faster combustion in conjunction with the increased oxygen levels.

3. Nitrous Increases Air/Fuel Density

When nitrous oxide is injected, it instantly changes from a liquid to an extremely cold gas. The nitrous vapors chill the temperature of the intake charge, including the gasoline, by as much as 65 degrees F. As you probably learned back in "Horsepower 101," a colder, denser intake charge promotes greater combustion and increased horsepower production.

It's important to clear up one common misconception about nitrous: Nitrous is not a fuel and does not increase power by itself. Nitrous oxide is a great way to add the necessary oxygen to burn more gasoline. However, nitrous oxide is not combustible by itself.

To gain power, you must add more fuel or risk engine failure. The way you introduce more fuel to the intake charge depends largely on the type of nitrous system you choose. You'll find a wide range of styles for carbureted and electronically fuel-injected engines. Cheater systems, piggyback systems, plate systems, and fogger systems are available. The bottom line is that all nitrous systems fit into one of three main categories: dry, wet, or direct-port systems. ■

horsepower. Additional fuel is delivered in one of two ways. The first way is to "trick" the OEM fuel-injection system into supplying more fuel to the engine. In these cases, the nitrous system is designed to modify your factory computer's fuel curve to get the necessary fuel delivered to your engine. A second way is to increase the fuel pressure to the injectors by applying nitrous pressure from the solenoid assembly when the system is activated.

Wet Nitrous Systems

Wet nitrous systems come with their own fuel components to introduce additional fuel to your intake system. Wet systems include a separate fuel solenoid and nozzle, which spray the fuel at the same location as the nitrous. In most carbureted applications, the fuel and nitrous is introduced just below the carburetor. In fuel-injected systems, the mixture is sprayed just ahead of the throttle body.

Wet nitrous systems mix nitrous and fuel at a common injector where both are sprayed into the intake port. American Muscle explains, "The wet nitrous kit mixes nitrous with the fuel directly. This mixture is then sprayed into the intake tube near the throttle body. Many Mustang tuners prefer the wet kit because it's easier to deal with. After all, the PCM controls the air/fuel ratio. Normally, the tuner simply chooses how much timing to give the engine.

"Also, with a wet nitrous kit there is no need to upgrade your Mustang's injectors. Because the nitrous is mixed directly with fuel, there is no need to upgrade the injectors as there is no need for additional fuel over what is regulated for any one given time. You also don't run the risk of a failed sensor like the mass airflow sensor."

The downside to wet nitrous is that if it is not installed properly or it is poorly tuned, it results in a nitrous backfire/explosion, which can do significant damage.

A dry nitrous system is a standalone system that operates separately from the fuel system and is injected separately from the fuel. Dry nitrous is safer than wet and best for the beginner.

Direct-Port Nitrous Systems

The last type of nitrous system is the direct-port system. This system introduces the nitrous and fuel mixture directly into each engine cylinder. Generally, these systems inject nitrous and additional fuel together through a common nozzle. Because individual nozzles are placed above each cylinder, direct-port systems are the most accurate and most powerful. They have more tuning capabilities than other styles of nitrous systems because each nozzle can be adjusted to control the nitrous and fuel flow to the individual cylinders.

The drawback to direct-port nitrous systems is the complexity of the installation. They are typically the most complicated system to install because they require the intake manifold to be drilled and tapped to accommodate each nozzle. That's why these systems are usually reserved for race vehicles.

Nitrous oxide is one of the more popular power adders for race vehicles and street rides alike. It's generally affordable, easy to install, and delivers a power boost when you want it and normal engine operation when you don't. The result is less stress on your engine, better overall drivability, and superior fuel economy over cylinder head porting, supercharging, and other power adders.

Squeeze Easy?

Although some refer to nitrous oxide or "squeeze" as free power, it is not. Anytime you can press a button and get 100 to 500 "free" horsepower at wide-open throttle you're playing a game of Russian Roulette. If your electronic engine control isn't in a proper state of tune for nitrous oxide operation, the damage you do to your engine can be permanent. This is why you must choose, install, and tune a nitrous oxide system to your engine's best benefit. Too much nitrous and not enough fuel or perhaps too much timing and you destroy the engine in a nanosecond; it's that simple.

If you intend to run large amounts of nitrous oxide, meaning anything beyond 100 to 150 hp, you need to design and build your Coyote for greater amounts of power. A stock Coyote handles a 100- to 150-hp shot of nitrous oxide and stays together. Anything beyond 100 to 150 hp calls for forged pistons, heavy-duty I- or H-beam rods, and more generous clearances. You need more generous clearances because, with nitrous, combustion temperatures go skyward and reciprocating mass grows accordingly.

A typical basic 100- to 150-shot nitrous system can net you anywhere from 90 to 130 hp and roughly 100 to 150 ft-lbs of torque depending on atmospheric conditions, bottle temperature, and your Coyote's state of tune.

Supercharging

Manufacturers are making it easy to supercharge high-performance Fords these days. There are basically two types of supercharger systems available for the Coyote: positive displacement and centrifugal. Choice depends on what you want a supercharger to do and how you want it packaged. Positive displacement blowers are generally a drop-in replacement for the factory induction system and are located at the engine's valley. Centrifugal blowers are mounted on the front of the engine and become part of the accessory drive system along with associated ducting. It can be debated endlessly which system is best for your Coyote engine. Much of it boils down to personal choice.

Vortech has long been the supercharger of choice for late-model Ford enthusiasts. This is the V-3 Si Vortech blower system with air-to-air intercooler, which can be installed over a weekend and have you back on the road Monday. (Photo Courtesy Christopher Campbell)

Here's the good-looking V-3 Si system from another angle in the 2015 Mustang GT. Although all this plumbing looks overwhelming, this is a simple system to install. And you just can't beat the sound of a Vortech blower. (Photo Courtesy Christopher Campbell)

Centrifugal Superchargers

Vortech leads the pack when it comes to centrifugal blower technology for the Coyote. The centrifugal supercharger has long proven to be one of the most effective means of reaching increased power without making major engine modifications. You can bolt these guys on your Coyote and make quick power during a weekend. Power comes from compressing air before it enters combustion chambers. Pressurized air fills cylinder bores and mixes with atomized fuel. This results in improved cylinder filling, allowing more air and fuel to be burned in the combustion cycle, with dramatic increases in torque and horsepower.

Vortech centrifugal superchargers operate on fundamental and proven turbomachinery principles, first described by Euler's turbomachinery equation, which was developed in the 18th Century. This principle relates the work imparted to a fluid by an impeller to the change in angular momentum of the fluid. Over the past century, the centrifugal compressor has evolved and found its way to become the most efficient and reliable means for delivering charged air at high pressures.

Advanced Compressor Stage

Vortech's compressor stages have evolved considerably in more than 20 years of experience and thousands of production superchargers. All Vortech compressors incorporate sophisticated impeller designs, coupled to a parallel wall diffuser, with a progressive scroll, or volute exit stage, as air leaves the compressor. Impellers employ advanced aerodynamic features such as optimized inducer blading, splitters, and in some cases, exit rake and backsweep. Each of these elements depends on the particular pressure/flow objectives. Rather than a simple change of blower speed to effect different "models," each Vortech supercharger is optimized aerodynamically so that best performance is attained for a specific vehicle application.

In order to effectively take advantage of impeller effort, flow must be efficiently diffused so that pressure rise can be generated with minimal flow losses. The diffuser is optimally matched to the impeller flow physics; many iterations are tested and verified until maximum efficiency is achieved with each supercharger design, in this case for the Coyote. Finally, a matched volute (manifold) effectively collects and diffuses further, resulting in additional pressure rise and improved performance.

Here's the Vortech V-3 Si blower as a standalone. You do have a choice of three basic Vortech blowers depending on how much power you want and how much boost your Coyote can stand. And don't kid yourself, the V-3 Si has plenty of huff for a stock Coyote and you can expect 600 to 630 hp from this supercharger. However, power comes at a price. If you plan on pushing your engine above 600 to 630, understand the failure risk. When you get beyond these numbers, you need H-Beam rods and forged pistons. (Photo Courtesy Christopher Campbell)

Complete Vortech supercharger systems are available for manual transmission vehicles only at press time. Automatic transmission models are being developed. These blower systems for the Coyote are good for 605 hp and are 50-state smog legal. Complete, fully calibrated supercharging systems are available for the 2011–2016 5.0L Mustang GT, featuring the V-3 Si centrifugal supercharger with air-to-air charge cooler.

This complete, smog-legal system boosts the 2011–2014 Mustang GT to 605 hp and 473 ft-lbs torque with 7.5 to 8.5 psi from the V-3 supercharger at the factory redline. For 2015–2016, we're talking 630 hp and 483 ft-lbs torque with 7.5 to 8.5 psi from the V-3 supercharger. Vortech's 2011–2016 Mustang 5.0L Coyote GT Supercharging Systems are available as either a complete, fully calibrated bolt-on, or as a V-7 tuner kit for custom installations at up to 1,200 hp.

The new Mustang system uses Vortech's V-3 Si supercharger. Continued development in Vortech's lab resulted in the V-3 Si. The "i" stands for improved, with its new, patented oil control system and a state-of-the-art centrifugal compressor.

Centrifugal superchargers make more pressure and flow than a positive displacement–type blower and are more efficient.

Vortech V-3 Si Supercharger

Vortech is going to briefly walk you through the installation of its 2015–2016 Mustang GT Intercooled V-3 Si supercharger system. Although the 2015–2016 Mustang GT differs from the 2011–2014, installation is basically the same.

Vortech Tuner Kits and Upgrades

The High-Flow Competition Air Inlet Upgrade adds 20 to 40 hp on top of a 605/630 hp V-3 Si installation, and even more power when used with higher boost and more aggressive tuning. For higher-horsepower custom-tuned installations I recommend a tuner kit, which does not include a fuel pump, fuel injectors, or PCM/ECU programmer. This requires you to provide custom calibration and the required fuel components.

The V-3 Si supercharger included with the tuner kit is capable of up to 775 hp on modified vehicles. Tuner kits with the V-2 Ti compressor stage are also available and allow for up to 850 hp with the right modifications. Tuner kits are also available with the 1,000-hp V-7 JT supercharger for high-performance racing vehicles.

Vortech System Components and Features

- V-3 Si compressor with 3.60-inch-drive pulley
- Manifold boost pressure, 7.5 to 8.5 psig at redline on stock Coyote engine
- Supplied SCT programmer re-flashes the PCM/ECM with a safe custom Vortech calibration for 91-octane pump gas
- Fuel system upgrade includes fuel rail spacers and high-flow replacement fuel injectors
- Air intake assembly includes:
  - High-flow roto-molded ducting; mates to OEM air box and some aftermarket "CAI" MAF/inlet assemblies
  - OEM replacement K&N panel filter
  - Silicone sleeves and reducers
  - Stainless-steel clamps
  - PCV and breather hose provisions for both automatic and manual transmission applications
- Replacement engine coolant pipe and hose assemblies
- Engine coolant reservoir replacement assembly
- Dual plate supercharger mounting system includes idlers, drive belt, and all hardware. Mount features multiple-position idler location for a wide range of belt and pulley fits.
- Discharge components include:
  - High-flow air/air charge cooler, 24 x 13 x 3.5–inch cooler core
  - Mandrel-bent 3-inch aluminum charge tubes for high flow and minimal weight
  - Stainless-steel clamps
  - Silicone sleeves
  - 98-mm MAF housing configured for "blow-through" use. Integrated air-straightener upstream of the MAF housing.
  - Vortech Maxflow Race Bypass Valve with filter

Vortech Supercharger Pulleys

- Six-rib pulleys: 2A036-348, 2A036-340, 2A036-333, 2A036-312
- Eight-rib pulleys: 2A038-348, 2A038-333, 2A038-312, 2A038-300

Vortech Competition Air Inlet Assembly with Filter

- 4FQ112-060
- Large high-flow duct with oversized K&N filter element
- Minimum restriction for high-flow competition use
- Sealed air box
- Adds 20 to 40 hp

Fuel Pump Booster

- 5A102-029: The Maxflow fuel pump booster increases voltage to the fuel pump for increased flow to the injectors. FPB2 is microprocessor controlled and is preprogrammed for the new 5.0.
- 5A102-030: The FPB1 Maxflow fuel pump booster is like the 2 version but has a fixed voltage increase without programmability. Can be operated with a pressure switch.

High-Flow Fuel Injector Kit

Optional high-flow fuel injector kit, 8F160-046, includes adapters and spacers for direct replacement of OEM injectors. This kit is 50-state smog legal. Complete systems are smog legal per California Air Resources Board (CARB), per CARB Executive Order D-213-32. Available with complete street-legal systems sold and installed by a Vortech Top-Tier Installer. This package is not available with tuner kits. ■

Vortech V-3 Si Supercharger Installation

1 *This Vortech support bracket bolts directly to the engine first. Then come pulleys and spacers, along with the supercharger support bracket. (Photo Courtesy Christopher Campbell)*

2 *Here's the support bracket, which bolts directly to the Vortech V-3 Si. Note the belt routing and pulley locations. The drive belt is routed through the two brackets to the supercharger drive pulley. (Photo Courtesy Christopher Campbell)*

3 *This is the Vortech 87-mm throttle body, which is factory calibrated and ready to go. All you have to do is plug, play, and tune. (Photo Courtesy Christopher Campbell)*

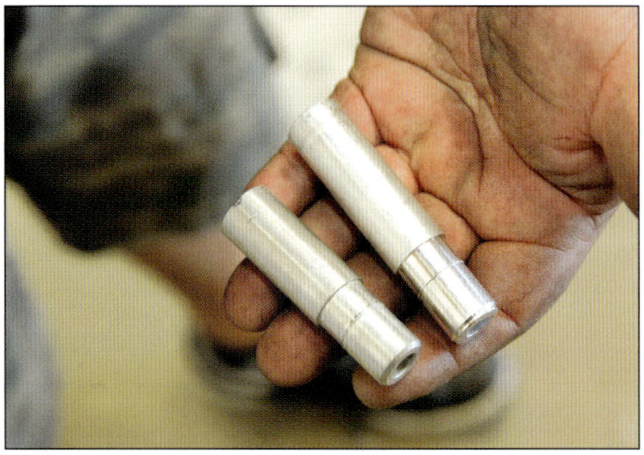

4 *Once injector plugs are disconnected, four 10-mm hex nuts hold the fuel rails to the intake. Remove these and the entire rail assembly with injectors comes out. (Photo Courtesy Christopher Campbell)*

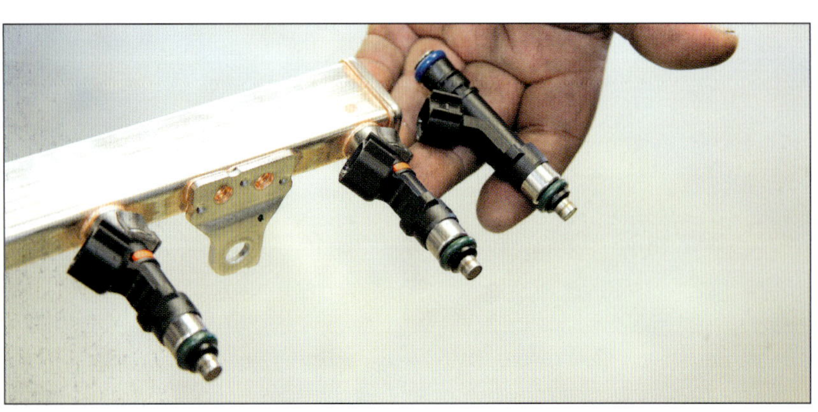

5 *With Vortech boost comes the real need for more fuel. Stock Coyote injectors are 24 lb/hr. The V-3 Si calls for EV-14 47 lb/hr injectors along with professional dyno tuning. (Photo Courtesy Christopher Campbell)*

6 The Vortech V-3 Si is installed at this time and the drive belt is looped around the pulley. Installation is simple. (Photo Courtesy Christopher Campbell)

7 Belt installation is tricky because it gets tight in there. The main thing is to be sure the belt routing is correct. Fortunately, belt tension is automatic once you have it on the pulleys. (Photo Courtesy Christopher Campbell)

8 The several air intake ducts are next. Begin at the throttle body and work your way outward. (Photo Courtesy Christopher Campbell)

9 This is the stock air cleaner housing with a K&N filter for improved filtration and airflow. The stock air cleaner works with the Vortech V-3 Si supercharger, seriously. You may also want to consider a BBK cold-air kit. (Photo Courtesy Christopher Campbell)

10 The mass air flow (MAF) sensor and duct are installed and connected as shown. Make sure all ducts are dovetailed into one another and void of leaks. (Photo Courtesy Christopher Campbell)

11 The air-to-air intercooler is easy to install once you have removed the front fascia, which is easy. It fits in front of the air conditioning condenser and radiator. (Photo Courtesy Christopher Campbell)

12 *Ductwork from the intercooler installs as shown here, connecting to the Vortech V-3 Si blower. (Photo Courtesy Christopher Campbell)*

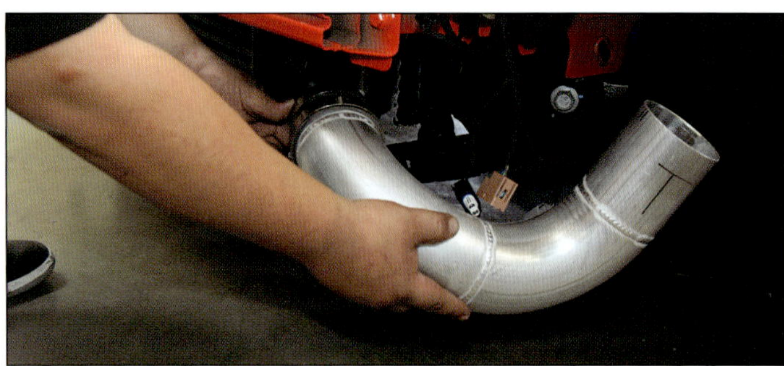

13 *More intercooler ductwork is shown here on the left-hand (driver) side. Vortech's instructions make light work of this operation. Vortech provides you with all of the information you need to complete the installation. (Photo Courtesy Christopher Campbell)*

14 *On the right-hand (passenger) side is this discharge duct with bypass valve (also known as a wastegate), which vents excess pressure to keep boost safe. (Photo Courtesy Christopher Campbell)*

15 *This is the Vortech V-3 Si intake duct from the air cleaner and MAF duct. (Photo Courtesy Christopher Campbell)*

16 *These check valves are for evaporative emissions function and are tied to the Vortech V-3 Si system. They must be installed for proper function. (Photo Courtesy Christopher Campbell)*

ROUSHcharger

There are three speedy paths to power. One is compression ratio, another is nitrous oxide, and the other is boost via supercharging or turbocharging. You get compression when you mechanically build it into an engine. Building in compression takes time and money. It can also be destructive. Nitrous is surely productive and you can get there via a simple bolt-on and proper engine tuning. However, nitrous carries with it a certain amount of risk if you don't know what you're doing.

Supercharging has always been a bolt-on path to power, and lots of it. However, supercharging does not come cheap. It also requires in-depth knowledge of how supercharging works, along with a professional tune once the system is installed. The ROUSHcharger Phase 1 positive displacement supercharger (421823) can boost performance to 670 hp/545 ft-lbs of torque for the S550 2015–up Mustang GT 5.0L Ti-VCT V-8. The Roush and Ford Racing 2.3L Phase 1 calibrated ROUSHcharger Kit is part of the TVS (Twin Vortices Series) line of superchargers developed by Roush, which raises the bar for performance and reliability. Eaton's TVS technology delivers more power and better fuel economy in a smaller package, which is what makes the ROUSHcharger good bang for the buck. This is the same caliber of quality and performance you get in a Roush Mustang.

The ROUSH R2300 TVS supercharger is a roots-type positive displacement supercharger that features twin four-lobe rotors that are twisted 160 degrees. By comparison, the original Eaton supercharger rotating assembly featured three lobes twisted 60 degrees. The fourth lobe and the additional twist, when combined with newly-redesigned air inlet and outlet ports, gives you greatly enhanced thermal efficiency, higher volumetric capacity, higher operating speeds, a smoother, more efficient flow of air into the engine, and improved noise and vibration characteristics.

Unlike turbocharging, the Roush R2300 2.3L supercharger provides instant throttle response void of lag and can generate abundant power throughout the engine's entire power band. Galpin Auto Sport (GAS) in North Hills, California, understands the power of both Roush and Ford Motor Company. This is why GAS suggested the ROUSHcharger to a

Here's the complete ROUSHcharger kit for the 2015–up Coyote V-8, 421823, about to be installed on a 2015 Mustang GT at Galpin Auto Sports (GAS) in Southern California. The 2011–2014 kit is similar. The difference between these kits is that the 2015–up has Charge Motion, which has to be bypassed when you install the ROUSHcharger. Everything imaginable is included in this kit, including spark plugs and injectors.

Roush and Ford Performance Racing Parts have teamed up to develop this OEM-calibrated supercharger system. The ROUSHcharger boosts performance to a staggering 670 hp/545 ft-lbs of torque for the all-new 2015–up Ford Mustang 5.0L V-8. The Roush and Ford Racing 2.3L Phase 1 Calibrated Supercharger Kit is part of the TVS (Twin Vortices Series) line of superchargers developed by Roush Performance.

Tools for the Job

- 1/4- and 3/8-inch-drive ratchets with extensions
- Metric and standard socket sets (short and deep recommended)
- 1/2-inch-drive ratchet or breaker bar
- Metric and standard wrench sets
- 3/8-inch-drive torque wrench (7 to 35 ft-lbs range)
- Short Phillips-head screwdriver
- 5/8-inch fuel line removal tool
- t-20 Torx bit screwdriver or socket
- 5/16-inch drill bits and drill motor
- Coolant (meeting factory Ford specification for 2011 Mustang GT)
- 6-inch scale, tape measure, or other measuring device
- Assembly lubricant (white lithium grease or petroleum jelly)
- Electrical tape
- Sharp knife or razorblade
- Solder and soldering iron
- Heat gun or small torch for heat-shrink tubing
- Tie straps (zip ties)
- Trim pad tool (for pushpin removal)
- Fender cover (2)
- Medium-strength thread locker: Loctite 242 (blue) or equivalent

customer who decided to install the R2300 on his 2015 Mustang GT. Because safety was paramount to the customer, they opted for better brakes and suspension from GAS, yielding the ultimate street Mustang rocketship.

GAS invited me into its shop for a look over the shoulder of technician Daniel Torres, who performed the complete R2300 ROUSHcharger installation, run-in, and road test. It was learned during this installation that this is not an installation to be hurried. It must be performed with patience in step-by-step fashion following Roush's instructions carefully. If you're tempted to sidestep the instructions, don't. Any detail missed is courting disaster and stands to void your warranty. When installation is complete, you must ship your PCM/ECU to Roush for programming. Never operate your supercharged Coyote engine without the Roush tune.

Supercharger Need to Know

Misinformation about the function of supercharger bypass systems abounds. The ROUSHcharger is a positive-displacement supercharger, or air pump. As long as it is rotating, it is always pumping air. During low demand or high manifold vacuum operation (i.e., idle, deceleration, and light-throttle cruise), the air pumping action is undesirable because it creates unwanted heat and noise. The bypass circuit, when open, prevents any overpressure at the supercharger and allows air to circulate through the rotors; it allows the supercharger to "idle" freely during these high-vacuum/low-pressure conditions. This results in reduced noise, and by reducing heat buildup in the intake, significantly improves street and strip performance.

As throttle demand increases, the bypass circuit is closed, resulting in maximum performance from the supercharger. The bypass circuit is never used to limit or control boost during full-throttle operation, and defeating or altering the bypass function does not result in improved performance in any condition, and results in poor drivability. You also risk engine damage in the process.

When your ROUSHcharger installation is complete, ship the PCM and its contents to ATTN: PCM FLASH, Roush Performance, 39555 Schoolcraft Road, Plymouth, MI 48170. Upon receipt of the PCM, a customer service representative will contact you to arrange payment and return.

Acronyms and Terms

ACT: Air Charge Temperature Sensor (From the factory, this function is integrated into the MAF sensor. With this kit, a separate ACT sensor is installed into the intake manifold.)

ETC: Electronic Throttle Control

MAFS: Mass Airflow Sensor

PCM: Powertrain Control Module (aka ECM, ECU, PCU, EEC, and more)

PCV: Positive Crankcase Ventilation

TPS: Throttle Position Sensor

VMV: Vapor Management Valve (aka Evaporative Emissions Canister Purge Valve)

Breakout Point: A place in an electrical harness where the wiring for an individual component leaves (breaks out of) the main harness to attach to an individual component.

ROUSHcharger Installation

When you're installing your ROUSHcharger you're not just installing a supercharger, you're changing the vehicle's entire induction and engine management system. This means you have to make the electronic engine control modifications Roush calls for in its instructions.

Step 1: First, locate the Throttle Position Sensor (TPS) (six-pin) connector and harness at the front of the right-hand cylinder head (passenger side). Using a depinning tool, pop out the locking tab and remove the six-pin connector from the engine wiring harness. Depress the red locking tab and separate the empty female 1 x 6 connector from the new TPS/ETC Extension Harness (131114A595). It is used in the next step.

Step 2: Fit the new Roush-provided six-pin connector with the yellow/violet wire in position 1, the blue/green wire is in position 2, the brown wire is in position 3, the blue/orange wire is in position 4, the yellow wire is in position 5, and the green/violet wire is in position 6. Install the red plastic lock into the connector to secure all six wires in place. Connect the TPS/ETC Extension Harness (131114A595) from Hardware Kit E (1315-TVSHKE) to the newly installed six-pin TPS connector. The wire colors on each side of the connector pair should line up. Route the harness along the main wiring harness to the rear of the left-hand-side (driver) cam cover. Use tape or zip ties to secure the extension harness to the main harness.

Step 3: Locate the Evaporative Emissions Canister Purge Valve electrical connector (two-pin) at the front of the right-hand (passenger's side) cylinder head. Using a depinning tool, remove the connector from the purge valve harness. Depress the locking tab and separate the empty female 1 x 2 connector from the Evaporative Emissions Canister Purge Valve Extension Harness (13119G866). This connector replaces the connector removed in the previous step. Carefully pull the white locking tab forward to allow wires to be installed into the connector. Fill the new connector to where the white/brown wire is in position 1 and the green wire is in position 2. Depress the white locking tab to secure these wires.

Step 4: Connect the Evaporative Emissions Canister Purge Valve Extension Harness (13119G866) to the newly installed connector. Wire colors on each side of the connector pair should line up. Route the revised harness along the main wiring harness to the rear of the right-hand-side (passenger) cam cover. Use tape or zip ties to secure the extension harness to the main engine harness.

Step 5: Next, locate the IMRC sensor connector (light gray) at the rear of the right-hand-side (passenger) cylinder head. Connect the IMRC sensor connector into the ACT wiring harness (1315-12A690), found in Hardware Kit E (1315-TVSHKE). Route the Roush extension wiring harness to the right-hand-side (passenger) cylinder head. Install the connector block (1315-14A464) found in Hardware Kit E (1315-TVSHKE) of your ROUSHcharger Kit, into the IMRC three-pin sensor connector (dark gray) located at the back of the left-hand-side (driver) cylinder head.

Step 6: Once you have modified the TPS and VPV connections, remove the wiring harness retainer and clip on the engine harness. Route both Roush extension harnesses along the engine harness. Secure them in place with zip ties. Again it is suggested you wrap and protect your harness with Powerbraid from Painless Performance. It protects better than the factory wrap and looks sharp.

Finally: If you're doing a 2015–up 5.0L Coyote with CMCV, there are factory connections you have to disconnect and seal because CMCV is being eliminated with the ROUSHcharger installation. Next, pry up the engine harness retainers at the right-hand side of the engine and release the ground. Strip the wrap back. You're going to have to relocate the ground wire. Install the pump ground wire with the existing ground wire near the right-hand strut tower and retighten.

1 ***Installation of the ROUSHcharger at GAS begins with removal of the factory 2015–up Charge Motion intake manifold. It is strongly suggested you take detailed pictures of your factory set-up before disassembly. This coupled with the ROUSHcharger installation instructions make it easy. Did you remember to disconnect the battery?***

2 *Locate the six-pin Throttle Position Sensor (TPS) connector and harness at the front of the right-hand-side (passenger) cylinder head. Using a proper pin removal tool, pop out the locking tab and remove the connector from the harness. To do this properly, you must consult Roush's instructions and follow them in great detail. Instructions walk you through the process of electrical connection changes.*

3 *Pay strict attention to the Roush instructions and proper TPS wire/plug repositioning. The factory female connector plug is replaced with the six-pin connector provided in the ROUSHcharger kit. The six-pin TPS plug receives wire re-positioning, which is explained in great detail in the Roush instructions. Here, wires have been repositioned and the plug is ready for use.*

4 *Here's the complete TPS installation and extension harness per Roush Performance, along with the connection.*

5 *The two modified TPS and evaporative emissions canister purge valve harnesses and extension harnesses are blended into the factory electronic engine control harnesses. It is suggested that you use PowerBraid wire wrap from Painless Performance to integrate and protect these harnesses.*

6 *Intercooler pump power comes from this terminal at the underhood fuse box. When you connect the pump and relay, do not overtighten the nut.*

7 *The evaporative emissions canister purge valve is transferred to the ROUSHcharger as shown. This solenoid valve is easily mistaken for an IAC (idle air control) solenoid. However, the Coyote and most drive-by-wire electronic engine control systems are not equipped with an IAC. Idle speed is controlled by the PCM/ECU via the throttle motor.*

8 *The ROUSHcharger comes with 47lb/hr EV14/US Car pencil-style injectors to meet the demands of this 2.3L Roush blower. However, you need more. Once installation is complete your PCM/ECU requires a Roush tune to get everything on the same page.*

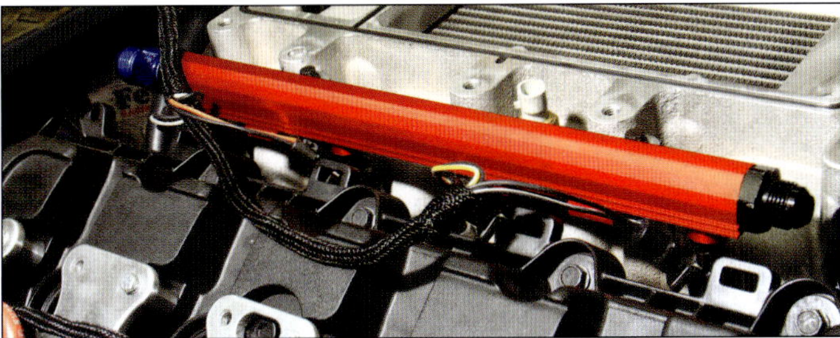

9 *The aftermarket offers a wealth of billet and stainless-steel fuel rails for the Ti-VCT Coyote. Russell, Earl's, and BBK can set you up with braided hoses, fittings, and lines to support the rails.*

10 *Gasket technology has come a long way and the ROUSHcharger lower intake and intercooler are no exception. These high-tech silicone seals provide a positive bond between surfaces with virtually no chance of leakage. Check out the alignment pin for a perfect fit.*

11 *The 2015–2017 Coyote cylinder head is different from the 2011–2014 head. It has the extended intake port flange for the CMCV system, which entered production for 2015. The ROUSHcharger does not have the clearance issues you experience with the 2011–2014 stock intake. Note that GAS had to swing the knock sensor plug inboard to clear the manifold.*

12 *Torres sets the Roush lower intake manifold/intercooler in place. This is an easy manifold to install, thanks to thoughtful engineering, better gasket technology, and alignment. It is impossible to get this wrong. Torque these bolts in crisscross fashion to 12 ft-lbs (8-12 Nm) in one-third values. Never overtighten.*

13 *The fuel rail and injectors are next, and the aftermarket offers plenty of fuel rails to choose from. GAS is going with the stock fuel rails on this one. Don't forget to lube the injector O-rings prior to installation.*

14 *Daniel installs the ROUSHcharger R2300. Contact surfaces have been checked for debris and cleared for installation.*

15 ROUSH-charger bolts are torqued crisscross to 25 ft-lbs (18 Nm). This is performed in one-third values.

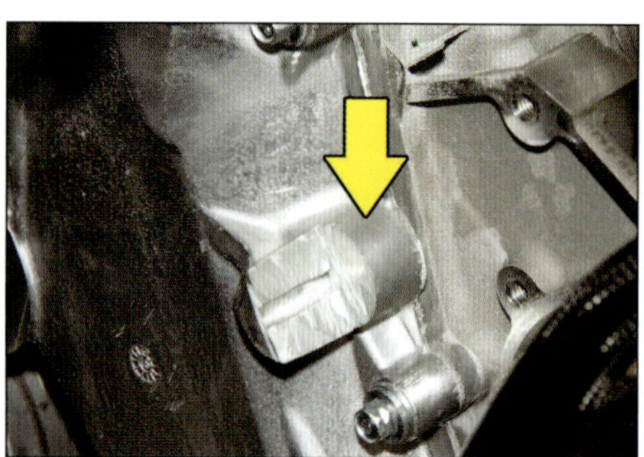

16 This Boss on the front timing cover must be cut as shown to make way for the ROUSHcharger drive package.

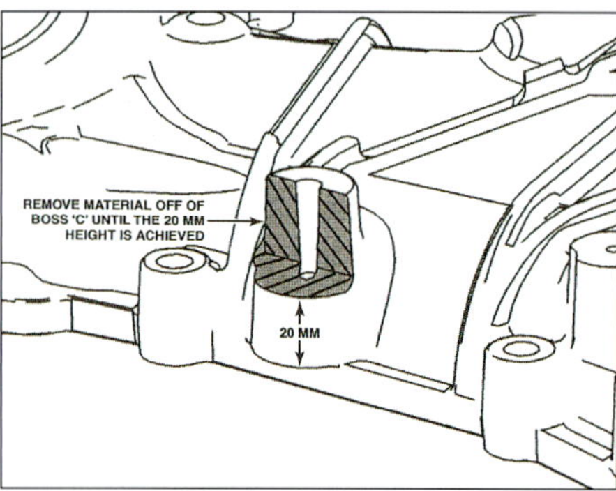

17 This Roush illustration demonstrates how the Boss should be cut, with 20-mm left as shown (arrow). (Photo Courtesy Roush Performance)

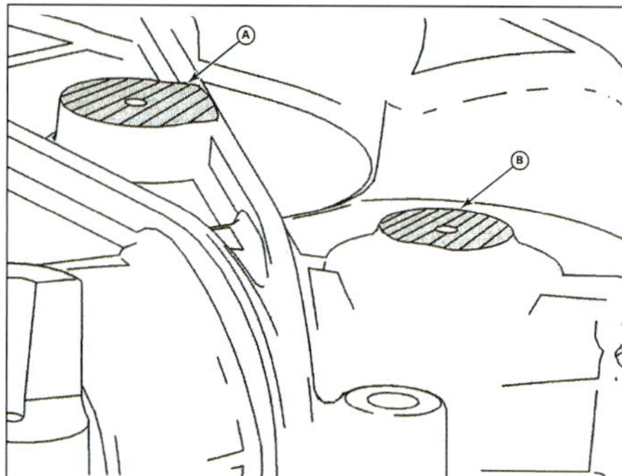

18 The shaded/lined surfaces A and B must be lower than or equal to this rib height on the front timing cover. (Photo Courtesy Roush Performance)

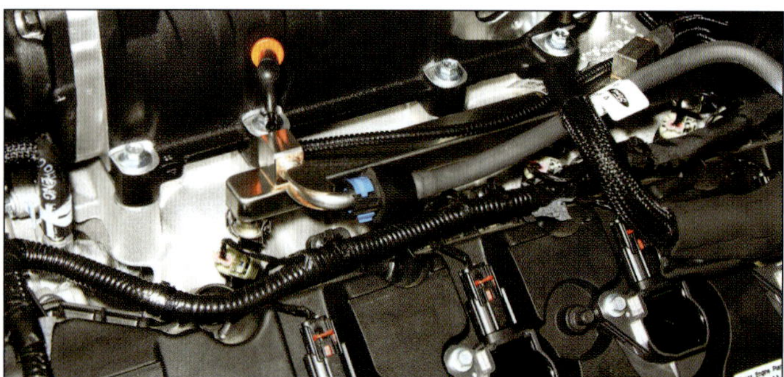

19 The fuel line and wiring harness should look like this on the left-hand (driver) side when installation is complete.

20 The twin blade throttle body and spacer are installed next; nothing to think about here because Roush has thought of it all for you. The throttle motor and TPS are already installed and synched, making plug and play installation easy.

21 Here is a closer look at the TPS and VCV harnesses and how they're secured to existing harnesses and hoses.

22 Positive crankcase ventilation plumbing is secured next. These are easy quick-connect fittings. All you have to do is click them into place. This is the time to think about an oil separator kit for your Coyote. PCV oil ingestion issues with the Coyote engine can cause engine damage at high RPM. Oil/air separators for the Coyote are available from Ford Performance as well as from JLT and Moroso.

23 This is the upper front-end accessory drive (FEAD) bracket, which is fastened to the front timing cover as shown. This cast-aluminum bracket supports the ROUSH-charger idler pulleys. Install the upper FEAD Bracket (1314-8B653U) using one M8 x 1.25 x 57 bolt, three (black) M8 x 1.25 x 60 bolts (11127083), and two M8 x 1.25 x 84 bolts (W704752) from Hardware Kit C (1315-TVSHKC). Torque the bolts to 18 ft-lbs (25 Nm).

24 Install two idler pulleys (953045) on the machined posts of the upper FEAD bracket. Secure the pulleys using two M8 x 1.25 x 28–mm idler bolts (R18020060) with washers found in Hardware Kit C (1315-TVHSKC). Torque bolts to 18 ft-lbs (25 Nm) with a 13-mm socket. Then, loosely install the FEAD Tensioner Bracket Assembly (13118B603) on the front timing cover using two M8 x 1.25 x 120–mm bolts (N811329) found in Hardware Kit C (1315-TVSHKC). Install the lowest bolt into the casting prior to positioning it in vehicle, in order to clear the sway bar (Mustang GT only).

25 The Low Temperature Radiator (LTR), or intercooler, is next. If you have a performance-pack car, remove the two outboard bolts on the factory radiator support bracket (as viewed from below the vehicle). Install the LTR (1315-8K229) and secure the LTR into position with the two M8 x 16–mm bolts included in Hardware Kit H. Install two J-Clips (W520823) on both frame rail ends. Some trimming of the J-Clip may be required to install the J-Clip through the hole in the frame.

26 The LTR hose is connected next as shown. This is a tricky hose to get to. Use long duckbill pliers to install the clamp.

27 *Here's the intercooler pump, which is installed on the right-hand side. Using the intercooler pump bracket (1315-8C4191) as a template, place the pump bracket against the frame behind the wiper-fluid-reservoir mounting bracket as shown. Mark the holes for drilling and remove the intercooler pump bracket. The bracket is placed on the outside of the frame behind the windshield-wiper-pump-reservoir bracket, making it easy to drill the holes. When installed, the intercooler pump and bracket are mounted on the inside of this section of the frame.*

28 *Reinstall the radiator cooling fans and secure to the radiator as shown, taking care to ensure all connections are completed.*

29 *Install the hose to the intercooler degas bottle inlet using the provided clamp (CT19X12) from Hardware Kit G (1315-TVSHKG). Install the hose to the intercooler cooler outlet using the provided clamp (CT19X12) from Hardware Kit G.*

30 *Here's what your coolant recovery reservoir (left) and intercooler degas bottle (right) should look like. Although this is a coolant recovery reservoir, Roush calls it a "degas" bottle. It serves as a place to vent gasses and relieve any pressure.*

31 *The intake ducting and cold-air package are installed last. All of these components are provided in the ROUSHcharger R2300 kit.*

This Galpin Auto Sports 2015 Mustang GT coupe includes this 725-horse 5.0L Coyote with a 2.3L twin-screw front-feed Whipple supercharger, huge intercooler and plenum, and a 132-mm throttle body. The Whipple front entry system offers less intake restriction because it is a straight shot in. Front entry systems do not call for multiple 90-degree bends or one sweeping 180-degree bend before the supercharger inlet, which causes unequal rotor filling and lower volumetric efficiency. Of course, there are many different opinions about superchargers and which approach works best. Positive displacement superchargers such as the Whipple yield plenty of real boost for demanding power plants such as the Coyote. It is easily one of the more popular superchargers.

Check out Edelbrock's new E-Force Supercharger System for 2011–2014 and 2015–2017 Coyote engines. This complete, easy-to-install system went in excess of 700 hp in Edelbrock's dyno labs on top of a Ford Performance Racing Parts Aluminator Coyote. (Photo Courtesy Edelbrock)

Meet the Kenne Bell Twin-Screw Mammoth supercharger for Ford's 2015–2017 5.0L Ti-VCT Coyote V-8. This is a pristine blower package with all kinds of intercooling; however, it is not for the faint of heart. It is quite an involved system. You must take your time and pay strict attention to instructions . When properly installed and tuned, the Kenne Bell system makes real power. (Photo Courtesy Kenne Bell)

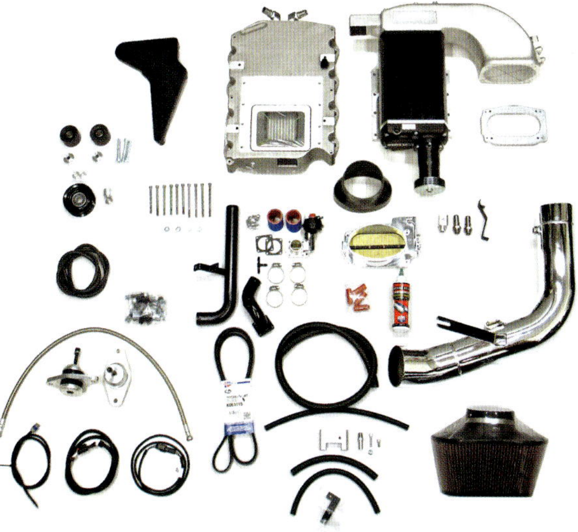

Here's the Kenne Bell Twin-Screw Mammoth system for the 2015–2017 Mustang GT spread out for you to see. What makes the Mammoth more efficient than a typical twin-rotor Roots blower is its screw-type design, which delivers more boost and at cooler temperatures. This efficiency does not come cheap, or easily. This is one of the more complex systems we've seen, and for good reason. It is well thought out, squeezing as much power from the Coyote as possible. Everything is here to get the job done. Be prepared to spend a couple of days with this install. (Photo Courtesy Kenne Bell)

Edelbrock E-Force Boost

For quite some time the only way you could get Edelbrock E-Force was if you purchased the entire Edelbrock E-Force Aluminator Coyote crate engine. Now you can buy the bolt-on E-Force supercharger kit from Edelbrock and be ready to romp in a weekend. Edelbrock's best people managed to get more than 700 hp from the E-Force positive displacement supercharger on top of a Ford Performance Racing Parts Aluminator crate engine. If you're going to supercharge your Coyote with the Edelbrock E-Force it is suggested you keep boost conservative or opt for Edelbrock's crate engine package, which is factory ready for 700 hp with Manley rods and Mahle forged pistons.

Kenne Bell Superchargers

Few companies are more serious about supercharged power than Kenne Bell. Kenne Bell's twin-screw liquid-cooled superchargers are a nice compact package for your Coyote's midsection. These systems tend to be more complex; however, they're well worth the learning curve and expense for the power you get.

On the Kenne Bell website you find options for your 5.0L and 5.2L Coyote engine. The basic Kenne Bell 2.8/2.8LC supercharger packages can net 750 to 1,150 hp. The upscale Kenne Bell 3.2, 4.2, and 4.7L superchargers take you to the moon at 800 to 2,000 hp. However, none of this stuff comes free. When your horsepower goal is more than 600 it is strongly suggested you build a Coyote engine ready for this kind of power. You're going to need a sleeved Coyote block, Eagle H-beam

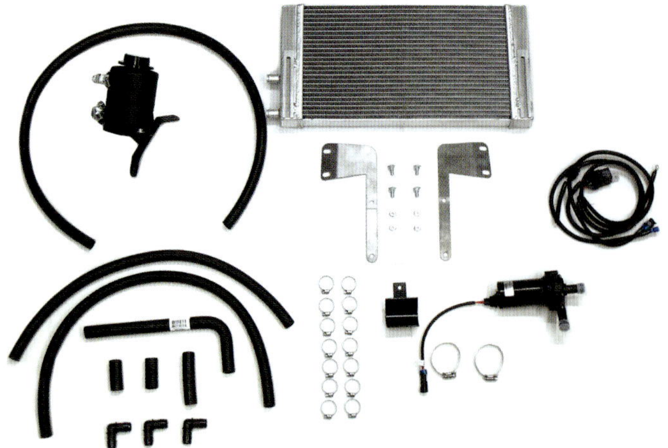

Here's the Kenne Bell air-to-water intercooler with pump and reservoir, which is installed in front of the air conditioning condenser and radiator. (Photo Courtesy Kenne Bell)

rods, Mahle forged pistons, and a steel core oil pump. Ideally, you have CNC-ported cylinder heads from Total Engine Airflow, available from Summit Racing Equipment. You most surely have to have a support system (brakes, suspension, and tires) to handle the power, including your own driving skill.

Kenne Bell clearly has a solid handle on "Twin Screw" supercharger technology. When Shelby was planning the "World's Most Powerful Muscle Car," he selected the ultra-efficient Kenne Bell 2.8H Kit to power the 725-hp Super Snake. Later on, the 3.6LC (Liquid Cooled) was enlisted for the new 800- and 850-hp versions. Then, 1,000-hp Shelbys with Kenne Bell's 4.2. As far back as 2010, prior to the Coyote's introduction, Kenne Bell stunned the supercharger world with patented liquid cooling, seal pressure equalizer, and the external spring bypass valve. In 2015, Shelby again chose the Kenne Bell 2.8 for the 750-hp 5.0L Super Snake. Saleen also opted for the Kenne Bell 2.8 for its 750-horse Mustang GT.

When you've chosen the Kenne Bell twin-screw supercharger be ready for the labor involved and the close attention to detail required. You have to remove your Mustang's front fascia for liquid cooler access. This is a simple task involving the replacement of plastic rivets if any are damaged during removal. Front dress installation is straightforward with a simple serpentine belt drive for the supercharger and accessories. As long as you follow Kenne Bell's detailed instructions with care you can install this system in a weekend.

Another important consideration is smog laws in your state. You must have a street legal smog system to make it through an emissions test. Each and every state has its own policy. Make sure the Kenne Bell system, and others, are street legal in your area.

Kenne Bell Supercharger Installation

1 *To clear the Kenne Bell supercharger, the hood insulation blanket must be removed. (Photo Courtesy Kenne Bell)*

2 *The front fascia and radiator support cover must be removed to install the intercooler. These items are easy to remove and reinstall thanks to plastic press-in fasteners. (Photo Courtesy Kenne Bell)*

3 *Wheelhouses must be removed to make way for liquid cooler ductwork. Again, this is easy to accomplish thanks to press-in plastic fasteners. Ford has begun using these fasteners for ease of assembly. They are normally a one-time-use fastener, so you have to buy replacement fasteners. (Photo Courtesy Kenne Bell)*

5 *Here's why the front fascia must be removed. The Kenne Bell intercooler installs here in front of the air conditioning condenser, which puts this guy out front into the heat-extracting slipstream. (Photo Courtesy Kenne Bell)*

7 *Here's the 2015–2017 Mustang GT's power distribution panel located underhood. This is a remarkable improvement to the Mustang's electrical system because it is easy to access electrical connections, fuses, circuit breakers, and relays. (Photo Courtesy Kenne Bell)*

4 *The washable air filter goes here in the left-hand (driver) wheelwell ahead of the wheelhouse. This is a cold-air induction system, which only adds to power. (Photo Courtesy Kenne Bell)*

6 *The intercooler pump is positioned here to the right (driver's seat reference) of the intercooler. Power comes from the main power panel and fuse box. Power comes on with the ignition, which means no power with the ignition off. (Photo Courtesy Kenne Bell)*

8 *This is the Kenne Bell intake manifold and intercooler. The technician is removing the protective covering. Although coolant is pretty warm at 200 degrees F, compressed air from the supercharger runs even hotter and under a lot of boost. The intercooler cools the compressed intake charge from the Kenne Bell twin-screw. When you consider the external intercooler in front, the cool-down and power gain is remarkable. (Photo Courtesy Kenne Bell)*

9 *The Kenne Bell Mammoth supercharger bolts on top of the manifold and intercooler. (Photo Courtesy Kenne Bell)*

10 *This huge single-blade 168-mm throttle body offers drive-through service. What this means for you is real CFM when the butterflies are pinned. (Photo Courtesy Kenne Bell)*

11 *This is the 4.125-inch standard Kenne Bell supercharger pulley, which should yield around 6.0 psi. A smaller 4.000-inch pulley should get you 7.0 psi. Take it down to a 3.875-inch pulley and get 10.0 psi, according to CarTech author Richard Holdener. (Photo Courtesy Kenne Bell)*

12 *This is the bypass valve (also known as a wastegate), which vents excess boost back into the intake (arrow). The bypass valve prevents the unthinkable: excess boost and detonation. (Photo Courtesy Kenne Bell)*

13 *Look at this huge 4.000-inch intake duct, which, as shown here, is actually a prototype part. This ensures you have plenty of volume when it's time to open the throttle and get boost. (Photo Courtesy Kenne Bell)*

14 *Here's the intake duct underneath, where it leads to the washable/reusable air filter behind the fascia. The MAF sensor is located in the intake duct just above the air filter in the engine compartment. (Photo Courtesy Kenne Bell)*

15 *The intercooler expansion tank is mounted here on the left-hand (driver) side near the brake master cylinder. (Photo Courtesy Kenne Bell)*

16 *Also included are urethane engine mounts, which are considerably smaller than the factory high-absorption mounts. These mounts are adjustable, which means you can lower the engine just enough for hood-to-supercharger clearances. (Photo Courtesy Kenne Bell)*

Turbocharging

When it comes to power adders, Ford's Coyote isn't much different from the rest, including its 4.6L and 5.4L Modular cousins. Like supercharging or nitrous systems, what you choose for your Coyote project depends on how far you want to go and how much risk you're willing to take. There are several turbo systems out there, including complete systems and custom systems you can amass and build yourself.

Turbocharging is for those who are really serious about horsepower. You have to love turbocharging and you have to know something about it to do it successfully. Look to those who've turbocharged Coyotes successfully for your inspiration and good advice. If you're planning all-out 8-second quarter-mile performance you don't need this book to show you how to do it. For the rest of you, we're going to touch on the basics of Coyote turbocharging here to get you headed in the right direction for acceptable street and weekend off-road performance.

Look at what is available from American Muscle: the JPC Racing single-turbo-system tuner kit, which will get you a whopping 600 whp with as little as 6 pounds of boost on the stock bottom end with pump gas. If you're ready to step up to Eagle H-beam rods and Mahle coated and forged pistons, expect to get over 1,000 hp to the ground (depending upon custom tuning and fuel upgrades). The advanced design of this single turbo kit offers minimal spool time while also reducing exhaust back pressure to essentially provide the spool time of a twin-turbo kit with the overall power from a larger single turbocharger.

Here's the Hellion twin turbo kit from American Muscle for Ford's brute 2011–2014 Coyote V-8. What this means for you is a ground-pounding 600 to 1,200 hp to the pavement. The Hellion Mustang twin-turbo kit comes with two Precision 62-mm turbochargers, two Turbosmart 40-mm wastegates, two Turbosmart v-port bypass valves, two stainless four-into-one tubular headers, eight 47 lb/hr fuel injectors, a handheld programmer with a base tune installed, and all of the required parts and hardware needed to upgrade your mild-mannered pony. If you're running a stock bottom end, keep horsepower conservative at no more than 600. If you intend to reach for the stars, beef up the bottom end with Eagle H-beam rods, Mahle coated and forged pistons, and a steel-core oil pump.

Turbonetics and Innovative Turbo are among the most well known in the industry and where you should probably shop first. American Muscle is another option, as well as JPC Racing. If turbocharging is a must for you, get educated on turbocharging and turbo systems before running off in the heat of the day and spending a fortune. Know exactly what you want before spending a dime.

Some companies, such as UPR Products, make it straightforward to install a turbocharger system. UPR Products offers a twin-turbo system for the 2011–2014 and 2015–up Mustang GT. The top-mount twin-turbo kit is adjustable from 5 psi to more than 25 psi depending on your engine's status. A 5-psi tune makes more than 600 hp at the drive wheels with a stock Coyote bottom end. This kit can make more than 1,200 drive wheel hp with 25 psi if your engine is precision-built with H-beam rods and forged pistons.

There's also a new UPR Products Hellion twin-turbo system for the all-new 2015–up Mustang GT. This is a chassis-dyno-proven system where these folks made 949.26 hp and 806.87 ft-lbs of torque with a 2015 Mustang GT at the rear wheels at just under 7,000 rpm with a stock Coyote bottom end. This kind of brutal testing proves the kind of power this engine can make and stay together.

If you opt for a Ford Performance Aluminator crate engine, all you have to do is order the engine and drop it in prior to installing the Hellion twin-turbo kit. Watch compression while you're doing this. Boosted applications call for 9.5:1 compression.

Though UPR Products accomplished this feat with a stock Coyote bottom end, it is strongly suggested you spec your Coyote for the mission or order up a Ford Performance Aluminator crate engine built and tested for your street/strip agenda. If you're anticipating more than 600 hp, build for that power with heavy-duty I- or H-beam rods and forged pistons. Focus on improved cooling at the rear of your Coyote's cylinder heads and block with the cooling kit from Modular Motorsports.

While you're at it, cam accordingly with a cam and valvetrain engineered for boosted applications. Ford Performance and Comp Cams can help with camshaft packages engineered for boost applications, making it easier than ever to dial "blow" into your Coyote Mustang or F-Series truck.

UPR Products 2011–2014 Hellion Twin-Turbo System Components

- Twin Precision Billet 62-mm turbo (V-band inlet for easy installation)
- Twin Turbosmart 40-mm wastegates (V-band inlet for easy installation)
- Twin Turbosmart VEE port bypass valves
- Stainless four into one tubular headers, all American-made stainless piping
- Large vertical flow dual inlet intercooler
- Dual 3-inch downpipes (can connect to factory exhaust if desired)

UPR Products Hellion Twin-Turbo System Options

- 64-mm Precision CEA Billet turbos (ball bearing only), $1,820
- Ball bearing upgrade, $1,200
- 67-mm CEA Billet wheel turbos, $1,050
- Turbosmart E Boost 2 boost controller, $557.99
- Turbosmart E Boost Street boost controller, $314.99
- AEM wide-band oxygen kit, $220

Note: Prices subject to change without notice.

Gen III Induction Facts

The Gen III's intake manifold did not change much from the Gen II version with Charge Motion valving built in to change intake-runner length. What makes the Gen III decidedly different is its dual-injection system of both port fuel injection and high-pressure direct injection straight into the combustion chambers like a diesel engine.

It is easy to wonder why Ford opted for dual injection consisting of two different types of injection. Upon release of the Gen III engine, Ford said, "The car's 5.0-liter V-8 now features dual-fuel, high-pressure direct injection and low-pressure port fuel injection technology for increased power and efficiency."

The backstory to all this technology is the cleansing of intake valve faces, which tend to get coked up with carbon deposits when there's direct injection only. Car and truck owners with direct-injected engines have been faced with lost power and performance issues due to coked-up intake valves that limit airflow and cause drivability issues, which has resulted in expensive service repairs to clean valve faces. The port-injection element on the Gen III washes the valve faces and keeps them clean.

Dual injection is just that: two electronic fuel-injection systems working together to improve performance, offer efficiency, and improve emissions. Direct Injection is programmed as necessary to complement port injection and vice versa, depending on conditions, such as

The Gen III intake manifold had few changes from the Gen II. You still get the same healthy airflow along with Charge Motion that improves both horsepower and torque.

Charge Motion is the same as Gen II and functions the same way, changing intake runner length depending upon torque requirements.

The 80-mm drive-by-wire throttle body is virtually unchanged across a decade of production.

The direct-injection manifolds are positioned at the base of the cylinder heads for direct access to the combustion chambers much like a diesel engine. There are four injectors on each head with timed solenoid operation.

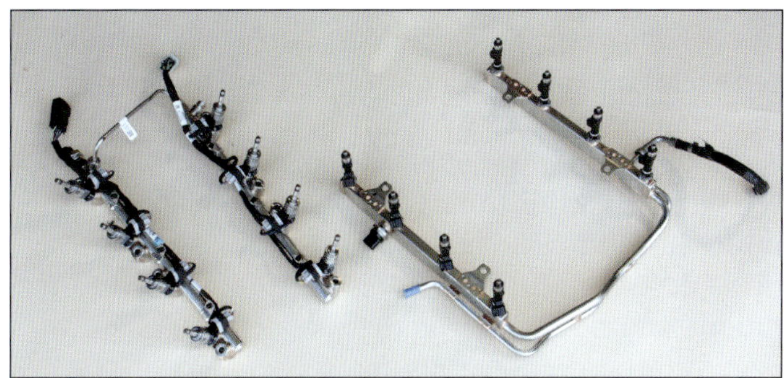

Dual injection is shown at a glance. On the left is the high-pressure direct-injection manifold with eight injectors that is hard-lined from the pump. On the right is the port-injection manifold with eight injectors. Port Injection is used at idle and at low-power conditions for both a smooth idle and efficiency. As RPM and load increase, both port injection and direct injection work together in a calculated blend to achieve both power and efficiency.

This is the cam-actuated, high-pressure, direct-injection pump.

The direct-injection pump sits on a follower, which is much like a roller tappet, that rides a separate cam lobe. This makes the Gen III Coyote right-hand exhaust cam different in that there's an additional cam lobe for the direct-injection pump.

With the cam cover in place, you can see how the direct-injection pump relates to the cylinder head. Also, note the unique #3 ignition coil configuration with an ignition lead to clear the direct-injection pump.

coolant/engine temperature, engine load, cold-start start-up, etc. The two systems are programmed to complement each other, utilizing the strengths of each system where applicable. If you could actually see direct injection function, you'd notice how it rolls in and out as you drive depending upon driving conditions and demands. For the most part, direct injection calls for very little maintenance. As necessary, service and clean both injection systems from time to time—primarily when you change spark plugs and the fuel filter (if so equipped).

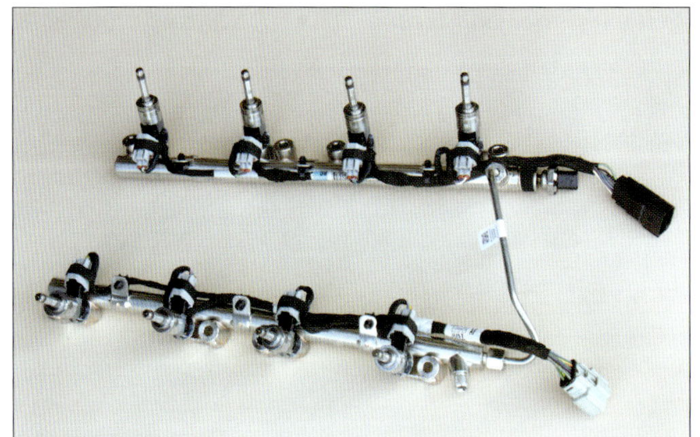

The direct-injection manifold has two leads that differentiate the right and left sides. Each injector is fired in time with the valvetrain and ignition system. Between the two manifolds is the high-pressure fuel line, which connects the two.

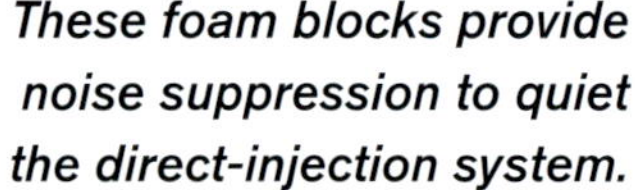

These foam blocks provide noise suppression to quiet the direct-injection system.

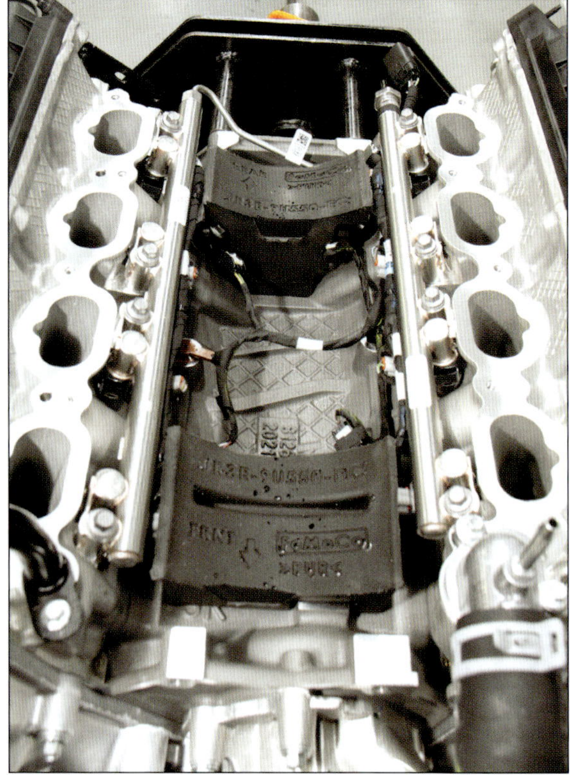

High-pressure direct-injection lines are one-time use only. They should not be reused. This means that every time they are disconnected, they must be replaced.

Ignition and Starting

The Coyote's electronic engine control, ignition, starting, and charging systems are advanced, state-of-the-art designs that are easy to maintain and tune. Electronic engine control (EEC), known as the Copperhead system, evolved from generations of systems originally born at the cusp of the 1980s. What makes the Copperhead system the most advanced to date is what it does. It has more responsibility and function than any other Ford EEC system in history. Copperhead manages fuel and spark curve, throttle function, transmission shift programming, and variable cam timing, just to scratch the surface of what it does.

Copperhead is very complex in what it does; variable cam timing alone involves tremendous amounts of memory/function. For 2011–2014, Ti-VCT was more a simple on/off function. It was either on or off. For 2015–up Ti-VCT is evolved so that variable cam timing rolls in and out in linear fashion instead of straight on/off. Ford powertrain engineers found a way to make variable cam timing even more driver friendly. Ford's Ti-VCT for 2015–2016 follows your foot on the gas and rolls valve timing in and out accordingly. Ford engineers weren't sure that 15 tables would have enough cam timing input, but they do. Ford's Copperhead system also manages to integrate the new ZF 6R80 6-speed transmission and engine into one highly efficient controller, which adds complexity to the mix.

The "One Touch Start" ignition key needs but a moment in the "start" position before handing function off to the PCM/ECU as aggressive deceleration fuel shutoff and torque-based deceleration when you come off the gas. These functions shut off the fuel during deceleration more often and

The 5.0L Ti-VCT Coyote and 5.2L Voodoo engines have the same coil-on-plug ignition system fired by the Copperhead electronic engine control system. Ford's family of electronic engine control (EEC-III, EEC-IV, and EEC-V) systems have led to the Copperhead system you have today in the Coyote and Voodoo "drive-by-wire" systems. What makes Copperhead different from its EEC predecessors is drive-by-wire technology along with coil-on-plug ignition and variable cam timing. It really is a complete engine and driveline electronic control system.

Ford Performance Parts offers the complete coil-on-plug ignition kit for the Coyote and Voodoo V-8s. The beauty of high-output coil-on-plug ignition is precision spark timing and long-term durability. If you're running higher-cylinder pressures with boost or nitrous you're going to need a hotter, more powerful spark to keep the fires lit. Each coil is fired in time with valve and piston-timing events to a point at which misfires virtually never happen, reducing hydrocarbon emissions and improving power.

Ignition coil service and replacement is easy on the Coyote. No ignition wires to sweat out. Only an 8-mm socket, plug coil disconnection, and removal. When you service the ignition remember to apply a dielectric compound to the boot for sealing and protection. These coils are life-of-the-engine durable.

This is the Coyote's ignition system one cylinder at a time. Each of these coils fires in perfect time with valve and piston events. Aside from precision and durability these coils are designed to keep moisture and dust out.

sooner than previous systems while coasting, on long downhill deceleration, and during mid-shifts with the new Getrag MT-82 6-speed manual transmission.

The Ti-VCT Coyote V-8 also features a new digital mass-air meter and universal exhaust-gas oxygen sensors, which report a finite numerical air/fuel ratio to something like the fourth decimal point, finer than a human hair so to speak. Previous systems weren't much more than rich/lean. But Ford had to tighten it up even finer to meet tougher Federal emission and fuel economy standards.

Ford engineers spent nearly a year developing the Coyote's electronic engine control function for the 2011 Mustang GT. It was a grueling, lengthy period of testing and programming that lasted the better part of 2008–2009 before they had a fully functioning Coyote in a Mustang test mule. Then they conducted more testing, in every environment imaginable from extreme Arizona desert heat to extreme cold and high altitude, to make sure it all shook out. The Coyote had to function properly under the very worst conditions. It is one thing to test an engine and its electronics in a laboratory and quite another to take it out there and shake it about the firmament on bumpy roads, open highway, stop-and-go traffic, mountain twisties, and more. By the end of 2009, Ford powertrain engineers had the Coyote in seamless smooth operation.

What made the Copperhead system challenging for Ford engineers was getting a drive-by-wire system to feel like a linear throttle cable. What does make drive-by-wire different is that ever-so-slight lag when you lean on the throttle. It isn't as quick as the humble throttle cable. There's a nanosecond lag and a certain amount of surging during throttle tip in. These dynamics vary from vehicle to vehicle. In time, drive-by-wire will be completely seamless.

Ignition System

The Coyote's ignition system does not have coil packs or ignition wires, just eight ignition coils and platinum-tip spark plugs to fire the mixture. The Copperhead PCM/ECU takes all of the known elements (driver input, speed, environmental conditions, and engine timing events) and turns them into a firing order cadenced in perfect time with piston and valve timing events to fire spark plugs at just the right moment.

Coil-on-plug ignition is undoubtedly the best ignition system innovation in automotive history. Eight high-energy ignition coils and deep-reach Motorcraft platinum-tip spark plugs extend deep into the middle of Coyote's four-valve chambers for more complete combustion. Ignition coil spark plug boots protect both plug and terminal from corrosion issues that can cause

Ti-VCT Coyote Firing Order

1 5 4 8 6 3 7 2

Traditional Ford V-8 pattern with cylinders 1 to 4, right bank; and 5 to 8, left bank.

The 5.0L Ti-VCT Coyote and sibling Voodoo is a plug-and-play electronics package. These two weathertight multiplex connectors plug right into the electronic engine control harness and PCM/ECU. If you're performing a swap on a vintage Ford or perhaps a 1979–1993 Fox-body Mustang, Ford Performance Racing Parts makes short work of a Coyote swap with a complete package and detailed instructions. This means complete, easy-to-install engine and transmission packages shipped right to your door. It has never been easier to perform an engine swap.

The Coyote's electronic engine control system is simple. The engine harness shown here consists of fuel injection and ignition along the fuel rails. The rest, which is not visible, goes to sensors and senders.

misfire. An umbrella boot completely covers the spark plug well to keep dust and moisture out. A weathertight Copperhead harness runs along the fuel rail, providing power to both ignition coils and injectors. Coils are fired in perfect time, as are injectors. Injector and ignition coil plugs are all positioned such that it is impossible to get them mixed up. The engine harness involves all of the sensors, senders, and evaporative emissions purge valve connections. It is impossible to get any of these connections mixed up because each component has a different multiplex plug.

It can be asked, how would you improve the Ti-VCT Coyote's ignition system? By upgrading to a more powerful aftermarket ignition coil from Ford Performance, MSD, Accel, or Granatelli Motorsports. A naturally aspirated Coyote lives happily with a stock Ford ignition coil. The more potent the spark the better, which is especially true in boosted applications.

If you're going to run boost or nitrous you're going to need an ignition coil and spark plug that can

Mustang GT Ford Performance Racing Parts Calibration System with High-Flow K&N Air Filter

- M-9603-MGTB
- Fits 2011–2014 Mustang GT
- Approximate peak increase of 16 hp and 7 ft-lbs on 93-octane fuel
- Up to 60 ft-lbs torque increase at 1,500 rpm
- Eliminates "skip-shift" on 2011–2012 Mustang MT-82 6-speed manual transmission

The kit includes:

- Ford Racing ProCal tool with performance calibration
- 2011–2014 Mustang GT high-flow K&N/Ford Racing air filter M-9601-MGT
- Premium (91 octane or higher) fuel only
- Due to multiple powertrain calibrations, online registration is required to receive ProCal calibration delivery tool after purchase
- Ford Performance Racing Parts does not ship ProCal tools directly overseas. Customers must make special arrangements with their Ford Performance Racing Parts Distributor
- Powertrain calibrations are developed and supported for U.S. and Canadian vehicles only
- This Ford Racing Power upgrade package is 50-state emissions legal and eligible for limited warranty when installed by a Ford or Lincoln Dealer
- Federal and state laws prohibit any person from installing aftermarket add-on or modified parts prior to the sale of a new motor vehicle

stand up to extreme cylinder pressures. You may also want a cooler spark plug that dissipates heat better than the factory range. Ford Performance Racing Parts, as one example, markets a one-range-colder spark plug for boosted/nitrous applications. The same can be said for MSD and Accel. Both have heat ranges you can work with.

Sending Unit

Although the Coyote's electrics are the most advanced in Ford history, some elements have never changed.

Electronic Engine Control

The Copperhead system takes engine and transmission function and ties them together into one seamless operation with the 6-speed 6R80 automatic. Of course, if you have the Getrag MT-82 6-speed manual this is where the Copperhead system leaves off, with the exception of vehicle speed, which affects speed sensor function. The ZF 6R80 6-speed automatic overdrive transmission is fully controlled by Copperhead; no throttle valve cables or shift kits to sweat out. The 6R80's many complex functions are controlled electronically.

The Coyote's many electronic functions are precise because Ford engineers have taken the "slop" out of engine control. It is needlepoint spot-on in every respect. Ignition and valve timing are precise, void of the variations we've seen in previous generations of engines. We old-timers can relate to "slop" in vintage Autolite/Motorcraft point-triggered distributors and even the electronic Duraspark ignitions. Distributors could not keep up with ever-changing driving conditions, nor could carburetors. I could only hope to keep spark timing and fuel mixture in the ballpark.

Copperhead is the sum total of all of its inputs, which give it the data needed to provide precision engine function. You have sensor function and feedback, which provides electrical resistance value to enable Copperhead to control engine function. Sensors are either resistance to ground (most sensors) or self-generation of electricity (oxygen sensors) to ascertain oxygen content in the exhaust.

Here's what you have for electronic engine control sensors:

- Throttle Position Sensor (1)
- Accelerator Pedal (1)
- Oxygen Sensors (2)
- Intake Charge Temperature Sensor (1)
- Mass Airflow (MAF) Sensor (1)
- Cylinder-Head Temperature Sensor (1)
- Cam Position Sensors (2 intake, 2 exhaust)
- Knock Sensors (2)
- Crank Sensor (1)

The Coyote's Copperhead control system does not have a MAP (Manifold Air Pressure) sensor or an IAC (Idle Air Control) solenoid. The PCM/ECU controls idle speed via the throttle motor. MAP function is incorporated into system programming.

Sensor function leads to PCM/ECU output to:

- Coil-on-plug ignition and timing
- Fuel injection timing and pulse width (fuel mixture)
- Variable cam timing (VCT)
- Fuel pump operation
- Throttle motor assembly
- Evaporative emissions purge valve
- Automatic transmission shift function

So how does this all work together? Copperhead system function takes input and turns it into proper output and engine/driveline operation. Unless you're a professional electronic engine control tuner much of how this thing works is going to be foreign to you, especially if you're thinking of the Ford EEC-IV and EEC-V systems. Copperhead drive-by-wire is a new approach to electronic powertrain control. Let's begin with the heart of the system known as the computer, brain, or controller. Ford calls this nerve center the Powertrain Control Module (PCM). Another popular term used by enthusiasts is Electronic Control Unit (ECU).

When Ford's electronic fuel injection, known as Sequential Electronic Fuel Injection (SEFI), became mainstream in the mid-1980s Ford located the PCM behind the right-hand kick panel. In the years since, Ford has made the PCM more easily accessible in the engine compartment either in the firewall or right out there in plain sight.

The Coyote's PCM is programmed two ways. If you're working with a factory original vehicle such as an S197 Mustang, S-550 Mustang, or F-Series truck, the PCM is programmed for a non-return fuel system. However, if you're doing a vintage Ford conversion swap the Ford Performance Racing Parts PCM is programmed for a return-style fuel system, which means you want to make provisions for a return fuel line back to the fuel tank. The reason for this is the use of a conventional fuel pressure regulator, which calls for a tank return. ■

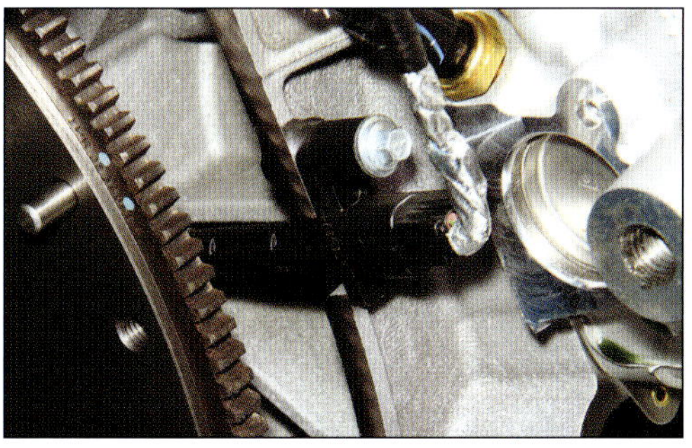

This is the crank sensor, which is triggered by the reluctor (shutter wheel) at the crankshaft. Replacement is easy with an 8-mm socket should replacement ever be necessary. You will likely not ever have to replace this sensor.

Shown are the right-hand-bank (passenger) VCT solenoid connectors. VCT gives the Coyote precision valve timing based on demand. The 2011–2014 VCT is different from the 2015–up VCT. For 2011–2014, valve timing is simple on/off. The 2015 and onward is more finitely modulated to driving demands.

Here's the left-hand (driver) side with cam covers removed. Visible are the cam reluctors inside and cam sensors outside. This is a Hall Effect trigger system that signals the PCM/ECU where cams are positioned/indexed. Note the sensor colors: Exhaust sensors are gray and intake sensors are black.

These are the Ti-VCT solenoid connections for variable cam timing. These solenoids modulate the VCT valves to advance valve timing. Each cylinder bank has two of these solenoid valves: one for intake and one for exhaust cam indexing. This is the left-hand (driver) bank.

Cam sensors are found at the rear of each cylinder head. This is the right-hand (passenger) side. These sensors are tied to the PCM/ECU to keep track of cam indexing. Note the foil insulation to protect wiring from heat.

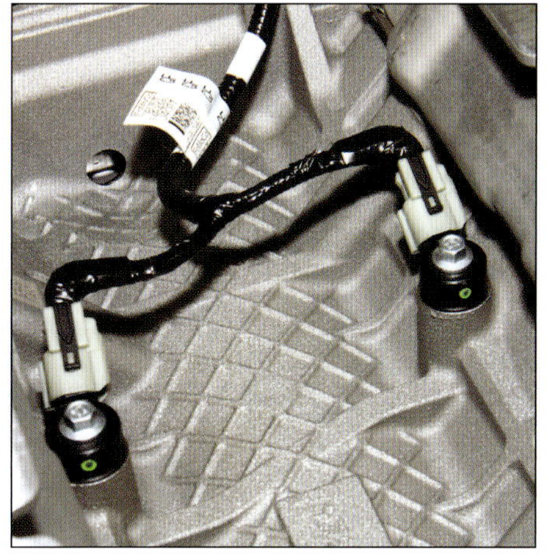

The Coyote's knock sensors are located in the valley, up close and personal to each cylinder bank. Ford has this dialed in so precisely that ignition timing and fuel curve are quickly corrected should spark knock occur.

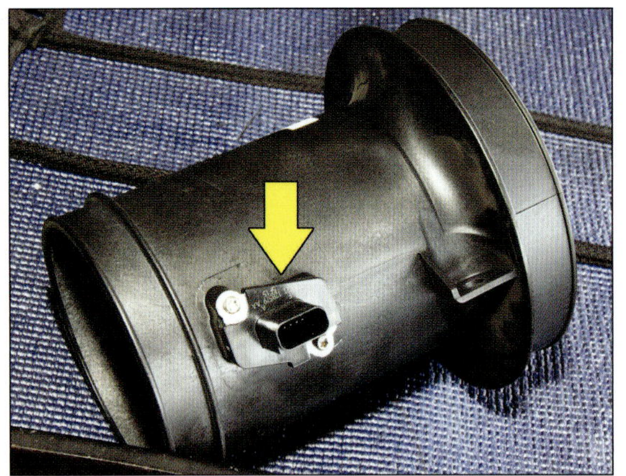

Here's the Coyote's MAF sensor, located in the intake duct. The MAF works hand in hand with the PCM/ECU's gang of sensors to keep ignition and fuel curves on track. The MAF enables you to perform constructive modifications on the Coyote and Voodoo without consequence. All you need is a qualified professional tuner. Never trust your Coyote to anyone less than a seasoned professional tuner. And remember, anyone can hang up a sign and call himself (or herself) a tuner. Investigate any tune shop thoroughly before entrusting them with your investment.

Modular applications in the past have normally included four oxygen sensors, with one ahead of each catalytic converter and one aft to gauge emissions before and after. The Coyote works the same way. There are two oxygen sensors for each bank, one ahead of the cat and one in the cat. This makes the Coyote both fuel efficient and clean burning.

Sending units and sensors still tend to operate on the principle of resistance to ground. This statement isn't true for all senders and sensors, but most of them. When you have high resistance to ground this means you have low current flow to ground. With high resistance, the instrument needle reads low. With low resistance to ground, the needle reads high. Using a cylinder head temperature or oil pressure gauge as an example, high temperature or high pressure creates low resistance to ground and a high reading.

Starting System

The Ti-VCT Coyote has the same basic starting system as the Modular

This is the cylinder-head temperature sensor, which contributes to the electronic engine control picture and temperature gauge.

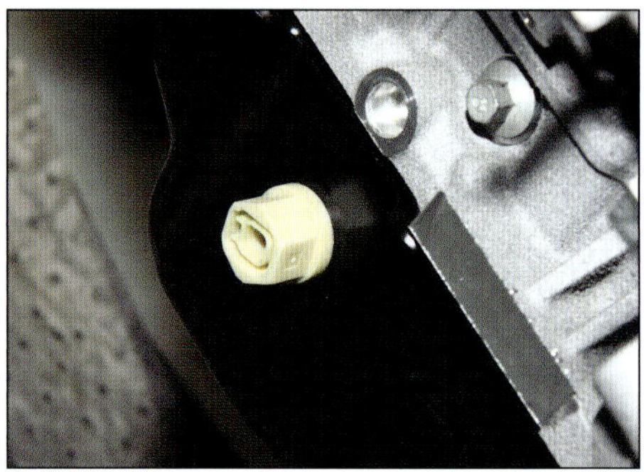

The oil level sensor is in the oil pan. Continuity via oil level determines whether or not you get a low oil level warning. These oil level sensors tend to leak regardless of what you do with them. They are vulnerable to temperature and vibration extremes.

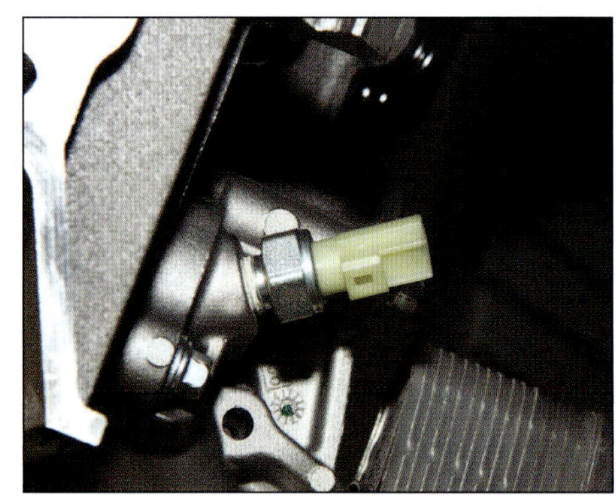

This is the oil pressure sender, which controls resistance to ground for the oil pressure gauge. The greater your Coyote's oil pressure the lower the resistance to ground, which affects gauge needle position. The lower the resistance, the higher the needle.

MSD Ignition markets these individual coil packs for coil-on-plug ignition. This is a true aftermarket ignition system with coils and wires for racing applications. However, you can run this system on your street Coyote. Boots are protected the same way as the stock coil-on-plug system.

Like its Modular predecessors, the 5.0L Ti-VCT Coyote has long-reach Motorcraft platinum-tip spark plugs. The main thing you want to be concerned with is heat range. Stock naturally aspirated Coyote engines don't need an alternative heat range. If you're going to supercharge, raise compression, or go nitrous. There's the Ford Performance Racing Parts M-12405-M50 spark plug, which is one heat range lower than stock. The M-12405-M50 is a colder plug engineered for higher-cylinder pressures. Suggested gap is in the .035-inch range for boosted applications.

The Coyote's starter is virtually the same as the 4.6L and 5.4L Modular. It remains a three-bolt reduction gear Motorcraft starter with an integral solenoid/drive. This starter package is easily adapted to vintage Ford Coyote conversions. Keep the original remote solenoid as a relay and route power to the starter and integral solenoid. You then have two solenoids doing the work. Ford Performance Parts makes it easy with this complete M-11000-C50 starter installation kit, which includes starter, hardware, and wiring harness.

Motorcraft 9G Alternator Specifications

- Minimum output: 96 amps at 650 rpm
- Maximum output: 156 amps at 6,000 rpm
- Pulley ratio (automatic transmission): 2.69:1
- Pulley ratio (manual transmission): 2.98:1
- Internally regulated

engine family from which it was born: a lightweight Motorcraft reduction gear starter with an integral solenoid. Power energizes the solenoid, which plays double duty; it energizes the starter and operates the starter drive engagement. This is a three-bolt starter just like you find on the 4.6L and 5.4L engines. If you're doing a Coyote swap into a vintage Ford you can run the factory starter solenoid as a means to getting power to the Motorcraft starter solenoid. You are, in effect, activating two solenoids this way. You may also eliminate the classic remote starter solenoid and get power directly from your vintage Ford's ignition switch via the "S" lead, which energizes the start solenoid down under at the starter.

Charging System

The Coyote utilizes a high-amp, internally regulated Motorcraft "9G" 150-amp alternator, which is more than adequate for most applications. Ford Performance Racing Parts offers you the 2012–2013 Boss 302 alternator, M-8600-M50B-ALT, which is an off-the-shelf piece designed specifically for high-RPM operation. Because the 9G is internally regulated, there's nothing to sweat out service-wise except regulator replacement, which is easy.

Ford no longer manufactures its own alternators. The 9G is manufactured by an outside supplier. It is available from the Ford Parts website for stock replacement. It is also available new and remanufactured from the aftermarket. Ford Performance offers you the Boss 302 alternator, M-8600-M50B-ALT, which is the better choice even if you're just doing a routine replacement.

Boss 302 Alternator Conversion

The Boss 302 Alternator Kit (M-8600-M50B-ALT) includes special high-performance components as used on the production 2012–2013 Boss 302 Mustang and is designed to operate at a higher-RPM range, according to Ford Performance Racing Parts.

Gen III Electronic Engine Control and Charging

The Gen III's electronic engine control is virtually unchanged from Gen I and Gen II. However, there are important changes that have come due to dual fuel injection—known as port fuel/direct injection (PFDI)—and the associated changes in electronics. There are additional parts to the engine wiring loom dedicated to dual fuel injection. The #3 coil-on-plug ignition coil is actually a remote coil with a lead to the spark plug due to interference issues with the direct-injection pump.

Boss 302 Alternator Conversion Kit

This fits the Mustang 5.0L Coyote engine and features the following:

- High-performance Boss alternator with one-way clutch to prevent belt hop during high-revving upshifts
- Higher-tension belt tensioner for belt security
- Larger pulley to slow the armature speed, reduce drag, and reduce power loss
- Also fits M-6007-M50, M-6007-A50NA, M-6007-A50XS, and M-6007-A50SC Ford Performance Racing Parts and Roush Performance crate engines
- Kit includes OEM Mustang Boss 302 alternator, tensioner, idler pulley, belt, and mounting hardware

The Coyote is fitted with a high-output state-of-the-art "9G" 150-amp alternator. Although this is a compact alternator it produces an outrageous amount of charging power. Its compact size makes it a good fit for the Coyote. If you intend to spin your Coyote high, consider the Ford Performance Racing Parts M-8600-M50B-ALT Boss 302 alternator conversion upgrade. Because high-output sound systems are so popular these days, you need to consult with an audio shop on charging system options should you opt for a high-wattage audio system. The stock alternator may not stand up to the demand.

Here's what you have for Gen III sensors:

- Throttle position sensor (TPS) (1)
- Accelerator pedal
- Oxygen sensors (2)
- Intake charge temperature sensor (1)
- Mass Airflow sensor (MAF) (1)
- Cylinder head temperature sensor (1)
- Cam position sensors (2 intake, 2 exhaust)
- Knock sensors (4)
- Crank sensor (1)

Through the miracle of electronics, the PCM (also known as the ECU, ECM, or computer) processes hundreds of millions of functions in a nanosecond with seamless precision. The TPS is a variable resistor like the volume control on your sound system. An electrical resistance value travels through the TPS to ground to get a given result from the PCM that controls the engine's many digital functions. It works in unison with the accelerator pedal potentiometer (variable resistor), oxygen sensors, intake charge temperature sensor, MAF, cylinder head temperature sensor, cam position sensors, knock sensors, and crank sensor to get specific actions from the PCM/ECU, which then dictates

The Ford Performance Racing Parts 5.0L Coyote Boss 302 alternator kit, M-8600-M50B-ALT, includes special high-performance components as used in the production 2012–2013 Boss 302 Mustang. They're engineered to operate at much higher RPM using a one-way clutch to prevent belt failure during manic upshifts. The belt tensioner has greater tension for better belt control at high RPM, and the larger-diameter pulley slows armature speed, which reduces drag and parasitic power loss. This is not a higher-amp alternator. It is designed specifically for high-RPM use.

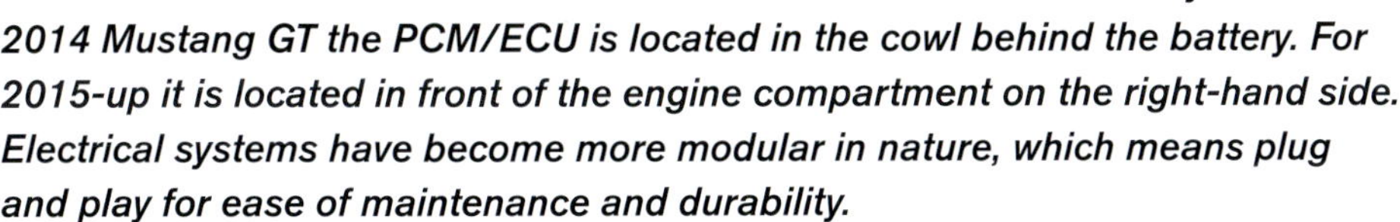

The Coyote's electronic engine control, known as Copperhead, is located closer to the engine these days instead of being inside the cabin. Access and service are easy. For 2011–2014 Mustang GT the PCM/ECU is located in the cowl behind the battery. For 2015-up it is located in front of the engine compartment on the right-hand side. Electrical systems have become more modular in nature, which means plug and play for ease of maintenance and durability.

Any time you make performance modifications to your 5.0L Ti-VCT Coyote or 5.2L Voodoo engine, it is strongly suggested you put it in the hands of a trusted electronic engine tuner. Some aftermarket software programs work quite well, but not all of them. Check out the chat rooms and forums to see what people's experiences are. Most tune shops use existing off-the-shelf software to tune, which doesn't mean they know what they're doing. You want a tuner who can interface with your Coyote's Copperhead system and dial in spark and fuel curve based on dyno numbers. This is a 2014 Mustang GT being retuned at GAS after an exhaust system change.

Here's one example of the modular nature of Ford electrical systems today. This is the 2015 Mustang's main fuse and relay box, located underhood for easy access.

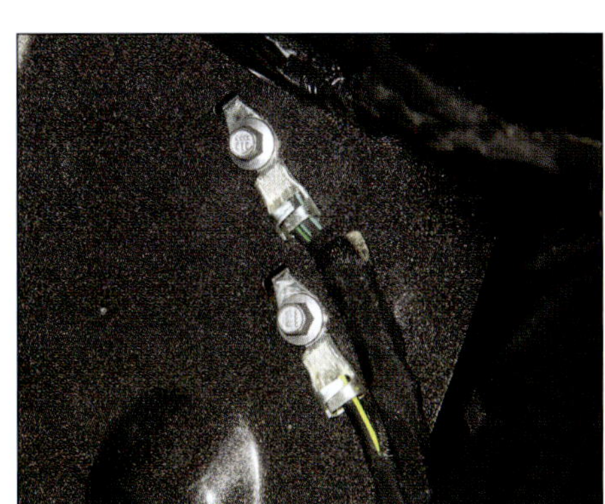

It may not seem like a big deal, but proper grounding is everything to proper PCM/ECU function. If you examine new Fords closely you see grounding everywhere to ensure solid negative ground continuity. The black and black with yellow stripe has been Ford's ground identity for more than a half-century.

air/fuel delivery and ignition timing. The PCM receives electrical feedback (signals) from these sensors to compute fuel delivery and ignition timing.

As the PCM receives feedback from these sensors, it uses that information to compute hundreds of thousands of decisions per second: fuel-injector timing and pulse width (spray) into each cylinder timed with the intake valve. It is programed to fire spark plugs in a timed sequence. It advances or retards spark timing as conditions warrant. It even controls

The Gen III's ignition system is a carryover of the Gen II system with a few exceptions. The Copperhead system operates in much the same fashion as it has since 2011 with the Gen I, with updates to the programming as Ford has refined the system with Charge Motion and other updates. This can be termed a failsafe ignition system that's water and dust tight at the plugs. Cam position sensors have been moved to the valve covers at the back (arrows). Cam phaser solenoids toward the front of the valve cover control intake and exhaust phaser function (arrows).

Each independent ignition coil is easy to service and not any different on the Gen III engine. Carefully unplug the harness from the coil and pull the coil. Use dielectric compound at the terminal to keep it moisture- and contaminant-free.

automatic transmission shift events based on driving demands.

When the PCM, sensors, fuel and ignition, and transmission are working together as a team, the result is smooth and efficient performance that is better than the carburetor and distributor ever were.

However, PCMs are genius when all is well, but when they or any part of the system malfunction, the result is startling. A worst-case scenario can leave you stranded and waiting for a tow. Most of the time, the problem is a faulty sensor or poor connection. If the oxygen sensor isn't working properly, the PCM will go into open loop or "limp home" mode, and your Coyote will perform poorly along with the illumination of the "check engine" light.

The Coyote's "Copperhead" system is pretty sharp. Ford has gone to extremes to make sure you don't wind up on the roadside. What's more is that function is so good there's rarely a performance issue. Because onboard diagnostics are so good, Copperhead will tell you what's wrong and be very specific about it. All you need is a reader, which can be found anywhere online. Any reputable automotive repair shop can read the PCM and learn quickly what the problem is. It has never been easier to troubleshoot, tune, and get back on the road.

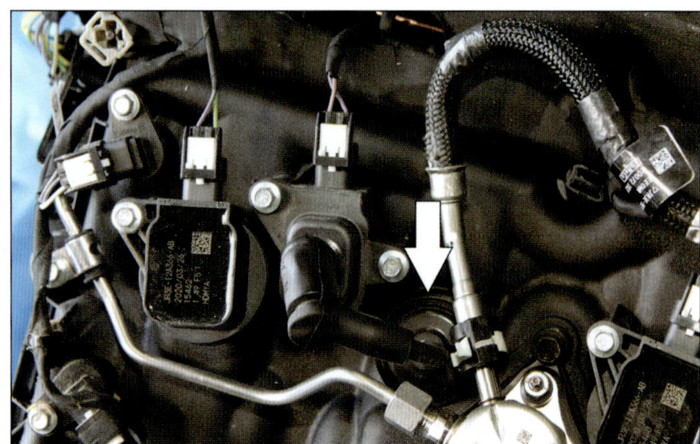

The #3 ignition coil is an obvious difference for the Gen III. The coil is separate from the boot and connected via an ignition cable to clear the direct-injection pump.

The Gen III Coyote has four knock sensors versus two on the Gen I and Gen II engines. This is critical due to a greater compression ratio on the Gen III.

Exhaust

The Coyote's exhaust system is just as critical to power and efficiency as the rest of the engine and driveline package. Headers might not seem like much of a big deal in the big performance picture, but exhaust scavenging is important and was a great area of focus for Team Coyote.

The Coyote has short tri-Y headers that were painstakingly thought out and executed by Ford engineers. These guys had to fight for them because it was everything to closing the power gap. Bean counters didn't want them because they're twice as costly to produce as cast-iron exhaust manifolds, yet crucial to emissions, power, and fuel economy.

Because the Coyote's factory shorty header is unique with its equal-length style, it has enabled the Ti-VCT to produce some 400 ft-lbs of torque. You can get horsepower all day long. Torque is another story and a huge challenge for engineers and product planners. Enthusiasts always want more horsepower, but torque is what gets your mojo on. Torque should be your priority on the street.

Exhaust Refinement = More Power

Although Ford's best engineers did an incredible job of exhaust system refinement there's always room for improvement. It begins with a great aftermarket exhaust system if you're seeking an easy upgrade. It is challenging to beat Ford's factory Coyote headers. However, BBK, JBA, Ford Performance Racing Parts, and a host of others produce short- and long-tube headers for the Coyote. Your challenge is to determine which ones yield the greatest benefit for your Coyote. In Chapter 12 I test three header types on a 2011–2014 Ford Performance Racing Parts crate engine and give you the results.

Although long-tube headers are time-proven in terms of power, they aren't always recommended for street applications. They aren't

When Ford was developing the Ti-VCT Coyote, engineers focused their energy on heads, cams, and valvetrain. However, after engine development was on the home stretch, their attention turned to improved exhaust scavenging. Exhaust system research and development was one of the toughest duties that Ford engineers had before them. Exhaust manifolds had to be shorty tubular headers and they had to be packaged to capitalize not only on horsepower, but also on low- to mid-range torque.

On the left-hand (driver) side you can see a similarity to the right-hand (passenger) side. It is all about the scavenging of hot gasses and the velocity necessary to draw four exhaust pulses into the collector at high speed. When you have the right amount of valve overlap you get good scavenging and the resulting torque.

Here's a closer look at the right-hand (passenger) header being installed at Performance Assembly Solutions in Livonia, Michigan. These shorty headers are included with your Ford Performance Racing Aluminator crate engine, which demonstrates just how effective these scavengers are.

Catalytic converters were once considered stifling to performance, but not anymore. Ford engineers looked at every aspect of the Coyote's exhaust system. The end result is low-restriction single-stage cats with two O2 sensors. One O2 sensor is ahead of the cat while the other is in the cat. This enables the system to keep an eye on catalytic converter and engine function.

always SMOG legal either. Any header you select for a street Coyote should be SMOG legal where you live. Ideally, you choose stainless or a ceramic-coated header. Chrome tends to rust with time and use, which makes it one of the least recommended choices.

Borla

Borla offers at least three muffler types for Coyote Mustangs and F-150s: Touring, S-Type, and Atak. Touring offers a soft throat, which is good for cruising. S-Type gets a little louder with less restriction. Atak is downright loud and snarly, a straight-through muffler void of restriction. Borla mufflers have always been the industry "loud" in all their many forms. And that's the Borla trademark.

Stage 3 Motorsports

Stage 3 Motorsports puts a nice system together for the 2011–2016 Mustang. When it comes to achieving the sound that's right for you Stage 3 Motorsports offers a nice selection of mufflers and systems. From a raspy race car sound to a deep and throaty muscle growl, these folks appear to have it covered. All Mustang exhaust systems come from top-quality manufacturers such as Magnaflow, Flowmaster, JBA Exhaust, Bassani, and Borla, and can give your Mustang additional horsepower and torque. Stage 3 also has high-performance headers and performance mid-pipes, which can yield a nice throat. Keep in mind that most long-tube headers and aftermarket mid-pipes require custom tuning to get their full power gains and avoid engine damage. Get a pro tune immediately after changing the exhaust system.

Roush Performance

Roush Performance is another good source for Coyote exhaust systems, with everything from headers to mufflers, which improve high-end horsepower primarily. While you are shopping, check local smog laws to make sure these exhaust system mods are legal for your area.

A Broader Brush

As you shop exhaust systems think about why you are upgrading your exhaust system. Are you doing it for sound, performance, or both? Most mufflers, regardless of what manufacturers tell you, are engineered more for sound than performance. It is more the headers and mid-pipes that yield performance gains. When you're shopping catalytic converters look at flow/restriction. Not all performance cats are performance cats. Not all X-pipes improve performance and sound. Header selection affects performance more than anything else. In addition, long-tube headers aren't already better than shorties unless you're going to all-out racing and high-RPM operation. Shorty headers are the champions of good low- and mid-range torque. Not all manufacturers call them shorty headers. Some call them "tuned length."

Ford Performance Racing Parts Power Pack

GAS recently allowed access for the installation of a Ford Performance Racing Parts Power Pack exhaust system, which also includes a tune package you can dial in when the exhaust system is installed. GAS is a Ford Performance Racing Parts dealership tied directly to Galpin Ford/Lincoln in the heart of the San Fernando Valley of Southern California. GAS is only the latest innovation from Galpin Ford.

The Ford Performance Power Pack is a nice, affordable exhaust upgrade for 2011–2016 Mustangs and Mustang GTs, and it takes about an hour to install. GAS can do this for you or you can perform the installation in your garage or driveway. The result is more power and a snarly bark when you crack the throttle. You need to get a professional performance tune when you install this system.

I decided to look in at GAS where technician Daniel Torres is installing Ford Performance Racing Parts' Power Pack for the 2011–2014 Mustang GT. The Power Pack promises 16 hp and 60 ft-lbs of torque along with a throaty sound at the tips. Installation begins with installation of the K&N/FPRP air filter and Pro Cal tune package. Ford Performance also includes a new oil filter. Unlike many of its competitors, the Ford Racing Power Pack is 50-state emissions legal under CARB EO D598-12. If it can pass tough California emission requirements, it can pass anywhere.

Ford's introduction of the 2005 S197 Mustang made exhaust tuning easier because you don't need a muffler shop to replace mufflers and pipes. Mufflers bolt on the end of the exhaust system at the tailpipe, which makes muffler tuning easier. The stock muffler is held on with an aerospace clamp. For a quick replacement, you simply loosen the clamp to free the muffler.

The S197 Mustang's mufflers are secured with aerospace clamps and mounted on soft rubber hangers with easy-to-access hardware. This is a new 2014 Mustang GT brought in to GAS for the Ford Performance Racing Parts Power Pack. The low restriction K&N/FPRP serviceable air filter has already been installed and the Pro Cal tune dialed in.

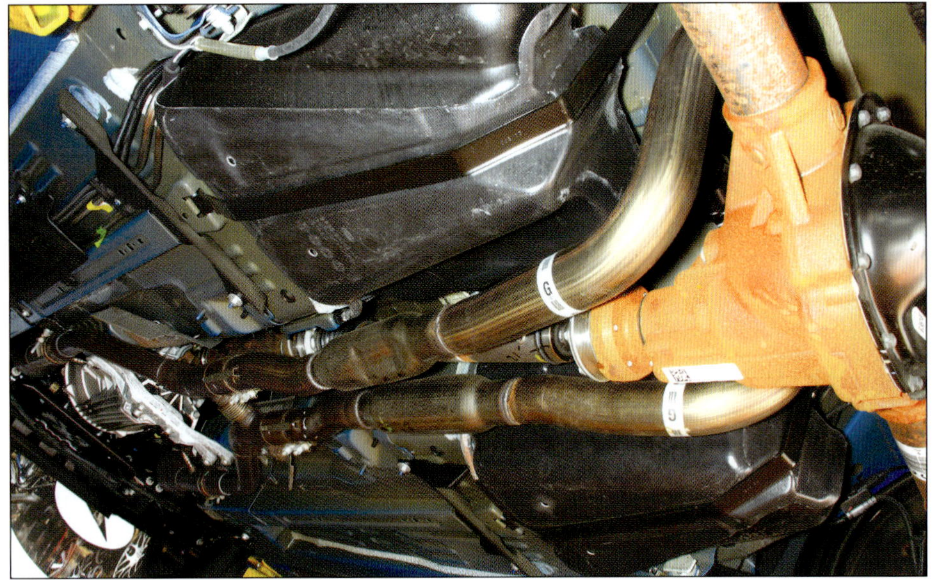

For 2011–2014 the Mustang GT has these resonators, which soften the Coyote's aggressive bark. They reduce and even eliminate resonance. These must be disconnected to replace the stock Mustang mufflers.

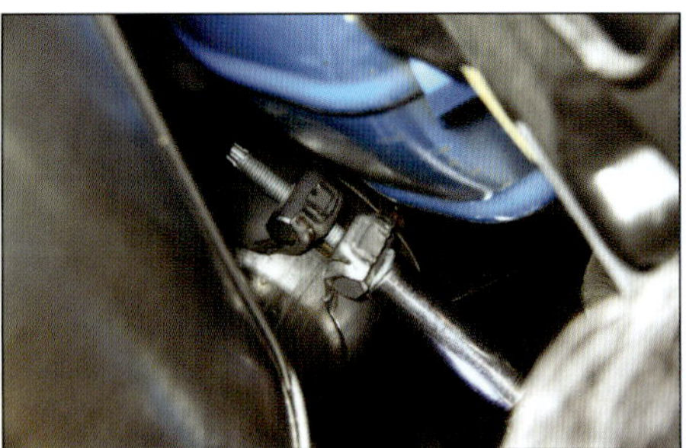

Back in the day, you had to visit a muffler shop to do an exhaust swap. Not anymore. Mustang GT has these simple aerospace exhaust clamps that make it easy to replace mufflers and pipes. One of the greatest S197 innovations has been these easy-to-service clamps, mufflers, and pipes. You can swap mufflers all day and listen to different exhaust symphonies. It's that easy.

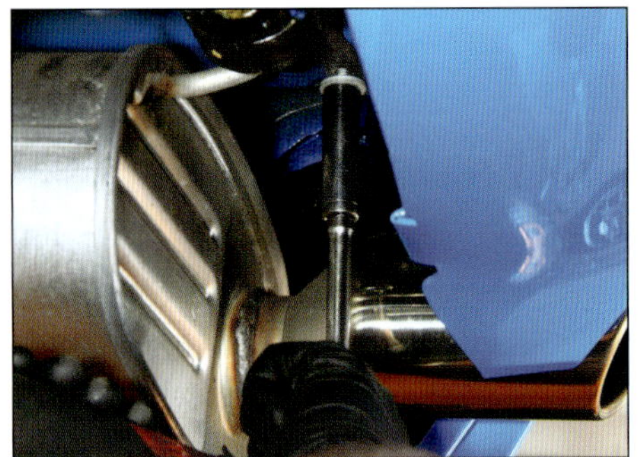

Soft rubber and steel hangers are unbolted from the frame rails, which frees up the mufflers. These brackets can be tricky to get to because it gets tight. Overall, access is straightforward.

Daniel Torres disconnects the resonators long enough to free up mufflers and tailpipes. This is easy to do.

Constructed from durable mandrel-bent aluminized 409 stainless steel for superior corrosion resistance and improved exhaust flow, the FR GT500 axle-back exhaust system features the same chambered muffler design found on the brute Shelby GT500s. These mufflers are finished with dual 4.000-inch-diameter polished 304 stainless-steel tips for a deep, throaty exhaust burble.

After mufflers are installed and clamps secured, these GT500–born and bred mufflers look and sound sharp. When Daniel fired this GT's Coyote it delivered a bark you could hear for blocks. GAS offers a complete inventory of Ford Performance Racing Parts for Coyote-powered Fords along with installation.

The installed Ford Performance Racing Parts mufflers look sharp and net a powerful bark, which is the Coyote's trademark.

Corsa 3.0-Inch Cat-Back System

CORSA Performance entered the exhaust business in 1998 and decided to rewrite the rulebook for what a performance exhaust should be. It introduced its own RSC (Reflective Sound Cancellation) Technology. RSC allows CORSA Performance to selectively target and eliminate resonant frequencies that cause that headache-causing drone in high-performance applications by reflecting sound waves out of phase, while custom tuning the exhaust note.

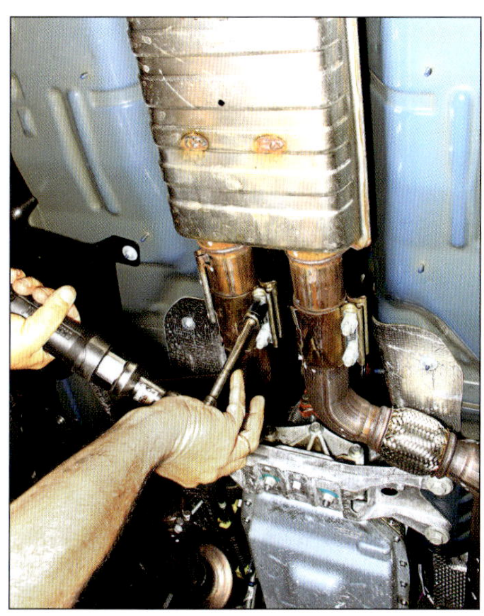

Look at this huge factory resonator on the 2015–2016 Mustang GT. The S550 Mustang's factory exhaust system is one gigantic system consisting of this huge resonator, pipes, and mufflers. The factory system is heavy and takes two people to remove.

When you get past resonator disconnection at the catalytic converters it's time to look at muffler and tailpipe security and how these guys are mounted. What makes the S550 Mustang different is the fully independent suspension and exhaust plumbing routed underneath the differential and axle shafts. Mufflers have hangers, as do the tailpipes.

Marlo's Frame & Alignment/Fly-Ford Racing provided a close look at the Corsa's 3.0-inch Sport Cat-Back stainless exhaust system that they were about to install on a customer's 2015 Mustang GT. This system is considerably lighter than the factory dual exhaust system because the heavy resonator is deleted.

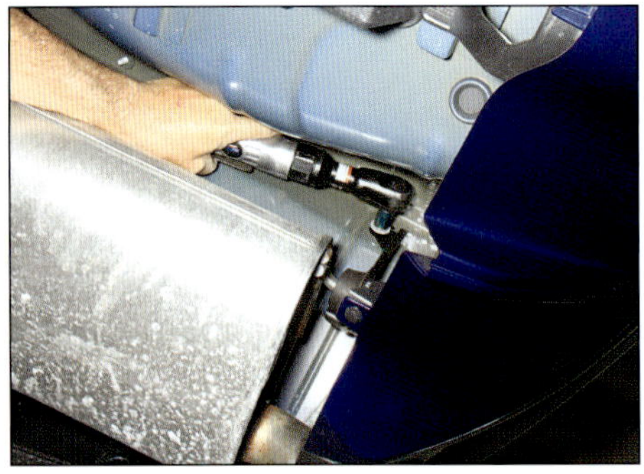

Mufflers are secured with two soft-mount brackets each, like this. It's a good idea to take pictures of your system before removal. It is easy to get these brackets backward when it's time to reinstall. Mufflers and pipes do not line up if you install these brackets backward.

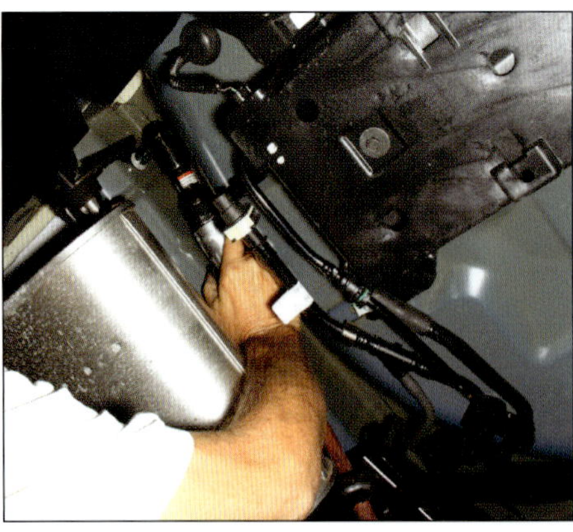

It is remarkable how easy these mufflers are to remove. As with the Ford Performance 2011–2014 exhaust system just mentioned, aerospace pipe clamps make it easy to disconnect mufflers and pipes and install new.

Tailpipes are secured at this central mount at the differential. When you consider the Mustang GT's dual exhaust system on the S550, it makes you wonder why this approach wasn't adopted earlier. Much of the reason for this change comes from the new S550 Mustang's independent rear suspension, which was a good change.

It takes two people to remove the S550 Mustang's dual exhaust system because it is all one huge assembly from the resonator amidships to the mufflers in back. Much of the weight can be credited to the resonator, which is very heavy.

These 2½- to 3-inch adaptors are fitted to the catalytic converter pipes. The aerospace exhaust clamps secure the adaptors and are easily removed should maintenance be required. Pipes sized 2½ to 3 inches allow exhaust gas expansion and improved scavenging.

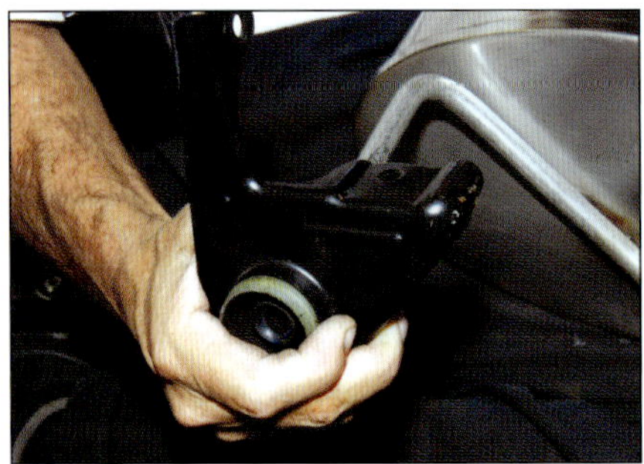

The S197 and S550 Mustangs employ state-of-the-art exhaust hangers, which take noise and vibration isolation to new heights. Where it gets tricky is forgetting how these hangers were installed to begin with. It's a good idea to mark them or take photos before disassembly.

Exhaust clamps are fitted to the pipe ends as shown. What makes Corsa different is the hourglass balance pipe between the cats and tailpipes. It eliminates the weight of the stock resonator, along with unwanted resonance.

The Corsa RSC mufflers and pipes are installed as shown. Corsa delivers outstanding quality when you look beyond drone cancellation technology. These good-looking stainless pieces will outlast your S197/S550 Mustang.

The first place to hang these pipes is the central mount. This takes the stress out of labor because the pipes are in place and you only have to add mufflers.

Polished exhaust tips are among the last installation steps and are fully adjustable. These tips are also available in black.

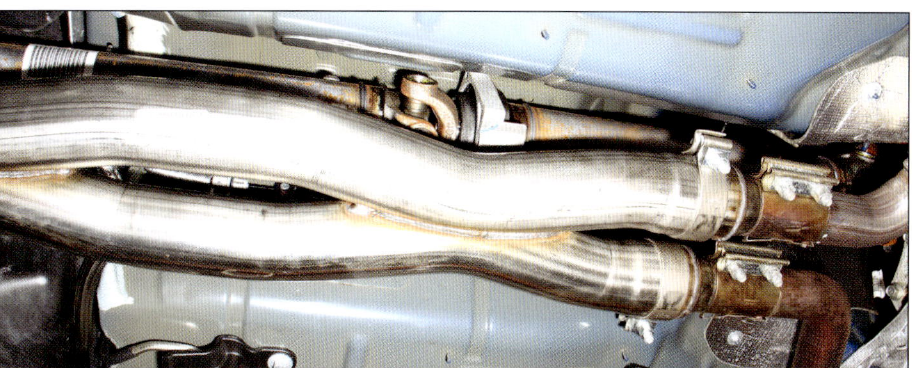

Here's the hourglass X-pipe balance assembly that blends exhaust pulses, eliminates resonance, and improves power.

The complete Corsa system is not only an improvement in performance, but also a weight loss program that eliminates the heavy factory resonator. There's a lot more room underneath now.

The Corsa RSC system is installed and adjusted. Check it out. The Corsa difference is all about throat; the raw throat sound of these stainless mufflers and the exhaust plumbing that feeds them. This is a sound you can hear when you crack the throttle.

Cool Corsa polished tips or black. The choice is yours. These 4.000-inch tips amplify the Coyote's bark, yet they're not bothersome in the cabin. This is the 14332 single polished tip system. You may opt for quad tips in polished or black. You can even order the tips alone.

Every CORSA Performance exhaust system for the S197 and S550 Mustangs and F-Series trucks takes into account OEM design, desired performance output as well as interactions of the entire exhaust system. Think of each CORSA system as a custom application for the vehicle for which it was designed. Rarely are any two exhaust systems featuring RSC Technology the same.

BBK Performance

BBK Performance offers a broad array of exhaust products from headers to mufflers. For off-road use only, BBK offers cat eliminators that go straight through to the X-pipe, tailpipes, and Vari-Tune mufflers. The BBK Performance 2015 Mustang GT test mule shows you what's possible from your GEN 2 Coyote with charge motion induction. You will see numbers from BBK's Tuned Length headers with cats and again with full-length headers without cats. BBK is using its own stainless long-tube headers, which for this testing eliminate the catalytic converters in off-road use only. BBK also offers high-flow cats for the long-tubes for street and race use. BBK Performance exhaust components are made right here in the United States in Southern California.

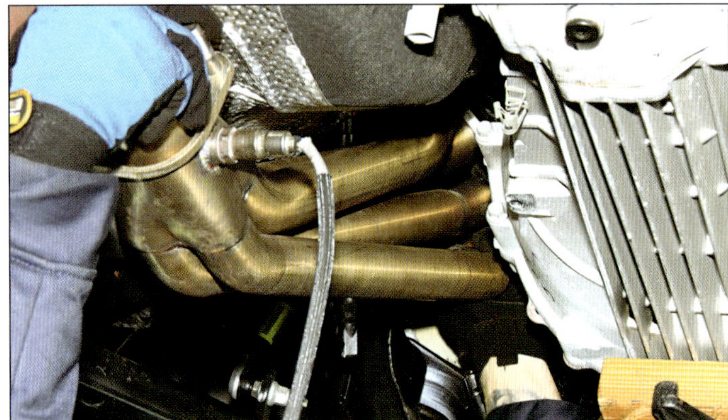

Stainless BBK long-tube headers are used for this exercise because they yield horsepower over torque. And horsepower is what we're going for.

These BBK "L" pipes transition into the factory resonator from long-tubes for off-road use. Note the proper location of the oxygen sensors.

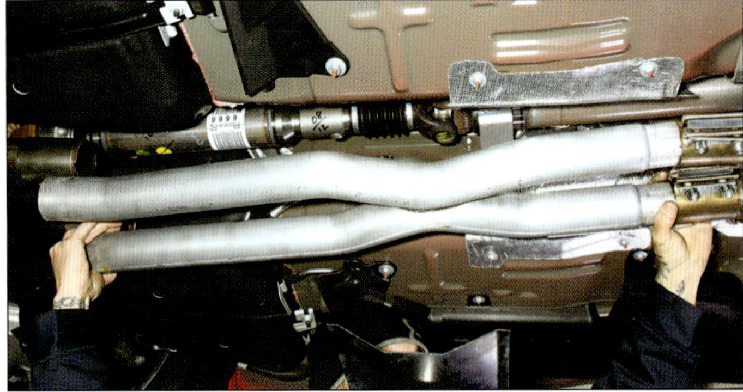

The factory resonator can be eliminated for this BBK Performance hourglass-shaped X-pipe, which mixes up the exhaust pulses and improves scavenging, giving the BBK system a nice bark.

This is the BBK Performance Vari-Tune muffler, which enables you to custom tune the mufflers without swapping mufflers. You can tune both flow and noise levels with this feature, then dyno tune.

CHAPTER 10

Cooling

Coyote's cooling system focuses close attention to exhaust valve cooling as well as other high-heat areas of the engine. Ford calls this "cross-flow" cooling, which is different from the conventional cooling for which the 4.6L and 5.4L Modular engines are known. Cross-flow cooling routes coolant up through the block, where it enters cylinder heads at the exhaust valves for excellent heat transfer and reduced operating temperatures. Coolant runs through a long manifold cast into the cylinder head at the exhaust valveseats. It then flows toward spark plugs, intake manifold, and block before heading back to the radiator. This keeps detonation issues to a minimum and durability high. Gone is the mid-valley coolant tube that consumes so much space in the 4.6L and 5.4L engines.

When you examine the Coyote's cooling system it can get confusing. There is what looks like two thermostat housings: one on top of the intake manifold on the left-hand (driver) side and another at the left-hand (driver) cylinder head in front. There's only one thermostat, which is located at the left-hand (driver) cylinder head where coolant flows from the radiator into the block. In a conventional cooling system, coolant flows into the block from the radiator. The thermostat controls flow out of the engine. With the Coyote, coolant flow remains from the radiator through the bottom hose. However, the thermostat controls flow into the engine instead of out of it.

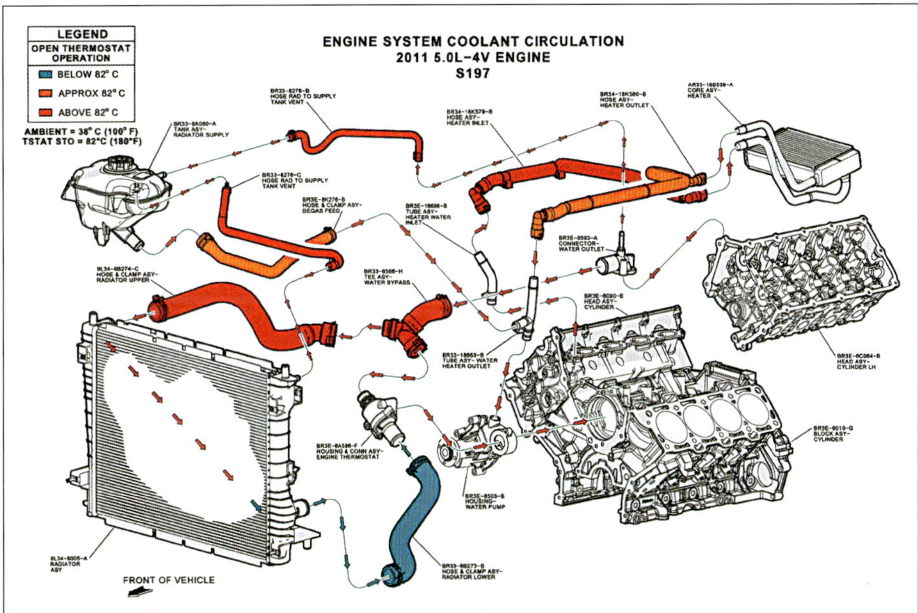

This illustration shows the Coyote cooling system's function and component location. The cooling system function begins with coolant leaving the radiator at the bottom and going into the engine via a lower radiator hose and water pump. Coolant enters the engine at the left-hand (driver) cylinder head at the thermostat and reaches exhaust valves on both heads first before flowing into the rest of the engine. Coolant exits the engine at the coolant neck on top and flows back to both the radiator and a return to the engine at the "Y"-pipe. The logic behind Coyote cooling system function is recirculation of coolant via the "Y" for faster warm-up and more generous coolant flow. The thermostat opens at 180 degrees F, allowing coolant flow from the radiator. (Illustration Courtesy Ford Performance Parts)

The Coyote's cooling system is simple in scope, as shown here. Coolant recirculates within the engine in a conventional fashion via the plastic "Y"-pipe when the thermostat is closed. When the thermostat opens, fresh coolant flows into the engine from the radiator via the lower radiator hose. Hot coolant exits the engine via the "Y"-pipe and upper radiator hose.

Here's a closer look at the plastic "Y" connector and two radiator hoses. The thermostat is located here (arrow) where coolant flows into the engine's left-hand (driver) cylinder head and makes its rounds through heads and block back to the "Y"-pipe and radiator.

Although this resembles a thermostat housing, it is the coolant neck at the left-hand (driver) cylinder head where coolant exits to the "Y"-pipe and upper radiator hose to the radiator.

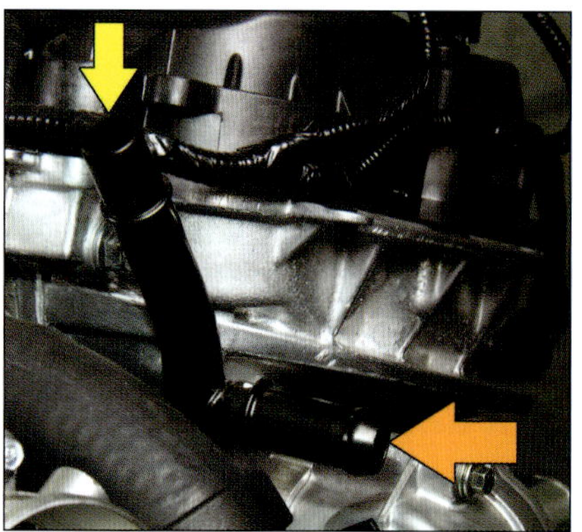

Heater hosepipe connections are incorporated into the cylinder heads in front as shown here. This is the left-hand (driver) side with the cockeyed "Y"-pipe. The top pipe at 12 o'clock (yellow arrow) is coolant flow from the heater hose. The lower pipe (orange arrow) is from the coolant expansion tank at the radiator. When you add coolant, it flows from the tank to this inlet pipe.

This is the heater hose connection at the right-hand-side (passenger) cylinder head (arrow). Coolant flows out of the engine via this pipe back to the heater core.

This is the water pump pocket at the front of the Coyote's aluminum block.

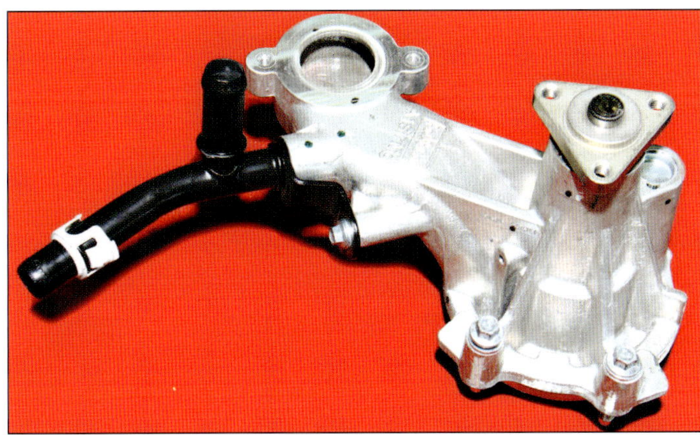

The Coyote's high-flow water pump does a very efficient job of moving coolant through this engine. Instead of an old-fashioned gasket, the Coyote's water pump uses an O-ring, which seals very well and will last for the life of the water pump.

Here's a close-up of the Coyote's water pump O-ring seal, which eliminates old-fashioned gaskets, making replacement a snap. This sealing approach isn't new to the Coyote. It dates back to the 4.6L and 5.4L Modular engines and is very effective. The only help this seal requires is lubrication, and the pump slips right in. This high-efficiency impeller aggressively moves coolant through the Coyote's water jackets.

Although the Coyote cooling system appears complex with its cluster of hoses and plumbing, it really is a simple system with clear priorities. The focus is the hottest segments of the engine and heat transfer to the radiator and atmosphere. Moreover, this is a system designed to prevent hot spots that come from coolant cavitation (trapped air) in the system. All air pockets are vented via the "Y"-shaped hose package at the front of the engine.

Cooling Improvements

How do you improve on an already great cooling system? Modular Motorsports Racing offers the head cooling kit, which improves coolant flow at the rear of Coyote engines. One weak link in the Coyote has been excessive cylinder pressures and temperatures from boost and nitrous, resulting in extraordinarily high engine temperatures at the back of the engine. The Modular Motorsports Racing head cooling kit reduces the risk of engine failure. Under more normal operating conditions, the Coyote enjoys more than adequate cooling and doesn't need the head cooling kit.

Another improvement for the cooling system is the Meziere electric water pump, if you're searching for hair-splitting increases in power. Engine-driven water pumps consume a certain amount of power, especially at high RPM. On the street or for weekend racing, the benefit of an electric water pump is debatable. For all-out racing, where every second counts, it's a measurable improvement. A high-flow coolant pump for the Coyote engine is not available at press time, although I expect that to change in time.

Coolant Servicing

When you are servicing your Coyote with coolant you must ensure that all water jackets are

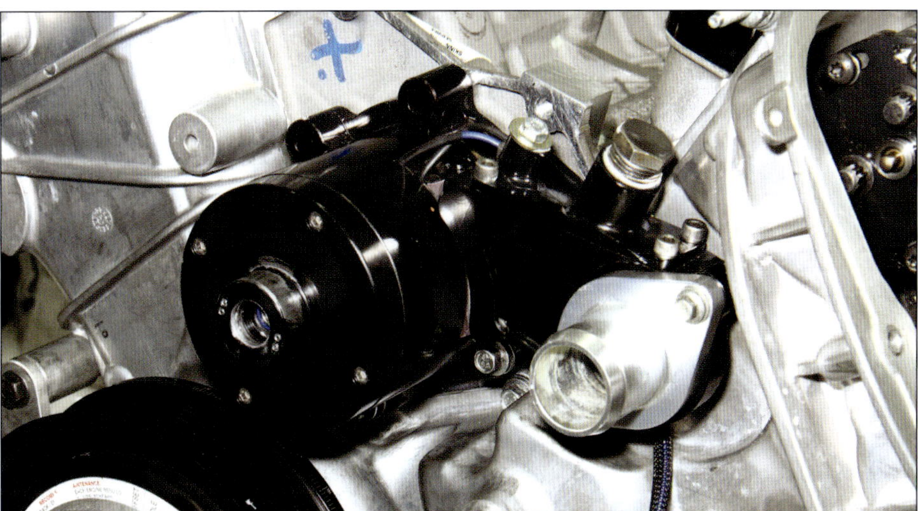

Electric water pumps such as this eliminate power losses from engine-driven water pumps. These electric pumps make more sense in racing than they do for street use, although you can use them on the street.

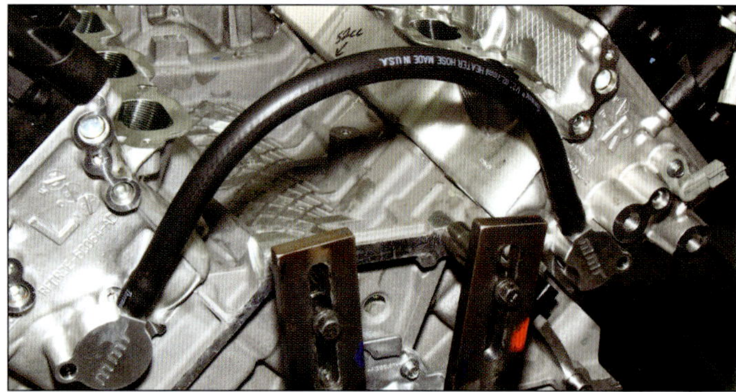

The Coyote's only cooling issue, which can also be considered a weakness, is hot spots at the back of the block and heads, primarily, under high boost or nitrous. If you are running a lot of boost or nitrous, cylinders number-4 and -8 can fail due to extreme heat in these areas and insufficient cooling. The result is blown-out cylinder walls and catastrophic engine failure. Modular Motorsports offers this kit designed to improve coolant circulation at the back of the engine, which saves cylinder walls.

Ford engineers made sure the Coyote had adequate cooling from the factory. At press time, the aftermarket hasn't answered the call to any great degree for a high-capacity radiator. However, Ford Performance Racing Parts brings you the M-8005-M8 high-efficiency radiator in the 2015–2016 Mustang GT. It offers greater cooling capacity and is a simple drop-in swap.

The Coyote's thermostat works in a conventional way. However, it is located at the inlet to the engine instead of the outlet. Flow is achieved through extensive computational flow dynamics (per Ford) and thoughtful engine architecture. This is a revised cooling approach called cross-flow cooling. The older 4.6L and 5.4L Modulars are series cooled, with coolant rising from the block into the back of the head, then flowing forward through the head and out into an external crossover tube in the valley and the thermostat.

Here's a closer look at the Coyote's two-stage thermostat, also known as a two-valve thermostat. The two-valve (or two-disc) function is designed to precisely regulate coolant flow and temperature. If you're going to run an aftermarket 170-degree F thermostat in your Coyote, this should only be done with a performance tune and never a stock tune. Stock Coyote engines do not need a low-temp thermostat.

Granatelli Motorsports brings Coyote buffs this aluminum coolant recovery tank for the 2015–2016 Mustang GT, which is a nice touch and looks better than the plastic factory reservoir. (Photo Courtesy Granatelli Motorsports)

This is the M-8005-MBR high-capacity radiator from Ford Performance Racing Parts. What makes this radiator better than the base Coyote heat exchanger is GT350-style capacity. This radiator is original equipment in the 2015–2016 Shelby GT350. (Photo Courtesy Ford Performance Parts)

filled with coolant. I have heard from engine builders and tuners that the Coyote engine's water jackets are challenging to fill due to the engine's cooling system design. Some builders say they fill the Coyote's cooling system via the heater hose tubes to ensure both sides of the engine are filled with coolant. Then, they add remaining coolant at the radiator/expansion tank. Coyote engines are known for hot spots, even after the initial coolant fill, which tends to yield fluctuating coolant temperatures until coolant occupies all cooling passages throughout the engine.

Gen III Cooling System Refinements

When Ford engineers revisited the Coyote's cooling system, which was exceptional to begin with, they looked at what a dual-injected engine was going to need to remain stable temperature-wise. Direct injection and a whopping increase in compression to 12.0:1 meant the cylinder head decks and head gaskets would have to be refined to keep head and deck temperatures safe.

Close examination of the head-gasket cooling passages shows a change in holes around the bores at the deck to better control temperatures at the hottest parts of the engine. What's more, cooling jackets are different compared with the Gen I and Gen II engine blocks. From a cooling standpoint, the Gen III is clearly the best evolution of the Coyote block. The block, coupled with better head gaskets, makes a strong case for the Gen III.

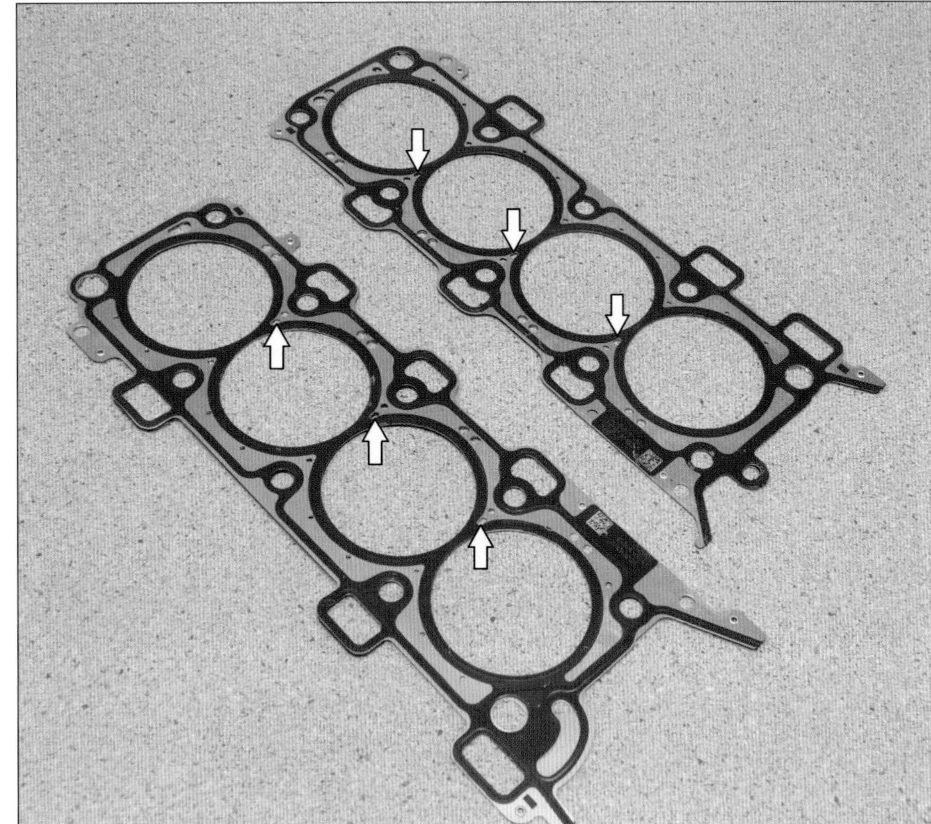

The Gen III head gasket shows finite improvements in cooling management (arrows). This is not an interchangeable head gasket with the Gen I and Gen II engines.

CHAPTER 11

Building the Coyote

Ford's Coyote engine mandates close attention to detail when you're building this engine from scratch. The Coyote is extremely unforgiving of carelessness, which is why I've looked to the expertise of seasoned Modular engine builders (Performance Assembly Solutions and L & R Custom Engines) to show you the way to a successful engine build. Performance Assembly Solutions builds crate Coyote engines for Ford Performance Parts. L & R Custom Engines is well known around Los Angeles for its vast experience with vintage and late-model engines.

Performance Assembly Solutions

What better place to learn about properly building the 5.0L Ti-VCT Coyote DOHC V-8 than Roush's Performance Assembly Solutions (PAS) in Livonia, Michigan. PAS builds high-performance Coyote crate engines for Ford Performance Parts. PAS begins with production 5.0L Ti-VCT Coyote engines shipped directly from Ford's Essex, Ontario, Canada, engine plant, which are uncrated and built to Ford's exact standards as Aluminator crate engines. These are factory-built engines with a warranty.

Forget what you know and believe about mass-production crate engines. PAS, Ford Performance Parts, and Roush are out to change your perception of crate engines by building the highest-caliber production crate engines in the world. When new 5.0L Ti-VCT engines arrive from the Essex Engine Plant across the Detroit River, they are the same production engines installed in new Mustangs and F-Series trucks.

To alleviate any chance of a flawed engine or warranty issues, Ford Performance Parts looked to PAS for precision engine building solutions. This is a system employing strict accountability every step of the way in which it is virtually impossible to miss a problem. If any phase of teardown and reassembly is overlooked, the computerized control system halts production until the problem is found and corrected. Each engine arrives from the Essex engine plant barcoded and assigned its own unique PAS identification code. As these engines arrive at PAS and are uncrated, they are checked in via the barcode and reassigned with a PAS barcode that

Coyote crate engines arrive from Ford's Essex, Ontario, engine plant fully assembled. They have been spin tested, but not fired.

Here's what makes a Ford Coyote an "Aluminator": Mahle forged and coated 9.5:1 or 11.0:1 pistons and Manley H-beam connecting rods. These components take a 450-horse engine and make it capable of withstanding 600 to 1,000 hp. These engines, with stock rods and pistons, can take 600 to 700 hp. However, if your goal is more than 600 hp, you are gambling with stock rods and pistons. With Mahle and Manley, these engines can tolerate 600 to more than 1,000 hp with a stock block.

follows the engine all through production. Each engine's identity can be traced back to the engine plant.

These 5.0L Ti-VCT engines are carefully disassembled as new never-been-fired crate engines. All parts and components are carefully documented and placed on a cart that is tied to the engine's barcode. All components that came out of the engine during disassembly will go back into the same engine. Forget barrels full of common engine parts and hurried slap-together production. PAS is a custom-engine-building operation that has an intimate assembly line where every technician has a job and has to sign his or her name to every phase of teardown and assembly.

I had the good fortune of working closely with Randall Harris, Travis Hopson, Eric Leach, and Shawn Staniszewski at PAS in 2015 for the original edition of this book. More recently (in 2022), John Torvinen, Frank Hoffman, and Will Clendenin invited me back to PAS for a fresh look at what the company is doing today. Quality standards haven't changed at PAS. Instead, the company has become even more regimented with what it has learned in the years since.

Think of PAS as a custom-engine-building shop that is able to produce crate engines on a mass scale. These engines arrive in stock condition and leave as engines ready for 600 to 1000-plus hp fitted with Mahle pistons and Manley H-beam connecting rods. PAS and Ford Performance Racing Parts will ship you an engine ready to go racing. You have the option of upgrading your Coyote in any way you wish: hotter cams, forced induction or nitrous, and more.

When these Coyote engines arrive at PAS, they are disassembled and built to Ford's tough standards with a warranty. The Ford Performance Aluminator engine is a fast solution to quick turnaround and the security of a warranty.

As all engines are disassembled, there is a strict documentation process in place that notates every phase of teardown and assembly with the accountability of barcode verification. It all becomes a matter of permanent record. Parts aren't haphazardly thrown into barrels and fed into a mass production line. Each part is measured, and those measurements are documented in a sophisticated computer system. These numbers are also documented on paper. Nothing is overlooked. In addition, each builder on the line has engine building down cold. All are seasoned engine builders.

Although the Coyote appears complex on the surface, it really is a simple engine to service. On an engine stand, it is simple and easy to assemble if you follow proper protocol. What you must understand is that the Coyote (and other Modular engines) is unforgiving of error. If you're doing it yourself, conduct your Coyote build by the book and pay close attention to detail. The economics of Ford Performance crate engines is such that it makes little sense to build the Coyote yourself. PAS and Ford Performance do it for you without the hassle of and risk of doing it yourself.

Mike Robinson, a PAS engineer, said in 2015 that the aspect that makes these Ford Performance Aluminator engines a cut above any other crate engine in the industry is a strict build and documentation process. This is a state-of-the-art quality control process that Ford employs in its plants. After teardown, each block is hot-washed, rinsed, and then dried with compressed air. Cylinder bores are wiped down with light oil to prevent corrosion.

The first phase of the build process includes measuring and inspecting every single component that goes into the Aluminator engine. New Mahle forged coated pistons and Manley H-beam connecting rods are inspected and checked after being dynamic balanced. Piston rings are inspected and gapped to each bore before being fitted to pistons. The same can be said for aluminum main and rod bearings, which are fitted and measured to precise tolerances. Aside from the Manley rods and Mahle forged pistons, Ford parts are used exclusively in these Ford Performance Racing Parts Aluminator engines.

When the measuring and calibration process is complete, the block is mounted on an assembly stand and enters the assembly line, where the identification bar code is scanned into the system and each step strictly documented. Every step is monitored and recorded into a PAS database. Instructions and specifications appear on a touch screen interface and must be acknowledged as complete by the operator prior to the system allowing continuation in the build process. In addition to the electronic sign-off process, the system also records all fastener torque data, the rolling torque data, and even the leak and cold test values.

Each crank is dynamic balanced to the Manley/Mahle reciprocating mass. Think of this as a custom-engine job shop on a mass production scale, only it's a small line with a family-like atmosphere in the heart of Livonia, Michigan.

Coyote Engine Building Specifications

Ford Performance Parts offers a complete line of high-performance Coyote crate engines for vintage and late-model Ford applications. These engines range from box stock to all-out race mills as the Boss 302 and Cobra Jet, which are engineered for both road and drag racing.

Ford Performance Coyote Crate Engine

- 5.0L 4V Coyote Ti-VCT 420-HP Crate M-6007-M50A
- High-performance 5.0-liter, four-valve Ti-VCT engine
- 420 hp at 6,500 rpm
- 390 ft-lbs of torque at 4,250 rpm
- 302-ci/5.0L displacement
- 3.630-inch bore x 3.650-inch stroke
- Aluminum block
- Forged steel crankshaft
- Forged steel powdered-metal connecting rods
- Hypereutectic pistons
- Aluminum cylinder heads, DOHC, four valves per cylinder, variable intake and exhaust camshaft timing
- 8-quart-capacity oil pan
- 11.0:1 compression ratio
- Tuned composite intake manifold
- 80-mm single-bore drive-by-wire throttle body
- Mustang GT 409 stainless-steel tubular exhaust manifolds
- Includes manual transmission engine harness and flywheel
- Vehicle harness and PCM not included
- Use Ford Racing's NEW wiring, PCM, and installation kit M-6017-A504V designed for street rod/project car installation
- Does not include alternator, for alternator kit see M-8600-M50BALT
- 5.0L Mustang engine cover kit available, see M-9680-M50
- Use Oil Line Adapter M-6881-M50 for applications requiring oil filter relocation
- Engine-mount Bosses and bellhousing mount pattern common to 4.6L modular engines
- Engines built after August 8, 2013, are equipped with a water pump using a three-bolt pulley pattern
- Engine weight: 444 pounds

5.0L Coyote Aluminator Naturally Aspirated M-6007-A50NAA

- Fits 2011–2016 Mustang GT
- 5.0L (302 ci)
- 11.0:1 compression ratio (nominal)
- Mahle hard-anodized forged pistons with Grafal low-friction coating
- Manley H-beam connecting rods with ARP 2000 bolts
- Boss 302 connecting rod bearings
- Forged steel crankshaft
- Uses production Mustang GT aluminum block, M-6010-A50L4V
- Large rear sump oil pan with 8-quart capacity features optimized oil drainback and windage tray to control oil and improve high-RPM performance
- Tuned composite Mustang GT intake manifold with production drive-by-wire 80-mm throttle body
- Four-valve-per-cylinder aluminum heads with roller-finger followers reduce friction
- Boss 302 valvesprings, M-6513-M50BR
- Mustang GT production camshafts
- Intake: 12-mm lift, 260-degree duration
- Exhaust: 11-mm lift, 263-degree duration
- Ford Racing engine cover kit, M-9680-M50
- Includes manual transmission engine injector harness
- Front cover is modified for Ford Racing Supercharger Kits
- For applications not using a Ford Racing Supercharger Kit, stock timing cover must be installed
- Includes colder heat-range-zero (0) spark plugs, M-12405-M50
- Includes Ford Racing oil filter, M-6731-FL820
- Includes billet steel gerotor oil pump, M-6600-50CJ
- Vehicle harness and PCM not included; use Ford Racing wiring, PCM, and installation kit M-6017-A504V designed for street rod/project car installation
- Does not include alternator, for alternator kit see M-8600-M50BALT
- Oil-line adapter M-6881-M50 available for applications requiring oil filter relocation

Coyote Engine Building Specifications *CONTINUED*

- Engine-mount Bosses and bellhousing mount pattern common to 4.6L modular engines
- Engines built after August 8, 2013, are equipped with a water pump using a three-bolt pulley pattern

5.0L Coyote Aluminator SC M-6007-A50SCA

- Fits 2011–2016 Mustang GT
- 5.0L (302 ci)
- 9.5:1 compression ratio for supercharged applications
- Mahle hard-anodized forged pistons with Grafal low-friction coating
- Manley H-beam connecting rods with ARP 2000 bolts
- Forged steel crankshaft
- Uses production 2011–2014 Mustang GT aluminum cylinder block
- Large rear sump oil pan with 8-quart capacity features optimized oil drainback and windage tray to control oil and improve high-RPM performance
- Tuned composite Mustang GT intake manifold with production drive-by-wire 80-mm throttle body variable runner control
- Four-valve-per-cylinder aluminum heads with roller-finger followers reduce friction
- Boss 302 valvesprings, M-6513-M50BR
- Mustang GT production camshafts
- Intake: 12-mm lift, 260-degree duration
- Exhaust: 11-mm lift, 263-degree duration
- Ford Racing engine cover kit, M-9680-M50
- Includes manual transmission engine injector harness
- Front cover is modified for Ford Racing Supercharger Kits
- For applications not using a Ford Racing Supercharger Kit, stock timing cover must be installed
- Includes colder heat-range-zero (0) spark plugs for supercharging, M-12405-M50
- Includes Ford Racing oil filter, M-6731-FL820
- Includes billet steel gerotor oil pump, M-6600-50CJ
- Vehicle harness and PCM not included. Use Ford Racing wiring, PCM, and installation kit M-6017-A504V designed for street rod/project car installation.
- Does not include alternator, for alternator kit see M-8600-M50BALT
- Engine-mount Bosses and bellhousing mount pattern common to 4.6L modular engines

Note: Due to 9.5:1 compression ratio, custom tuning is required for optimum performance

5.0L Coyote Aluminator XS M-6007-A50XS

- Fits: 2011–2016 Mustang GT
- 500 hp
- 5.0L, 302 ci
- 11.0:1 compression ratio
- Mahle hard-anodized forged pistons with Grafal low-friction coating
- Manley H-beam connecting rods with ARP2000 bolts
- Forged steel crankshaft
- Uses production Mustang GT aluminum cylinder block
- Ford Racing M-6675-M50BR 12-quart rear sump oil pan features optimized oil drainback and windage tray to control oil and improve high-RPM performance
- Ford Racing M-6600-50CJ High-Performance billet steel oil pump
- Ford Racing M-9424-M50CJ Cobra Jet tuned intake
- Ford Racing M-9926-CJ65 throttle body
- Four-valve-per-cylinder Boss fully CNC-ported aluminum heads with roller-finger camshaft followers
- Ford Racing M-6513-M50BR Boss valvesprings
- Ford Racing camshafts
- M-6550-M50BINT intake camshaft, 13-mm lift/263-degree duration
- M-6550-M50BEXH exhaust camshaft, 13-mm lift/290-degree duration
- Ford Racing M-9593-LU47 47 lbs/hr fuel injectors
- Ford Racing M-12A227-CJ13 high-RPM pulse ring
- Ford Racing M-6P067-M50B blue coil-covers
- Ford Racing M-12405-M50 heat-range-zero (0) spark plugs
- Ford Racing M-6731-FL820 oil filter
- Alternator kit M-8600-M50BALT
- Includes production Boss 302 crankshaft dampener
- Vehicle harness and PCM not included; use Ford Racing wiring, PCM, and installation kit M-6017-A504V designed for street rod/project car installation
- Engine-mount Bosses and bellhousing mount pattern common to 4.6L modular engines
- Headers not included
- Assembly plant lift brackets not included
- Premium fuel only!

Note: Custom PCM calibration required when installing M-6007-A50XS crate engine

Although these engines are designed specifically for the 2011–2014 Mustang GT as well as the 2015–2016 Mustang GT they're easily adapted to classic, Fox, and SN-95 applications using the electronics available from Ford Performance Racing Parts. ■

Coyote Engine Building Specifications *CONTINUED*

Engine

Displacement..4.957L (302 ci)
Bore ....92.2 mm (3.629 inches)
Stroke..92.7 mm (3.649 inches)
Firing order..1-5-4-8-6-3-7-2
Spark plug gap....................1.25 to 1.35 mm (.049–.053 inch)
Oil pressure at idle ....10 to 15 psi
Oil pressure at 2,000 rpm ....30–40 psi
Compression ratio ....11.0:1; 9.5:1 (supercharged
....FRP applications)
Engine weight ....431 pounds

Cylinder Heads

Combustion chamber volume................................54.5–57.5 cc
Intake valvestem diameter 6.015–6.044 mm (.2368–.2379 inch)
Exhaust valvestem diameter.. 6.015–6.044 mm (.2368–.2379 inch)
Intake valvestem-to-guide clearance.................. .020–.069 mm
....(.008–.0027 inch)
Exhaust valvestem-to-guide clearance .... .045–.094 mm
....(.0018–.0037 inch)

Intake valve head diameter (2011–2014)

Intake valve head diameter (2015–2017) ....37.0 mm
....(1.450 inches)

Exhaust valve head diameter (2011–2014)

Exhaust valve head diameter ....31.0 mm (1.220 inches)
....(2015–2017)
Valve face runout ....05 mm (.019 inch)
Valve face angle 3-angle
Intake valveseat width ....1.3–1.5 mm (.051–.059 inch)
Exhaust valveseat width................1.4–1.6 mm (.059–.063 inch)
Valveseat runout .... .04 mm (.016 inch)
Valveseat angle ....121/91/61 degrees
Intake valvespring free length ....51.32 mm (2.020 inches)
Exhaust valvespring free length ....51.32 mm (2.020 inches)
Intake valve perpendicularity ....3.0 mm (.118 inch)
Exhaust valve perpendicularity ....3.0 mm (.118 inch)
Intake valvespring compression force ....650 n
Exhaust valvespring compression force............................650 n
Intake valvespring installed height...........40 mm (1.5748 inches)
Exhaust valvespring installed height..........40 mm (1.5748 inches)
Intake valve installed force ....265 n
Exhaust valve installed force..265 n
Roller rocker ratio..2:1
Head gasket surface flatness ....025 mm (.001 inch) in any 25-mm (1.000 inch); .050 mm (.002 inch) in any 150-mm (6.000 inches) x 150 mm (6.000 inches); .1 mm (.004 inch) overall

Hydraulic Lash Adjuster

Hydraulic lash adjuster diameter ....12 mm
....(.472 inch) intake/exhaust
Bore clearance.................... .018–.050 mm (.0007–.0019 inch)
Hydraulic lash adjuster leakdown .... .45–3.0 seconds
....intake/exhaust
Collapsed lash adjuster gap................................ .35–.85 mm
....(.0137–.0334 inch)

Camshafts

Intake lobe lift ....5.963 mm (.2348 inch)
Exhaust lobe lift..5.488 mm (.2160 inch)
Cam journal diameter.....................28.620 mm (1.1267 inches)
Cam journal bore diameter .... 28.682–28.657 mm
....1.1292–1.1282 inches)
Cam journal to bearing clearance .... .025–.075 mm
....(.001–.002 inch)
Camshaft runout .... .04 mm (.0016 inch)
Camshaft endplay .... .15 mm (.0059 inch)

Cylinder Block

Cylinder bore diameter ....92.200–92.220 mm
....(3.6299–3.6307 inches)
Cylinder bore taper................................ .013 mm (.0005 inch)
Cylinder bore maximum out-of-round......... .010 mm (.0004 inch)
Main bearing bore inside diameter ....72.400–72.424 mm
....(2.850–2.851 inches)
Head gasket surface flatness (block) .... .0254 mm
.... (.001 inch) across any 38.1-mm (1.500-inch) surface

Crankshaft

Main bearing journal diameter.....................67.481–67.505 mm
....(2.657–2.658 inches)
Main bearing journal maximum taper......... .004 mm (.0002 inch)
Main bearing journal maximum out-of-round .... .006 mm
....(.0002 inch)
Main bearing journal-to-main bearing clearance.......... .025–.045 mm
....(.0009–.0016 inch)
Connecting rod journal diameter.................52.983–53.003 mm
....(2.086–2.087 inches)
Connecting rod journal maximum taper . .004 mm (.0002 inch)
Crankshaft maximum endplay.................... .28 mm (.011 inch)

Piston and Connecting Rod

Piston diameter..... 92.161–92.175 mm (3.6283–3.6289 inches)
Piston-to-cylinder wall clearance .025–.059 mm (.0009–.0023 inch)
Piston ring end gap, top .... .15–.25 mm (.0059–.0098 inch)
Piston ring end gap, middle........30–.55 mm (.0118–.0216 inch)
Piston ring end gap, oil control ... .15–.45 mm (.0059–.0177 inch)
Piston ring groove width, top . 1.220–1.250 mm (.0480–.0492 inch)
Piston ring groove width, middle..................... 1.220–1.240 mm
....(.0480–.0488 inch)
Piston ring groove width, oil control .... 2.530–2.560 mm
....(.0996–.1003 inch)
Piston ring width, top ....1.17–1.19 mm (.0460–.0468 inch)
Piston ring width, middle.......1.17–1.19 mm (.0460–.0468 inch)
Piston ring-to-groove clearance, top.................. .030–.080 mm
....(.0019–.0031 inch)
Piston ring-to-groove clearance, middle............ .030–.070 mm

Coyote Engine Building Specifications *CONTINUED*

.... (.0019–.0028 inch)
Piston pin bore diameter .... 22.004–22.010 mm
.... (.8663–.8665 inch)
Piston pin diameter ....22.004–22.010 mm (.8649–.8661 inch)
Piston pin length .... 60.7–61.0 mm (2.3897–2.4015 inches)
Piston pin-to-bore fit clearance........................ .004–.013 mm
.... (.0002–.0005 inch)
Connecting rod-to-pin clearance.. .003–.018 mm (.0001–.0007 inch)
Connecting rod pin bore diameter .... 22.003–22.015 mm
.... (.8663–.8667 inch)
Connecting rod length (bore to bore) ..... 15.7 mm (5.933 inches)
Connecting rod maximum allowable bend .. .038 mm (.0015 inch)
Connecting rod maximum allowable twist .050 mm (.0019 inch)
Connecting rod bearing-to-crankshaft clearance........................
....028–.069 mm (.0011–.0027 inch)
Connecting rod side clearance at crank........................ .325 mm (.0128 inch) standard play .500 mm (.0197 inch) maximum play

Cooling System

Coolant ....Motorcraft Orange antifreeze/coolant
Lubrication..
Engine oil.................................Motorcraft SAE 5W-20 synthetic
.... Motorcraft SAW 5W20 premium blend ■

Teardown to final build is performed by just four to six people positioned along an easy-to-manage production line where there's solid communication between phases. One phase physically hands off to the next and people actually talk to each other. If there's a snag in the assembly process the problem is flagged, a meeting is called, and they find a fix.

Block assembly begins with a ring end gap in each cylinder. A lot of builders gap rings to one cylinder bore and completely disregard the rest. Not PAS or FPRP. Rings are match gapped to each cylinder, and then installed on each piston. Assembled pistons are assigned to a specific cylinder. When the steel forged crank is seated, capped, and torqued to Ford specifications endplay is checked and notated.

As new Mahle pistons and Manley rods are stuffed into the block they are checked for proper fit at the crank journal, seated, and torqued to Ford specifications. Freedom of crank movement is checked with each bore. When all eight piston and rod assemblies are installed and torqued, a rolling friction test is conducted and it either passes or fails. The technician listens for abnormal sounds as the short-block rolls over. This phase of assembly receives a torque reading, which is documented into the system. Each main and rod bolt has been torqued and marked with a green marker to document this assembly procedure.

When the short-block is complete, it is moved along the line to the next phase, at which cylinder heads, valvetrain, and pan are installed. Because these crate Coyote Aluminators have never been fired, gaskets and seals are intact and can be reused. Anything marginal is discarded and replaced. Next, the oil pump pick-up tube and windage tray are inspected and installed. Ford has incorporated the windage tray and pan gasket into one convenient piece for the Coyote. After the oil pump is fitted and aligned with the crankshaft without any side loading, it is torqued to specifications, ensuring the O-ring has been lubricated and properly fitted. You will notice that the Coyote engine utilizes RTV sealer at joints and seams where the oil pan meets the block and where cylinder heads and timing cover come together. This is normal and it ensures a true seal.

Cylinder head and block deck surfaces are inspected for damage and debris before the gasket goes on and heads are secured. Because stock cylinder head bolts are torque-to-yield, they are not reused. This means they are stretched and not as strong as they were, hence no reuse. If you are using ARP bolts they are not torque-to-yield and may be used again. In any case, you should install new hardware at the main caps and cylinder heads with any Coyote rebuild. These are critical areas of your Coyote's assembly and should get the greatest attention.

The Coyote's cylinder-head bolts reach deep into the block instead of the block deck, which means you get a better, more consistent clamp load than with the rest of the Modular engine family and conventional pushrod V-8 engines. You may also use cylinder-head studs for even greater clamp strength. However, when installed in a vehicle, cylinder head removal could prove impossible with studs. The Coyote also employs better cylinder-head gasket technology for greater sealing. Bolt-on items, such as the oil filter adaptor and oil-to-water cooler, are installed next as you make your way around the long-block.

The PAS Aluminator Build

For this build, Performance Assembly Solutions in Livonia, Michigan, tears down a Coyote engine and builds an Aluminator.

Disassembly: Front Dress

1 *Disassembly begins the minute the engine is uncrated and enters the PAS production line. Think of a Ford Performance Aluminator crate engine as a custom-built factory production line piece.*

2 *The harmonic dampener is removed first and placed on a production cart that follows this engine and all its parts through the PAS Aluminator process.*

3 *The timing cover is carefully removed and placed in safe storage with all of the other parts. Each Aluminator crate engine and all its parts remain together throughout the entire process.*

Cam Assembly

1 *Ti-VCT components are carefully removed and put aside for later assembly. Cam phasers, which advance valve timing via switched and metered oil pressure, are removed.*

2 *Cam timing phasers are easy to remove and reinstall. In fact, if you're doing a cam swap, the engine must be in proper time with all marks and chain links lined up during disassembly.*

3 *Next, camshafts are removed next and placed on the production cart. These cams go back into the same engine during assembly.*

4 *Each Coyote engine is identified by this series of coded markings. Think of each Coyote block as an encrypted thumbprint that cannot be identified with any other engine.*

Final Disassembly

1 *The rear main seal holder and seal are removed next. These items are inspected closely during assembly to ascertain condition. No one wants a rear main seal leak.*

2 *The main caps are removed next. Pistons, rods, and cylinder heads have already been removed.*

3 *Parts aren't recklessly thrown into massive bins and used again during reassembly. Each engine is carefully disassembled and all of its parts placed on a numbered cart, which follows the engine throughout the assembly process.*

Short Block Building and Blueprinting

1 *New Mahle forged and coated pistons from Ford Performance Racing Parts are measured, bore-matched, and documented.*

2 *Manley H-beam connecting rods are preassembled with bearings and measured as shown here. Journals are also measured; then clearances are checked.*

3 *After all reciprocating mass has been checked, it's time to put it all together for installation in the new Coyote block.*

4 *Piston ring end gaps are checked and matched to each cylinder bore. Top rings are gapped .0059 to .0098 inch. Intermediate or secondary rings are .0118 to .0216 inch. Oil control rings are .0059 to .177 inch. Ring gaps are spaced 45 degrees apart. These specs are for naturally aspirated applications. Boosted applications call for greater ring end gaps.*

5 *Bare Coyote blocks are mounted on industrial engine-build stands and prepped for assembly. PAS opts for the Coyote's original aluminum main bearings and lubricates them generously with engine-assembly lube. The block has been power washed and sprayed with an anticorrosion lubricant.*

Crank and Main Bearings

1 *The Coyote's forged steel crank can take as high as 1,500 hp without breaking a sweat. The crank is set and then main caps are positioned as shown. Caps, which are numbered, should be positioned as squarely as possible with the block, and then bolts are snugged before applying torque.*

2 *Each main cap is numbered 1 through 5 and can be installed one way only. Main cap bolts are torqued in the proper order: outboard bolts first in numerical order from the center cap outward; then inboard main cap bolts in proper numerical order. Side bolts are torqued last in proper numerical order from the center cap outward.*

3 Main caps are electrically torqued to Ford specifications. This is a foolproof system with no chance of error. The electronic torque wrench is positioned and the trigger pulled. It gets the torque spot on, and it also records the torque.

4 Crankshaft endplay is checked and documented. If it doesn't measure up to standards, the block and crank are disassembled and each is checked to find the cause. The thrust bearing thickness at the number-5 main bearing cap is where and how you modify endplay.

Pistons and Rods

1 Mahle forged and coated pistons and Manley H-beam connecting rods are installed next, after the cylinder walls and rod bearings have been coated with assembly lube. Rods are seated to the crank journals, and then side clearances are checked once both banks are installed.

2 Connecting rod bolts are electronically torqued to Ford specifications and then side clearances are checked. Again foolproof electronic torque with documentation is used.

3 The connecting rod and main cap bolts are marked in bright green as they are torqued as a visual indication for final inspection to indicate that they have been torqued.

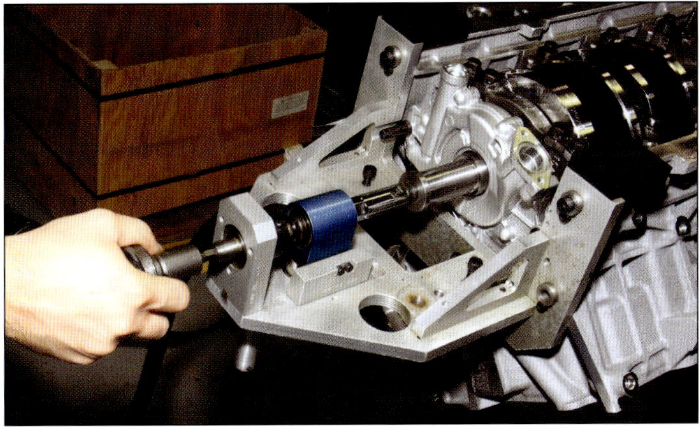

4 This is a mechanical rollover test to ensure that the bottom end turns freely and within specifications. If the short-block rotating assembly is too tight or there are abnormal noises it is rejected by the system and sidelined until the problem is corrected.

Oiling System Assembly

1 *The oil pump pick-up is fitted with this O-ring, which is lubricated with assembly lube and fitted to the crank-driven high-volume oil pump. There is no optional high-volume oil pump. The standard pump yields abundant volume and pressure. The only option is hardened steel pump internals, which are available from Ford Performance Parts.*

2 *The oil pump gasket and windage tray are one integral piece, which makes installation a snap.*

3 *RTV sealant is used in all joints in the Coyote. This is where the pan gasket/windage tray combo meets the rear main seal cap. The same thing happens in front where the pan gasket meets the timing cover.*

4 *The oil filter adaptor is installed next and torqued to specifications. Here, bolts are run down with a driver and then torqued to specifications.*

5 *The oil-to-water cooler is installed at the oil filter adaptor. Coolant flows through this cooler. Hot engine oil heat, which runs roughly 80 degrees hotter, is transferred to the coolant, which is cooler at 200 degrees F.*

Head and Cam Assembly

1 *High-tech composition cylinder-head gaskets are installed next. Note the cooling passages (arrows), which vector coolant close to the exhaust valves. The Coyote engine has a rather unconventional cooling system pathway that improves exhaust valve and cylinder cooling.*

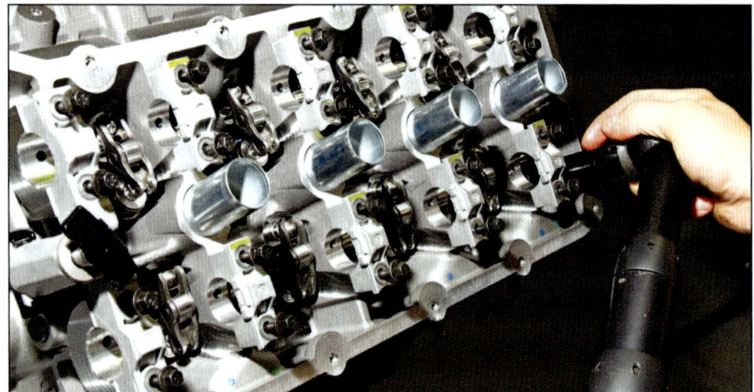

2 *As with the rest of the engine, cylinder-head bolts are torqued to Ford specifications in the pattern specified. This is an electronic torque wrench, which runs these bolts down to the proper torque. Torque, as well as torque-to-yield, is documented electronically into the system.*

3 Cam journals are generously lubricated with assembly lube and cams are set in place. Journal caps and bolts are installed and torqued electronically in a very specific order to proper specifications. These cam journal caps cannot be tightened haphazardly because of exact tolerances. The caps are tightened slowly in proper numerical order to prevent cam distortion. The rocker arms and followers (lifters) have been installed.

4 The cam journal bolts are snugged in proper order and then torqued to Ford specifications. Cams are then checked for freedom of rotation, but are not fully rotated because of valve-to-piston clearance issues.

5 The left-hand (driver) cylinder head cams are installed and timed like this. These "D"-shaped pockets are timing marks. Intake cam "D" (left) is located at six-thirty to seven o'clock. Exhaust cam "D" (right) is at ten-thirty to eleven o'clock. When the cam phasers are installed, some adjustment is required to get cams and sprockets lined up. If they do not fit, they are not properly lined up.

6 The right-hand (passenger) cylinder head cams are installed and timed per this image, with the exhaust cam (left) at five o'clock as shown and the intake cam (right) being at two o'clock. As with the left-hand (driver) cylinder head these "D" timing marks must be positioned as shown. When cam phasers are installed they should be a perfect fit. If they do not fit, cams and sprockets are not properly aligned. Again, some adjustment of the cams and/or crank is required to achieve perfect cam/sprocket alignment.

7 Here are the cam phasers/sprockets and secondary timing chains. The Coyote has just two types of phasers (intake and exhaust), which interchange from side to side. The exhaust phasers have two sprockets each. Secondary chains have timing links. The double link goes on the intake cam phaser (left). Single links are located at the exhaust cam phaser (right). This applies to both sides. Shown here is the right-hand (passenger) secondary sprocket package as seen from the engine. Note that the double link is on the left (intake) and the single link is on the right (exhaust).

8 Each camshaft has this blue filter to keep debris out of the cam phasers. It is extremely important to ensure that these filters are installed.

Timing Chain Assembly

1 *Main timing chains are installed next, after the secondary cam chains on top have been installed and properly timed.*

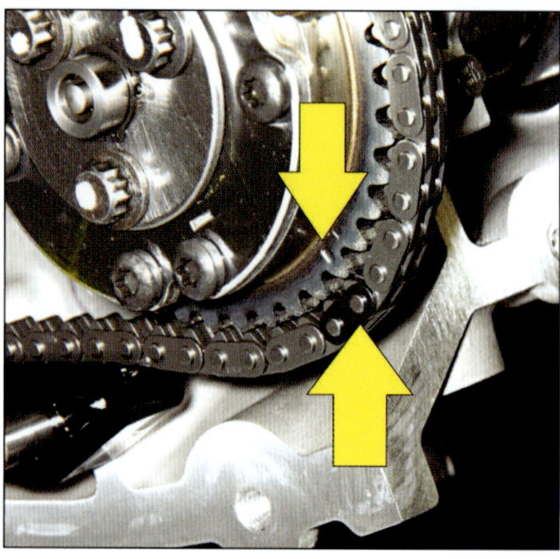

2 *This is the left-hand (driver) timing chain with the marks on top. The dark chain link is a timing mark as is the mark on the phaser.*

3 *Down below at the crank is the gear for the left-hand (driver) timing chain. Crank gear timing marks are in green at PAS. The chain timing mark is a dark link (arrow). The crankshaft keyway is at twelve o'clock.*

4 *Oil pressured chain tensioners are secured via this pin during assembly. After both chains are installed and properly timed, these pins are pulled, which provides chain tension.*

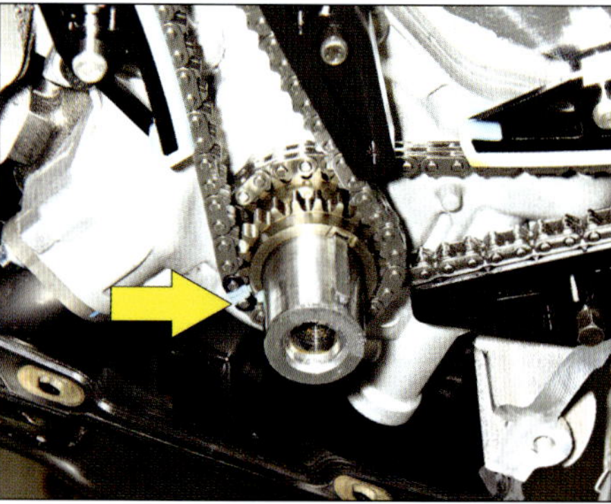

5 *The right-hand (passenger) timing chain is installed and timed as shown here. The dark chain link is the timing mark as are the green paint daubs.*

6 *Here's how the right-hand (passenger) cam chains are timed on top. The dark chain links should line up with the phaser sprocket timing mark as shown.*

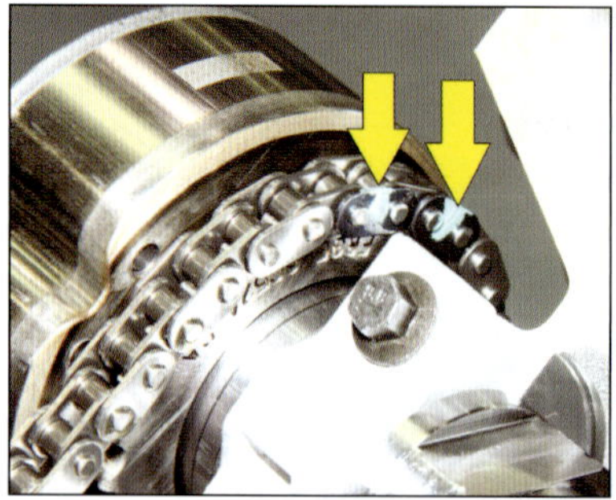

7 *Here's the secondary cam drive chain view and the double links on the left-hand (driver) side of engine. This is what you need to remember with the secondary chains: Double links and intake phaser sprocket marks go to the inside (intake side). Single links and phaser sprocket (dual sprocket) marks go toward the outside (exhaust side). If the cams and phasers are not in perfect alignment (in time) they will not go together. If the phasers do not seat on the cams they are out of proper time. Cams and/or phasers may have to be rotated slightly to get them in time.*

8 This Ford illustration demonstrates proper main chain timing. Links and timing marks should line up on phasers and crank sprocket. (Photo Courtesy Ford Performance Parts)

Final Assembly

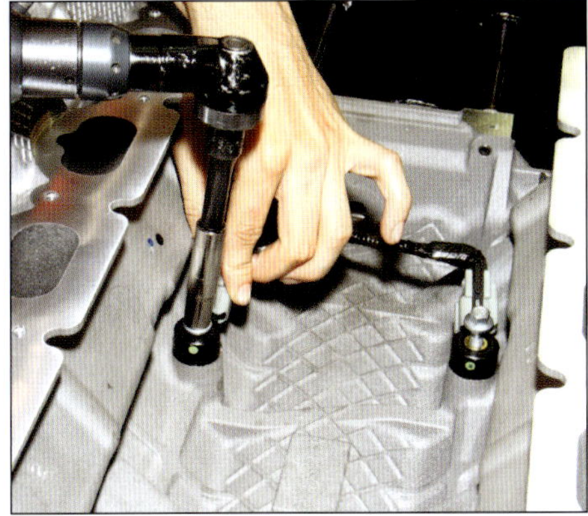

1 The knock sensors and harness are installed next. Each bank has one knock sensor.

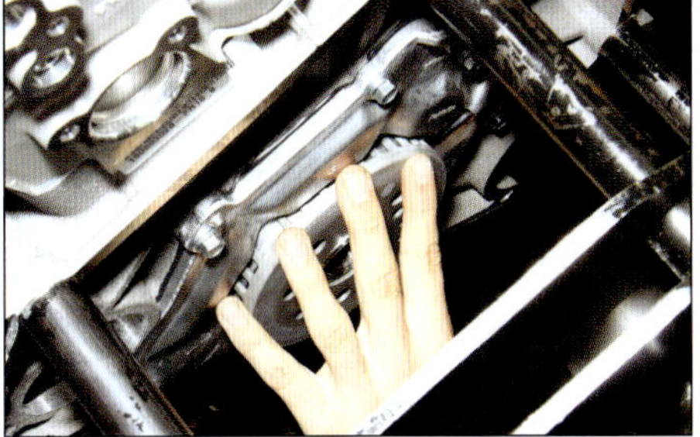

2 The crank trigger "reluctor" wheel is fitted to the crank as shown. The reluctor whizzes past the crank sensor, providing real-time PCM/ECU feedback for electronic engine control.

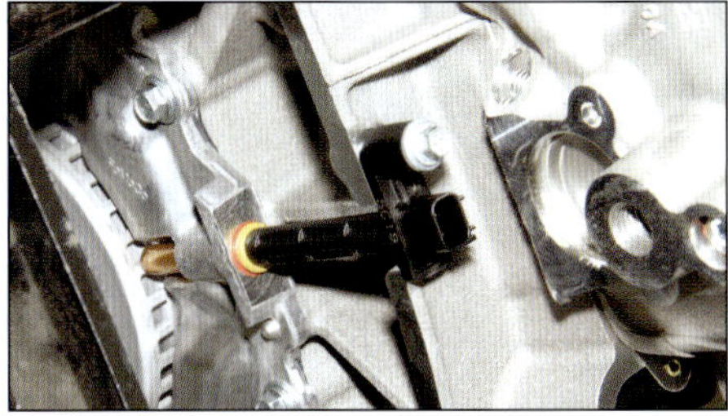

3 This is the crank sensor, which is a Hall Effect triggering system. Replacement is easy if you ever have to do it in a car. The reluctor wheel triggers this sensor. PAS technicians install these sensors as one of the final phases of engine assembly.

4 RTV sealant is used only at joints with leak potential. Gasket technology has come a long way since the days of cork and sealer.

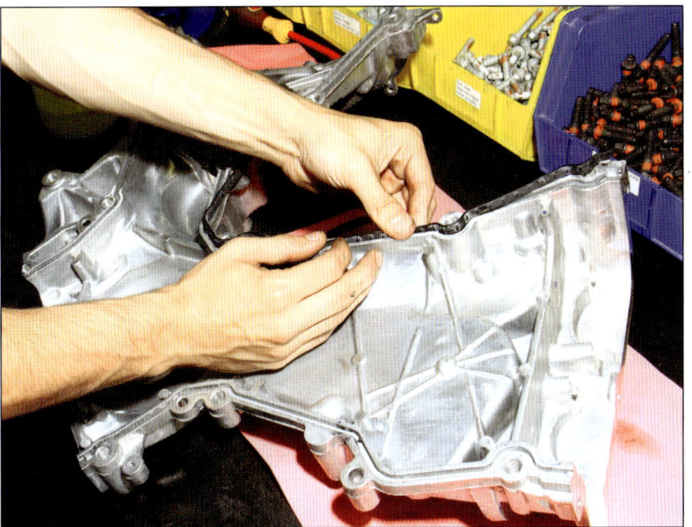

5 Modern gasket technology features a positive serpentine seal in the timing cover to eliminate messy and time-consuming gaskets. The seal is seated as shown.

6 *This is the crankshaft/harmonic dampener seal. As you can see, this seal has a garter spring, which mandates extreme caution. This seal should be packed full of engine-assembly lube so that the garter spring cannot be jarred loose during installation. You also want abundant lubrication on this seal during start-up to prevent damage. This seal leaks without the garter spring.*

7 *The timing cover is installed, making sure that all seal surfaces make solid contact with the heads and block. The cover bolts should be snugged and then tightened evenly to seat the cover.*

8 *The water pump and cooling system plumbing are installed next. The Coyote has an unconventional cooling system. The thermostat is located at the engine inlet instead of at the outlet on top; yet the system is set up to burp air out of the coolant at the plastic "Y" in the technician's left hand. The cylinder heads receive coolant first around the exhaust valves.*

9 *The harmonic dampener is installed next along with plenty of assembly lube at the crank and seal.*

10 *The induction system follows. This is a 2015 5.0L Coyote engine, which has Charge Motion actuators at the rear. Charge Motion was never factory installed on 2011–2014 5.0L Ti-VCT Coyote engines.*

11 *The PAS production line is an intimate affair in Livonia, Michigan. Think of the Ford Performance Aluminator engine as a custom-built mass-produced crate engine.*

L & R Automotive

I've shown you the Ford Performance Parts Aluminator build program. It is time to take it to a more personal level at L & R Custom Engine Building in Gardena, California, just outside of Los Angeles. L & R is going to build a Coyote, including all of the important machining steps you need to know to build a Coyote from scratch.

L & R Automotive was established in 1977 by Larkin Ranney Jr. Larkin worked for a number of engine rebuilders before he decided to venture out on his own nearly 40 years ago. Larkin felt that he could offer better service and product to the growing automotive industry.

Larkin opened L & R Automotive out of his home garage selling engine parts and contracting out machine work. As his business grew Larkin leased a building in which to keep inventory and do business. A few years later Larkin decided to do his own machine work so he could control quality. Starting with a single Sunnen rod heater Larkin built his own machine shop. As business grew, Larkin moved into a larger building and filled the place with machines. Today, L & R Custom Engine Building is currently in a 10,000-square-foot building fitted with the latest technology in the engine rebuilding industry.

Moreover, L & R Custom Engine Building is a family-owned and -operated business that enthusiasts around Los Angeles have trusted for decades. Larkin's sons Derek and Brent started working for the family business right out of high school. Derek Jr. (a third-generation Ranney) is now working in the business. L & R also has a great staff with abundant experience with every type of internal combustion engine imaginable. Ford's new 5.0L Coyote is no exception. L & R is going to show you how to build the Ford Coyote, including all of the important machining steps necessary to erect an engine that will serve you well. Let's get started.

L & R Custom Engine Coyote Build

Short Block Machine Work

1 *L & R Engines in Gardena, California, has its own Coyote specialists in-house. Andre Majeau will walk you through the important details of a Coyote build.*

2 *Here, a customer's Coyote block is bored prior to being torque-plate honed. L & R employs a Coyote/Modular–specific technician to build its Coyotes and Modulars because of the special care these engines require.*

3 *The honed block is ready for minimal milling on top and only as necessary. Deck trueness is important, as is deck thickness.*

4 *L & R is installing a new Ford Performance Racing Parts Boss M-6303-M50B steel crank in this Coyote, which is being dynamic balanced at this time along with new Eagle H-beam rods and Mahle forged and coated pistons. The Coyote is internally balanced.*

Short Block Blueprinting and Assembly

1 *L & R Custom Engines leaves nothing to chance. The Coyote calls for precise measurements in terms of tolerances. Although this is a new FPRP Boss, crank journals and bearings are mic'd to ascertain precise tolerances.*

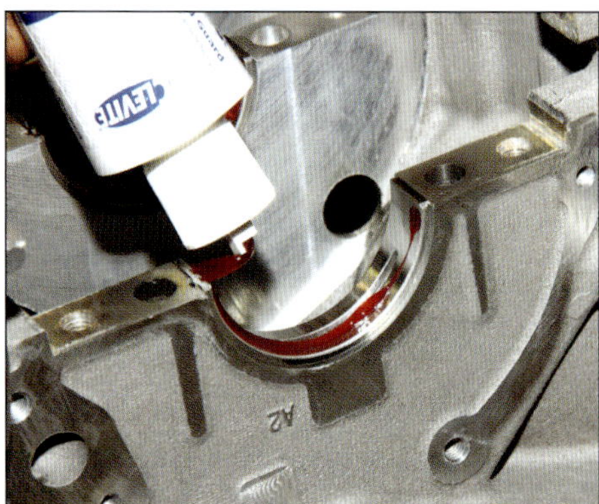

2 *Andre stresses the importance of generous amounts of assembly lube on the Coyote's main and rod bearings and journals. You can never have too much.*

3 *A fresh L & R Coyote block has been fitted with new aluminum bearings. Tri-metal bearings are not necessary in this engine, which tends to be old school. A Ford Performance Parts Boss crank is carefully positioned.*

4 *Pay close attention to oil cooling piston jets during assembly. Some Coyote builds with aftermarket H-beam connecting rods have been known to hit these oil-cooling jets. As you assemble your Coyote, make sure there is no interference. You must have a minimum of .060-inch clearance.*

5 Main cap bolts are torqued in one-third values to Ford specifications (see sidebar "Coyote Torque Specifications"). Outboard main cap bolts are torqued first in numerical sequence. Inboard main cap bolts follow in proper numerical sequence. Side bolts are torqued last in proper numerical sequence.

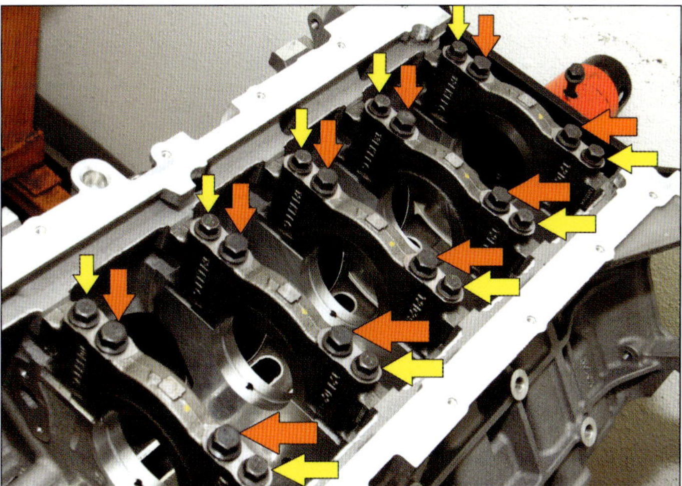

6 Main cap bolts are torqued as shown, outboard main bolts first from the center outward (yellow arrows). Inboard main cap bolts are torqued next from the center outward (orange arrows). Torque in one-third values. These are torque-to-yield bolts, which means you cannot use them again. Torque-to-yield is a measure of bolt stretch. If you are using studs or ARP bolts, torque-to-yield does not apply.

7 Main cap side bolts are snugged and torqued last, in proper order from the number-3 cap outward.

Rods and Pistons

1 L & R is using Mahle coated and forged pistons along with Eagle H-beam rods in this customer build. This provides durability in the 600- to 1,000-hp range.

2 If you are building a stock Coyote, you're going to use hypereutectic pistons. Stock hypereutectic pistons are marked in this fashion for proper installation. This dimple goes toward the front of the engine block.

3 Piston ring end gaps are checked top, middle, and bottom of the bore to allow for taper. Cylinder bores are nearly always narrower at the bottom, even when they have been bored and honed. Always allow for bore taper. It is better to have too much ring end gap than too little. Too little ring end gap puts you at risk for engine failure.

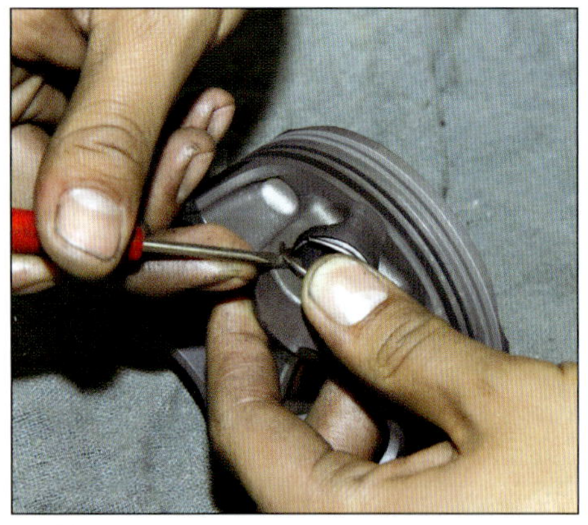

4 *Mahle coated and forged pistons are assembled onto Eagle H-beam rods. Most important here is C-clip security. Make absolutely sure the C-clip is deeply seated. Take care not to scratch the piston skirt or ring lands.*

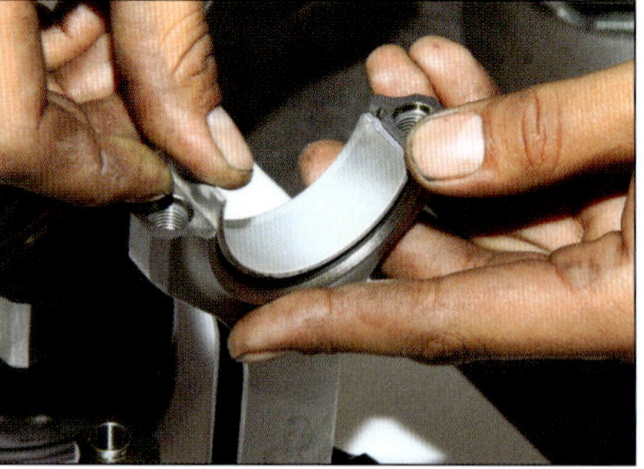

5 *Aluminum rod bearings are seated as shown. The bearing tang isn't there for security, but instead as a reference to ensure proper installation. Because skin oil is a contaminant, keep your fingertips off bearing surfaces. Note that Andre's fingertips are on the edge of bearing surfaces.*

6 *The Eagle/Mahle piston/rod combo is installed as shown using a piston ring compressor. All engine builders have their preferred methods. Cylinder walls and pistons should be coated with SAE 30–weight engine oil or assembly lube; never install dry.*

Cylinder Heads and Final Assembly

1 *Composition head gaskets are installed next after ensuring all deck surfaces are hospital clean. Andre has installed ARP studs for improved cylinder head security. Studs are the best choice for clamping power. Studs should never be bottomed out; instead, they should be just shy of the bottom of the bolt bore. If you're planning head removal in-vehicle, consider using head bolts instead because removal becomes impossible in the vehicle if you use studs.*

2 *You have two basic choices when it comes to Coyote oil pumps: original equipment high-volume or steel internals for extreme applications where durability is more critical. L & R has opted for a stock replacement oil pump for this street Coyote.*

Total Engine Airflow

L & R has opted for CNC-ported Coyote heads from Total Engine Airflow (TEA). Customers' heads were shipped to TEA in Ohio and received the complete work-up including a valve job and guides. Here's what you get from the TEA head:

Valve Job

All TEA valve jobs are engineered to optimize airflow and deliver outstanding power and durability. These valve jobs are blueprint exact, meaning all seat depths are equal from valve to valve and head to head.

Total Engine Airflow *CONTINUED*

Airflow

All TEA CNC-ported heads are properly hand blended in the critical areas and flow tested to ensure they perform as designed. All heads come with a flow sheet for your set of heads. This means that you know exactly what you are getting for your money.

Assembly

Every set of TEA CNC-ported heads is ready to install directly out of the box. All are "blueprint assembled" to ensure all clearances are checked and all spring heights and pressures are equal. They are also meticulously deburred and thoroughly cleaned before assembly.

Custom Options

Countless custom options can be performed on TEA Coyote cylinder heads. TEA has the experience and know-how to make sure they are performed properly. For instance, chamber volume is something TEA can mill to the customer's requested size. In some cases, they can remove extra material to make the chambers larger as needed. TEA also stocks parts from all the leading valvetrain manufacturers and can supply countless variations of valvesprings, retainers, and valve materials.

Experience

TEA's staff comprises veteran machinists with years of experience building cylinder heads and engines. TEA knows what will live and what doesn't. ■

L & R Custom Engines has chosen Total Engine Airflow CNC porting for this project. These are nice pieces that have been CNC and hand ported, and then properly set up for L & R Engines with Ferrea stainless-steel valves and stiffer Trick Flow Track Max valvesprings rated at 80 pounds.

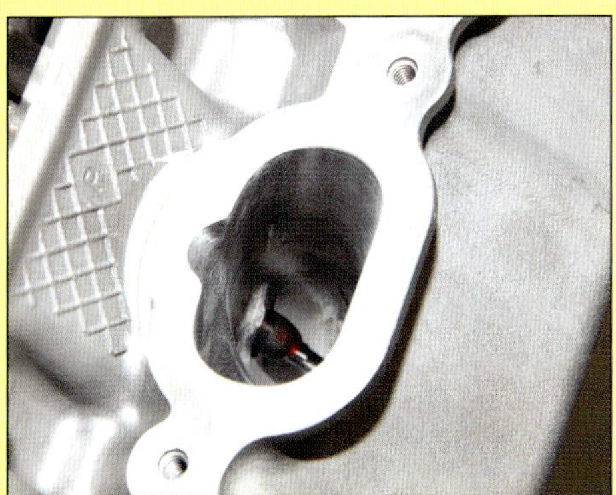

Total Engine Airflow heads does a nice combo job of CNC and hand porting. This is the intake port, which is 209-cc volume with a 1.460-inch Ferrea intake valve. The estimated air flow is more than 320 cfm and the maximum valvespring lift is .560 inch.

Exhaust port dimensions are generous at 89 cc with nice CNC and hand porting. Ferrea exhaust valves are 1.220 inches.

Total Engine Airflow 57-cc chambers cleaned up nicely, which eliminates sources of detonation.

Cylinder Heads and Final Assembly *CONTINUED*

3 *Coyote 12-mm hydraulic lash adjustors and rocker arms are inspected for abnormal wear or damage. These are extremely rugged pieces that can withstand 1,000 to 1,500 hp and upwards of 9,000 rpm or more.*

4 *The cylinder head torqueing sequence for the Coyote must be followed to the letter to ensure uniform gasket compression and deck contact; it must be performed in one-third values. The cam journal torque sequence is also critical (shown here) and must be followed to prevent cam distortion and engine damage. Slowly run these bolts down in proper numerical order from the center caps outward until the journal caps seat. Then apply proper torque and then torque-to-yield with factory bolts. These torque-to-yield bolts cannot be used a second time. You must install new bolts whenever you perform a cam swap.*

5 *The harmonic dampener should be lubed around the seal contact surface. Where the dampener meets the crankshaft, use a very thin film of Permatex's The Right Stuff to prevent oil leaks around the dampener.*

Coyote Torque Specifications

A Never have torque specifications been more critical than they are with today's all-aluminum engines and torque-to-yield fasteners. Torque specifications must be followed to the letter and in proper order. ■

Item	Nm	Ft-Lbs	In-Lbs
Camshaft journal caps	6 plus 45 degrees in proper numerical order	–	53 plus 45 degrees in proper numerical order
Camshaft journal mega caps	6 plus 45 degrees	–	53 plus 45 degrees
CMP sensor bolt	10	–	89
Catalytic converter to header	40	–	30
Clutch pressure plate	60 plus 60 degrees	46 plus 60 degrees	–
Connecting rod bolts	20 then 38 plus 105 degrees	–	177 then 28 plus 105 degrees
Coolant outlet bolts	10	–	89
Coolant outlet pipe bolt	10	–	89
Coolant pump bolts	20	–	177
Coolant pump pulley bolts	20	–	177
Main bearing cap bolts	20 all then 40 outer only then 65 inner only plus 90 degrees in proper numerical order	–	177 All then 30 outer only then 48 inner only plus 90 degrees (In proper numerical order)
Main bearing cap cross bolts	10 then 30 plus 60 degrees	–	89 then 22 plus 60 degrees
CKP sensor bolt	10	–	89

Coyote Torque Specifications *CONTINUED*

Item	*Nm*	*Ft-Lbs*	*In-Lbs*
Crankshaft pulley bolts	140 then loosen 360 degrees then 100 then tighten 90 degrees	–	103 then loosen 360 degrees then 74 then tighten 90 degrees
Crankshaft rear main seal plate	10 plus 45 degrees	–	89 plus 45 degrees
Cylinder head bolts	25 then 40 plus 90 degrees	–	18 then 30 plus 90 degrees
CHT sensor	11	–	97
Engine support insulator bolts	55	41	–
Engine support insulator bracket bolts and stud bolts	55	41	–
Engine support insulator nuts	63	46	–
Engine-to-transmission bolts and stud bolts	48	35	–
Exhaust header nuts	24 then 32	18 then 24	–
Exhaust header studs	25	18	–
Flexplate bolts	20 plus 60 degrees	–	177 plus 60 degrees
Flexplate inspection cover bolts	35	25	–
Flywheel bolts	20 plus 60 degrees	–	177 plus 60 degrees
Alternator B+ wire terminal nut	17	–	150
Alternator bolt and nut	48	35	
Ground strap-to-cowl bolt	10	–	89
Ground strap-to-RH engine support insulator nut	48	35	–
Heater hose support nuts	7	–	62
Ignition coil bolts	6	–	63
Knock sensor bolts	20	–	177
Oil cooler threaded fitting	58	43	
Oil filter adaptor bolts	20 plus 60 degrees	–	177 plus 60 degrees
Oil pan bolts	2 then 10 plus 45 degrees in proper numerical order from center out	–	18 then 89 plus 45 degrees in proper numerical order from center out
Oil pan drain plug	26	19	–
Oil pan stud bolts	10 plus 45 degrees		89 plus 45 degrees
Oil pan stud-to-bolt-to-wiring harness bracket nut	8	–	71
Oil pump bolts and stud bolts	10 large bolt first then 25 top stud bolt then 10 small bolt then 20 bottom stud. Next large bolt 45 degrees. Top stud 75 degrees. Small bolt 45 degrees. Bottom stud 60 degrees	–	89 in-lbs large bolt first then 8 ft-lbs top stud bolt then 89 in-lbs small bolt then 177 in-lbs bottom stud. Next large bolt 45 degrees. Top stud 75 degrees. Small bolt 45 degrees. Bottom stud 60 degrees
Oil pump screen and pick-up bolts	10	–	89
Oil pump screen and pick-up tube spacer	25	18	–
Primary timing chain tensioner bolts (on block)	10	–	89
Timing chain guide bolts	10	–	89
Timing cover bolts	25 plus 60 degrees; 10 at oil pan plus 45 degrees	–	18 plus 60 degrees; 89 at oil pan plus 45 degrees
Spark plugs	15	–	133
Thermostat housing bolts	10	–	89
Valvecover bolts	10 in proper numerical order from center out	–	89 in proper numerical order from center out
VCT sprocket assembly bolts	15 plus 90 degrees	–	133 plus 90 degrees

Coyote Crate Projects

Never has the Ford enthusiast enjoyed a better playing field than the exciting, emerging world of Coyote crate engines from Ford Performance Parts and the aftermarket in general. These engines are factory-backed with a 24-month/24,000-mile warranty and are ready for installation.

Why buy a crate engine? You buy a crate engine more for convenience than anything else, especially if you need fast turnaround or are building a vintage Ford and would like to avoid the hassle of having an engine built. The advantages of a crate engine are both durability and the warranty, should anything go wrong. What follows are crate engines either currently in production or discontinued that may be in remaining inventories or for sale from private sellers.

5.0L 4V Coyote Ti-VCT 420-HP Crate M-6007-M50A

- High-performance 5.0L, four-valve Ti-VCT engine
- 420 hp at 6,500 rpm
- 390 ft-lbs of torque at 4,250 rpm
- 5.0L (302 ci) displacement
- 3.630-inch bore x 3.650-inch stroke
- Aluminum block
- Forged steel crankshaft
- Forged steel sintered steel connecting rods
- Hypereutectic pistons
- Aluminum cylinder heads, DOHC, four valves per cylinder, variable intake and exhaust camshaft timing
- 8-quart-capacity oil pan
- 11.0:1 compression ratio
- Tuned composite intake manifold provides efficient air delivery and weight savings
- 80-mm single bore drive-by-wire throttle body
- Mustang GT 409 stainless-steel tubular exhaust manifolds
- Includes manual transmission engine harness and flywheel
- Vehicle harness and PCM not included
- Use Ford Racing's new wiring, PCM, and installation kit M-6017-A504V designed for street rod/project car installation.
- Does not include alternator (for alternator kit see M-8600-M50BALT)
- 5.0L Mustang engine cover kit available (see M-9680-M50)
- Use oil line adapter M-6881-M50 for applications requiring oil filter relocation
- Engine-mount Bosses and bellhousing mount pattern common to 4.6L Modular engines
- Specifications may vary. These features apply for engine code EG-397-AA. Engines are this build code or newer while supplies last.
- Engines built after August 8, 2013, are equipped with a water pump using a three-bolt pulley pattern
- Engine weight: 444 pounds
- Replaced by M-6007-M50C

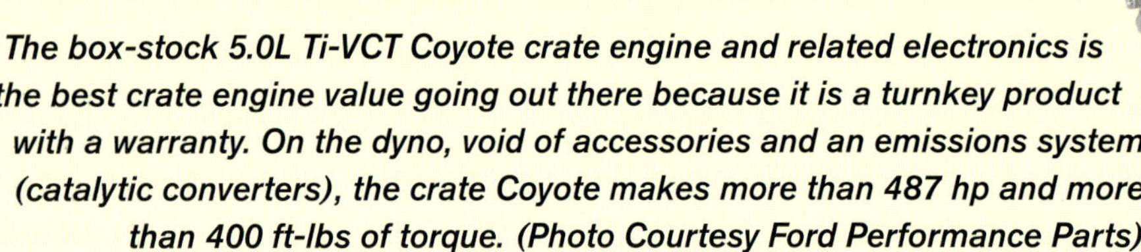

The box-stock 5.0L Ti-VCT Coyote crate engine and related electronics is the best crate engine value going out there because it is a turnkey product with a warranty. On the dyno, void of accessories and an emissions system (catalytic converters), the crate Coyote makes more than 487 hp and more than 400 ft-lbs of torque. (Photo Courtesy Ford Performance Parts)

5.0L 4V Coyote Ti-VCT 460-HP Crate M-6007-M50C (Gen III)

- 460 hp
- 420 ft-lbs of torque
- 12.0:1 compression ratio
- Hypereutectic cast-aluminum pistons
- Sintered steel connecting rods from the 2012–2013 Boss 302 Mustang
- Forged steel crankshaft
- Aluminum block featuring plasma transferred wire arc spray weld liner coated cylinder walls like the 5.2L GT350 Voodoo block
- Longer 12-mm head bolts for higher clamp load
- 10-quart-capacity oil pan
- Tuned composite intake manifold provides efficient air delivery and weight savings
- 80-mm single-bore drive-by-wire electronic throttle body
- Charge Motion variable runner control
- High-flow aluminum cylinder heads
- DOHC, four valves per cylinder
- Variable intake and exhaust camshaft timing
- Mustang GT 409 stainless-steel tubular exhaust manifold on the right side only
- Includes manual transmission engine harness and dual mass flywheel.
- For engines equipped with the automatic transmission engine harness and flexplate, see M-6007-M50CAUTO
- Engine-mount Bosses and bellhousing mount pattern is common to 4.6L Modular engines
- Vehicle harness and factory PCM not included
- Use Ford Performance M-6017-M50B control pack, which includes wiring, PCM, and installation kit for project car installation
- Does not include alternator (for kit see M-8600-M50BALT)
- 5.0L Coyote air-conditioning (for kit see M-8600-M50AC)
- 5.0L Mustang motor mount (for kit see M-6038-M50)
- 5.0L Mustang engine cover (for kit see M-9680-M50B)
- Engine weight: 445 pounds

5.0L Coyote Aluminator Naturally Aspirated M-6007-A50NAA

- Fits 2011–2017 Mustang GT
- 5.0L (302 ci) displacement
- 11.0:1 compression ratio (nominal)
- Mahle hard anodized forged pistons with Grafal low-friction coating
- Manley H-beam connecting rods with ARP 2000 bolts
- Boss 302 connecting-rod bearings
- Forged steel crankshaft
- Uses production Mustang GT aluminum block (M-6010-A50L4V)
- Large rear-sump oil pan with 8-quart capacity features optimized oil drainback and windage tray to control oil and improve high-RPM performance
- Tuned composite Mustang GT intake manifold with production drive-by-wire 80-mm throttle body
- Four-valve-per-cylinder aluminum heads with roller-finger followers reduce friction
- Boss 302 valve springs (M-6513-M50BR)
- Mustang GT production camshafts (intake: 12-mm lift, 260 degrees duration; exhaust: 11-mm lift, 263 degrees duration)
- Ford Racing engine cover (kit M-9680-M50)
- Includes manual-transmission engine injector harness
- Front cover is modified for Ford Racing supercharger kits
- For applications not using a Ford Racing supercharger kit, stock timing cover must be installed
- Includes colder heat range (zero) spark plugs (M-12405-M50)
- Includes Ford Racing oil filter (M-6731-FL820)
- Includes billet steel gerotor oil pump (M-6600-50CJ)
- Vehicle harness and PCM not included. Use Ford Racing wiring, PCM, and installation kit M-6017-A504V designed for street rod/project car installation.
- Does not include alternator (for kit see M-8600-M50BALT)
- Oil line adapter M-6881-M50 available for applications requiring oil filter relocation
- Engine-mount Bosses and bellhousing mount pattern common to 4.6L Modular engines
- Engines built after August 8, 2013, are equipped with a water pump using a 3-bolt pulley pattern

5.0L Coyote Aluminator Naturally Aspirated M-6007-A50NAB

- Fits 2018–present Mustang GT (Gen III)
- 5.0L (302 ci) displacement
- 9.5:1 compression ratio for supercharged applications (nominal)
- Note: Due to 9.5:1 compression ratio, custom tuning is required for optimal performance
- 12:1 compression ratio for naturally aspirated applications
- Mahle hard anodized forged pistons with Graphal low-friction coating
- Manley H-beam connecting rods with ARP 2000 bolts
- Forged steel crankshaft
- Production Coyote aluminum cylinder block
- Longer 12-mm head bolts for higher clamp load
- Large rear-sump oil pan with 10-quart capacity features optimized oil drainback and windage tray to control oil and improve high-RPM performance
- Tuned composite Mustang GT intake manifold with production drive-by-wire 80-mm throttle body
- Four-valve-per-cylinder aluminum heads with roller-finger followers to reduce friction
- Mustang GT production camshafts
- Includes Ford Performance colder heat range (zero) spark plugs for supercharging (M-12405-M50)
- Includes CM-6731-FL820 Ford Performance oil filter
- Includes M-6600-M52 billet steel gerotor oil pump
- Vehicle harness and PCM not included. Use Ford Performance wiring, PCM, and installation kit M-6017-M50B designed for street rod/project car installation
- Engine-mount Bosses and bellhousing mount pattern common to 4.6L Modular engines. Engine does not include engine harness or flywheel/flexplate
- Does not include alternator (for kit see M-8600-M50BALT)
- Does not include exhaust manifolds

Although the Boss 302 Coyote is no longer available from Ford Performance Parts, some inventories exist out there for those determined to find them. This is also an engine you can build yourself with off-the-shelf parts available from Ford Performance Parts. (Photo Courtesy Ford Performance Parts)

5.0L Coyote Aluminator SC M-6007-A50SCA

- Fits 2011–2017 Mustang GT (Gen II)
- 5.0L (302 ci) displacement
- 9.5:1 compression ratio for supercharged applications (nominal)
- Note: due to 9.5:1 compression ratio, custom tuning is required for optimal performance
- Mahle hard anodized forged pistons with Graphal low-friction coating
- Manley H-beam connecting rods with ARP 2000 bolts
- Forged steel crankshaft
- Uses production 2011–2014 Mustang GT aluminum cylinder block
- Large rear-sump oil pan with 8-quart capacity features optimized oil drainback and windage tray to control oil and improve high-RPM performance
- Tuned composite Mustang GT intake manifold with production drive-by-wire 80-mm throttle body variable runner control
- Four-valve-per-cylinder aluminum heads with roller-finger followers reduce friction
- Boss 302 valve springs (M-6513-M50BR)
- Mustang GT production camshafts (intake: 12-mm lift, 260 degrees duration; exhaust: 11-mm lift, 263 degrees duration)
- Ford Racing engine cover kit (M-9680-M50)
- Includes manual-transmission engine injector harness
- Front cover is modified for Ford Racing supercharger kits
- For applications not using a Ford Racing supercharger kit, stock timing cover must be installed
- Includes colder heat range (zero) spark plugs for supercharging (M-12405-M50)
- Includes Ford Racing oil filter (M-6731-FL820)
- Includes billet steel gerotor oil pump (M-6600-50CJ)
- Vehicle harness and PCM not included. Use Ford Racing wiring, PCM, and installation kit M-6017-A504V designed for street rod/project car installation.
- Does not include alternator (for kit see M-8600-M50BALT)
- Engine-mount Bosses and bell housing mount pattern common to 4.6L Modular engines

5.0L Coyote Aluminator SC M-6007-A50SCB

- Fits 2018–present Mustang GT (Gen III)
- 5.0L (302 ci) displacement
- 9.5:1 compression ratio for supercharged applications (nominal)
- Note: Due to 9.5:1 compression ratio, custom tuning is required for optimal performance
- Mahle hard anodized forged pistons with Graphal low-friction coating
- Manley H-beam connecting rods with ARP 2000 bolts
- Forged steel crankshaft
- Uses production Coyote aluminum cylinder block
- Longer 12-mm head bolts for higher clamp load
- Large rear-sump 10-quart-capacity oil pan features optimized oil drainback and windage tray to control oil and improve high-RPM performance
- Tuned composite Mustang GT intake manifold with production drive-by-wire 80-mm throttle body
- Four-valve-per-cylinder aluminum heads with roller-finger followers to reduce friction and allow for a more aggressive profile
- Mustang GT production camshafts
- Includes Ford Performance Parts colder heat range spark plugs for supercharging (M-12405-M50)
- Includes CM-6731-FL820 Ford Performance Parts oil filter
- Includes M-6600-M52 high-performance billet steel gerotor oil pump
- Vehicle harness and PCM not included. Use Ford Performance Parts wiring, PCM, and installation kit M-6017-M50B engineered for street rod/project car swap installations
- Engine-mount Bosses and bellhousing-mount pattern common to 4.6L Modular engines
- Engine does not include engine harness or flywheel/flexplate
- Does not include alternator (for kit see M-8600-M50BALT)
- Does not include exhaust manifolds

5.0L Coyote Aluminator SC M-6007-A50NAB

- Fits 2018–present Mustang GT (Gen III)
- 5.0L (302 ci) displacement
- 12.0:1 compression ratio for naturally aspirated applications (nominal)
- Mahle hard anodized forged pistons with Graphal low-friction coating
- Manley H-beam connecting rods with ARP 2000 bolts
- Forged steel crankshaft
- Uses production Coyote aluminum cylinder block
- Longer 12-mm head bolts for higher clamp load
- Large rear-sump 10-quart-capacity oil pan features optimized oil drainback and windage tray to control oil and improve high-RPM performance
- Tuned composite Mustang GT intake manifold with production drive-by-wire 80-mm throttle body
- Four-Valve-Per-Cylinder Aluminum Heads with roller-finger followers to reduce friction and allow for a more aggressive profile
- Mustang GT production camshafts
- Includes Ford Performance Parts colder heat range spark plugs for supercharging (M-12405-M50)
- Includes CM-6731-FL820 Ford Performance Parts oil filter
- Includes M-6600-M52 high-performance billet steel gerotor oil pump
- Vehicle harness and PCM not included. Use Ford Performance Parts wiring, PCM, and installation kit (M-6017-M50B) engineered for street rod/project car swap installations
- Engine-mount Bosses and bellhousing-mount pattern common to 4.6L Modular engines
- Engine does not include engine harness or flywheel/flexplate
- Does not include alternator (for kit see M-8600-M50BALT)
- Does not include exhaust manifolds

Ford Performance 5.2L Aluminator XS

When word hit the streets that Ford was bringing an intoxicating Shelby Mustang GT350 to market, enthusiasts wanted to know all about it. I happened to be behind a GT350 test mule in Arizona at a traffic light during field-testing. The car was camouflaged and sounded snarly nasty. The engineer cracked the throttle and there wasn't any doubt. It sounded unlike any Mustang in history. What I heard at that traffic light was the 5.2L Voodoo engine exclusive to the Shelby GT350 that was coming for 2015–2016. The flat-plane crank 5.2L engine

Roush Performance gives you the ability to get into a complete 5.0L RSC ROUSHcharger crate engine. Contact Roush Performance for pricing. Bank on at least 600-plus hp. In addition, you receive a Ford Performance Aluminator 24-month/24,000-mile warranty. (Photo Courtesy Roush Performance)

If you're ready to go racing or do a combination of weekday commuting and weekend racing, the Aluminator XS Cobra Jet crate engine M-6007-A50XS delivers 500 hp. It has a steel-billet gerotor oil pump, CJ short-runner high-RPM intake manifold, 1,517-cfm dual 65-mm CJ throttle body, competition high-RPM pulse ring, and 12-quart competition oil pan. (Photo Courtesy Ford Performance Parts)

5.2L Aluminator XS Specifications

- Fits 2011–2017 Mustang GT
- 5.2L (317 ci) displacement
- 570-plus hp
- 542 ft-lbs of torque
- 12.0:1 compression
- Shelby GT350 aluminum block
- Mahle forged pistons
- Manley H-beam connecting rods
- Coyote forged steel crankshaft
- Shelby GT350 CNC ported cylinder heads
- M-6550-M52 performance camshafts
- Shelby GT350 12-quart oil pan and pump
- M-9424-M50CJ Cobra Jet intake manifold
- M-9926-CJ65 Cobra Jet dual throttle body
- Ford Racing M-6675-M50BR 12-quart rear-sump oil pan features optimized oil drainback and windage tray to control oil and improve high-RPM performance
- Ford Racing M-6600-50CJ high-performance billet steel oil pump
- Ford Racing M-9424-M50CJ Cobra Jet tuned intake (preproduction intake manifold shown)
- Ford Racing M-9926-CJ65 throttle body
- Four-valve-per-cylinder Boss fully CNC ported aluminum heads with roller-finger camshaft followers
- Ford Racing M-6513-M50BR Boss valve springs
- Ford Racing camshafts
- M-6550-M50BINT intake camshaft (13 mm lift, 263 degrees duration)
- M-6550-M50BEXH exhaust camshaft (13mm lift, 290 degrees duration)
- Ford Racing M-9593-LU47 47-pound fuel injectors
- Ford Racing M-12A227-CJ13 high-RPM pulse ring
- Ford Racing M-6P067-M50B blue coil covers
- Ford Racing M-12405-M50 heat range (zero) spark plugs
- Ford Racing M-6731-FL820 oil filter
- Alternator kit M-8600-M50BALT
- Includes production Boss 302 crankshaft damper
- Vehicle harness and PCM not included. Use Ford Racing wiring, PCM, and installation kit M-6017-A504V designed for street rod/project car installation.
- Engine-mount Bosses and bellhousing-mount pattern common to 4.6L Modular engines
- Headers not included
- Assembly plant lift brackets not included
- Premium fuel only
- Custom PCM calibration is required when installing the M-6007-A50XS crate engine
- Although these engines are designed specifically for the 2011–2014 Mustang GT as well as the 2015–2017 Mustang GT, they're easily adapted to classic, Fox, and SN-95 applications using the electronics available from Ford Performance Parts.

Ford Performance Parts offers a 5.2L Coyote crate engine, which has just been announced at press time. Where the 5.2L Coyote differs from the GT350's flat-plane Voodoo is with its cross-plane crankshaft that is shared with the 5.0L Coyote. This means 5.2L (317 ci), 12.0:1 compression, 5.2L block with a larger bore, Mahle coated and forged aluminum pistons, Manley H-beam connecting rods with ARP 2000 bolts, M-6550-M52 block, CNC-ported heads, large race pan, and brute power. You may also build a 5.2L from scratch with Ford Performance parts. (Photo Courtesy Ford Performance Parts)

produced a European, buzzy throat like no other American muscle car had ever had.

Ford Performance decided to tap into the Voodoo's genetics to conceive the 5.2L Coyote crate engine. In addition, you can piece all of the parts together to build your own 5.2L Coyote if you'd like to do something different. What makes the crate 5.2L and all its components different is the absence of the flat-plane crankshaft. The 5.2L Coyote is a cross-plane crank mill with increased displacement. This means 5.2L (317 ci), 12.0:1 compression, 5.2L block with a larger bore yet the same stroke, Mahle forged-aluminum pistons, Manley H-beam connecting rods with ARP 2000 bolts, M-6550-M52 block, GT350 CNC-ported heads, and more. You're getting a Shelby-class crate engine except without the cross-plane crank.

Edelbrock E-Force Coyote

The Edelbrock E-Force Coyote is a complete supercharged engine package for your classic or late-model Ford project vehicle. The Edelbrock E-Force engine is a new, factory-fresh Ford Aluminator crate engine built for high-performance applications with a steel forged crankshaft, Mahle forged and coated 9.5:1 compression pistons, and Manley H-beam connecting rods. The 9.5:1 compression ratio allows for safe and reliable supercharged performance on 91-octane pump gas.

On top is the Edelbrock E-Force supercharger system, which is also scheduled to be a separate supercharger kit at press time. This great-looking system features Eaton TVS 2300-cc rotors, which provide unparalleled efficiency, whisper-quiet operation, and OEM reliability. This engine package comes complete with the essential E-Force supercharger kit including electric intercooler water pump, intercooler plumbing, and intercooler recovery tank, as well as fuel rails, 50 lb/hr fuel injectors, mass air flow sensor (MAFS) housing, and reusable air filter. It also includes all front-end drive accessories: water pump, alternator pulleys, idlers, tensioners, belts, and hardware. Pair with universal heat exchangers 15405, 15406, or 15407 for a complete installation. What this means for you is 700 hp with an OEM-style warranty.

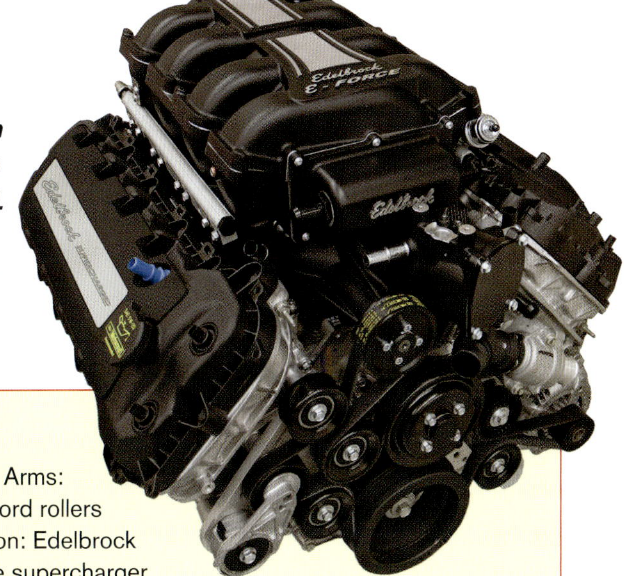

Edelbrock's E-Force Coyote is a drop-in supercharged package you can swap into your S197 or S550 Mustang over a weekend and have 700 hp available. This is also a nice swap for a classic Mustang or vintage Ford. Edelbrock also offers the E-Force supercharger kit for Coyote engines. The nice thing about the E-Force Coyote is its Ford Performance Aluminator status: forged pistons and H-beam rods down under for extreme durability. (Photo Courtesy Edelbrock)

Edelbrock E-Force Coyote Specifications

- Displacement: 5.0L (302 ci)
- Horsepower: 700 hp
- Torque: 606 ft-lbs
- Compression: 9.5:1
- Block: Ford Coyote aluminum
- Crankshaft: Forged steel
- Pistons: Mahle forged aluminum
- Rods: Manley forged H-beam
- Camshafts: stock Ford Coyote Ti-VCT
- Rocker Arms: stock Ford rollers
- Induction: Edelbrock E-Force supercharger system
- Cylinder heads: stock four-valve aluminum with Boss 302 valvesprings
- Supercharger finish: black powder-coated
- Warranty: 2-year/unlimited mileage

Proving the Coyote

Ford Performance Parts has provided me with a 2011–2014 M-6007-M50 crate engine to work with in JGM Performance Engineering's dyno lab in Valencia, California. I'm going to try everything from basic bolt-on parts to cam swaps and Ford Performance Parts Boss and Cobra Jet induction. I'd like to show you how you can improve on the Coyote in your Mustang GT or F-150 with easy bolt-on mods.

The big challenge for the aftermarket, including Ford's own Performance Racing Parts division, is how to make the Coyote more powerful while maintaining durability. Improvements come from larger throttle bodies and induction systems from Ford Performance Parts and Edelbrock. Ford Performance Parts and Comp Cams have a variety of cam picks for the Coyote that improve horsepower and torque.

As this book goes to press, no one in the industry is working on a cylinder head for the Coyote apart from existing castings and sophisticated CNC port work. Total Engine Airflow from Summit Racing Equipment, JPC Racing, Livernois, MMR, and a host of others offer CNC-ported cylinder heads for the Coyote. The web is rich with options. Regardless of the head you choose, you can count on improvements in horsepower and torque. Jim Grubbs has invited me into his dyno lab at JGM along with the Ford Performance Parts 5.0L DOHC Coyote. Let's get started.

JGM Performance Engineering's dyno lab in Valencia, California, is home to this Ford Performance Parts 2011–2014 5.0L Ti-VCT Coyote. This is a Ti-VCT Coyote void of the charge motion associated with the 2015–2016 engine. Simple modifications add up to big power gains. We start with 487 hp and 400 ft-lbs of torque out of the crate. Ultimately it is 591 hp and 420 ft-lbs of torque.

Extensive thought went into the Coyote's exhaust system. Bean counters were thinking cast-iron manifolds. Engineers and product planners were thinking tuned tubular headers. They managed to get them, against great odds. Exhaust tuning has been very influential to Coyote power.

Baseline Pull

The amount of power the Ford Performance 5.0L Ti-VCT Coyote engine pulled right out of its shipping

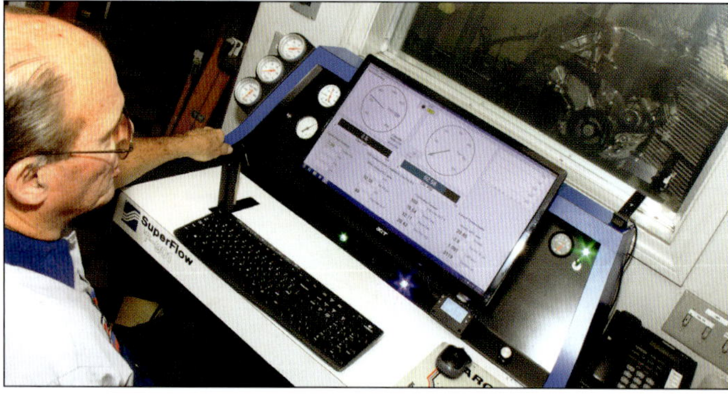

Jim Grubbs of JGM Performance Engineering has found that the Coyote's performance is stunning right out of the crate. Easy bolt-ons have netted eye-opening power gains. Jim began with a conservative redline of 6,500 rpm. By the time we wrapped up, along with a Ray McClelland tune, he had this thing at 7,600 rpm.

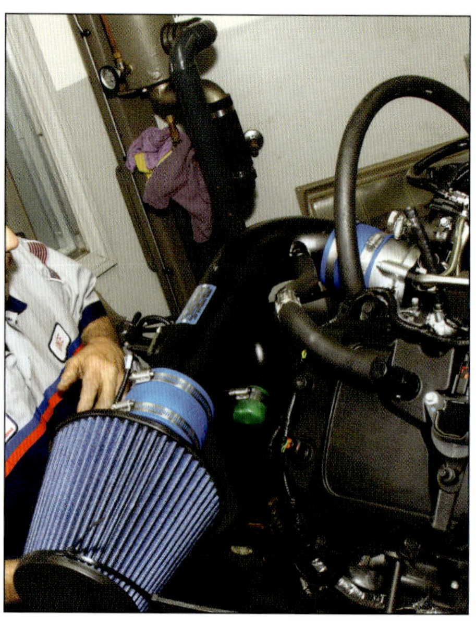

BBK Performance's cold-air kit netted more than 10 hp and comparable torque. Although 10 hp doesn't sound like much it must be figured into the big picture as a first step. It is the beginning of a path between 487 hp and 591.

crate is remarkable. This is not an Aluminator crate engine, which is more about durability than power. Ford Performance's Aluminator crate engines are torn down and built up using race-ready components on which you build power.

The Ford Performance dyno engine is an out-of-the-box Mustang GT engine, which means stock powdered-metal rods and hypereutectic pistons. I took this engine to 7,200 rpm initially just to see what it would do power-wise. JGM tried a couple of baseline pulls on its newly calibrated and digitized SuperFlow 901 for consistency. Our best numbers at the crank were 487.4 hp at 6,300 rpm and 416.47 ft-lbs of torque at 5,000 rpm.

Stock Intake with BBK Cold-Air Kit and Factory Shorty Headers

JGM suggested we conduct baby-step modifications to prove out the value of each modification. I installed BBK's cold-air kit just to witness the value of a simple cold-air kit. The best numbers at the crank were 498.3 hp at 6,800 rpm and 412.21 ft-lbs of torque at 5,100 rpm. Here's what happened.

We lost some torque but gained 10.9 hp with the BBK cold-air kit. This demonstrates a common sense approach to power. The Coyote is an easy engine with which to make power. However, power is gained step by step. Each individual modification, regardless of how small, contributes to big power gains over time.

Stock Intake with BBK Cold-Air Kit and BBK Shorty Headers

The BBK cold-air kit yielded 10 hp. BBK provided ceramic-coated shorty headers to complement the cold-air kit. Here are the numbers: 509.7 hp at 6,800 rpm and 417.70 ft-lbs of torque at 5,100 rpm.

BBK Performance ceramic-coated shorty headers brought 10 to 15 more horsepower and comparable torque. More remarkable was their performance against long-tube headers. We achieved 591 hp through these BBK tubes.

Jim and I ultimately ran four header types on the Ford Performance Parts base Coyote. Of the four, these BBK shorties provided the best street power curve. Just bolting these guys on netted another 11.4 hp and 5.56 ft-lbs of torque. Again, it all adds up to significant gains.

Stock Intake with BBK Cold-Air Kit and BBK Long-Tube Headers

The installation of BBK long-tube headers proves that there isn't always benefit to long-tube headers when compared to shorties alone. If you're going to long-tube headers, be prepared to change both induction and cam profile if you want serious gains in power. Also be prepared to visit a professional tuner. Here's how long-tubes stack up against shorties with no other modifications. Here are the numbers: 508.4 hp at 6,600 rpm and 417.19 ft-lbs of torque at 5,100 rpm.

Stock Intake with BBK Cold-Air Kit and JBA Long-Tube Headers

When we bolted on a set of ceramic-coated JBA long-tube headers, numbers came in lower in terms of horsepower and torque; this is another reminder of why a custom tune is so important to horsepower and torque numbers. You don't always gain power with an induction and exhaust

BBK shorty headers are an easy fit for 2011–2016 Mustangs, netting more power than expected. We managed to get 20 to 25 more horsepower just from a BBK cold-air kit and shorty headers.

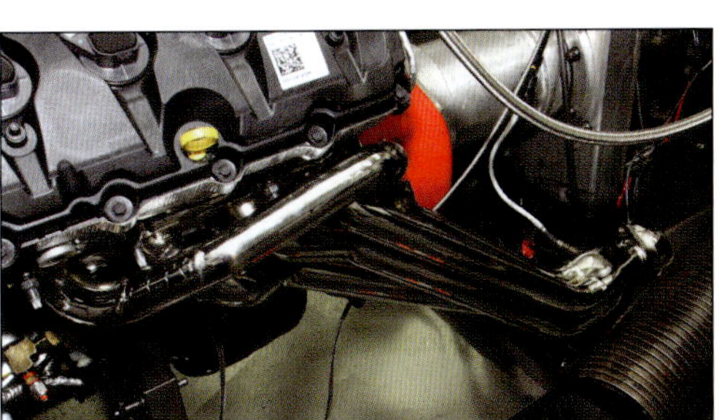

These are BBK Performance long-tube headers. Long-tube headers witness real gains when you complement them with a more-aggressive cam and induction system. If you're staying with stock cams and induction system, your money is best spent on BBK Performance shorty headers, cold-air kit, and a larger 87-mm throttle body. If you opt for all three you're looking at a 30- to 35-hp increase.

upgrade. You must have a custom tune to complement the parts upgrade, which makes the most of the upgrades. Here are the numbers: 497.9 hp at 6,800 rpm and 408.48 ft-lbs at 5,400 rpm.

JBA sent these ceramic-coated long-tube headers for Coyote dyno testing. As with the BBK long-tubes, power was about as expected with comparable horsepower and torque on a par with what you experience from shorty headers in the 510-hp range. Long-tube headers, especially on a late-model performance Mustang, make sense only if you intend to run hotter cams, CNC-ported heads, and a deep-breaking induction. Be mindful of smog laws in your area before buying long-tubes.

Stock Intake with BBK 87-mm Throttle Body and JBA Long-Tubes

When we installed the BBK 87-mm throttle body it actually lost horsepower but gained torque. This shows something about how to package induction and exhaust systems. With the BBK long-tube headers it gained torque but lost some horsepower. Ray McClellend of Full Throttle Kustomz in Fillmore, California, explains the importance of dyno tuning every time you change parts, regardless of how small the modification appears to be. Each upgrade changes the engine's dynamics. When we went to the BBK 87-mm

With header swaps out of the way the next bolt-on comparo is this BBK 87-mm throttle on the stock Coyote manifold.

Ford Performance's Boss 302 intake manifold as a single bolt-on swap doesn't necessarily increase power, but changes where power is made. The first Boss 302 manifold test was with the BBK 87-mm throttle body, which netted good street torque.

Boss 302 induction delivers a nice balance of street torque and high-RPM road course power. With Boss induction, including the 90-mm throttle body, BBK shorties, and a Ray McClelland tune, we managed to get 551 hp and 422 ft-lbs of torque.

The Ford 90-mm Boss and Dual Bore 67-mm Cobra Jet throttle bodies call for the use of the included adaptor harness from Ford Performance when a plug swap is necessary. When you transition to these induction systems, professional tuning is required.

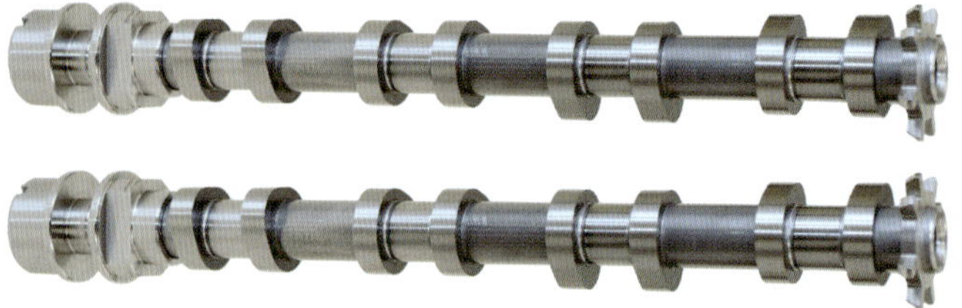

Ford Performance Boss 302 cams were used with the Boss induction system and BBK shorty headers. This netted more than 50 hp.

A Boss cam swap is time consuming and mandates your very close attention. Cam and front timing covers must come off to perform this swap. Get all of your timing marks where they belong before disassembly and the crank keyway at twelve o'clock. Lay the cams in per your Ford Performance instructions. If you get everything lined up, you cannot miss. Tighten the am journal caps slowly, beginning at the middle, and then torque in proper order. These bolts are torque-to-yield and cannot be reused.

throttle body and long-tubes the crate Coyote needed a professional tune, which would have gained both horsepower and torque. Here are the numbers: 498.4 hp at 7,000 rpm and 423.83 ft-lbs at 5,200 rpm.

Ford Performance Parts Boss 302 Intake with BBK 87-mm Throttle Body and JBA Long-Tube Headers

When we installed the Ford Performance Boss 302 induction with 87-mm BBK throttle body it woke the Coyote up with 22.2 more ponies but lost torque. This change proves what the Boss 302 intake manifold is all about. This is a great street and track manifold designed for the road course, which makes it a nice compromise between street and track. It comes on strong at high RPM on an engine that likes to rev. Here are the numbers: 520.1 hp at 7,000 rpm and 394.82 ft-lbs at 4,500 rpm.

JGM did a second pull with this combination after a brief cool-down and came up with these numbers: 524.4 hp at 6,900 rpm and 402.09 ft-lbs at 5,300 rpm.

Ford Performance Parts Boss 302 Intake with BBK 87-mm Throttle Body and BBK Shorty Headers

Exhaust tuning is a big part of how power is made. I have learned that long-tube headers do their best work at high RPM while shorties are better for low- to mid-range torque. When we went back to the BBK shorty headers the numbers improved across a broader RPM range. Torque was consistent. Here are the numbers: 528.2 hp at 7,000 rpm and 406.48 ft-lbs at 5,200 rpm.

Ford Performance Parts Boss 302 Intake with 90-mm Throttle Body, Boss 302 Cam Swap and BBK Shorty Headers

When we went to the larger Ford Performance 90-mm throttle body and Boss 302 cams it was apparent from the numbers that Ray McClelland was needed to tune the Coyote, which came in a pinch lower in terms of horsepower and torque. Whenever you change engine dynamics, such as a larger throttle and cams, you have to change air/fuel ratio and spark timing. The testing logic was, what can the average enthusiast get from just changing parts without a tune? Ray stresses that it does not work that way. Any time you change induction and exhaust you effectively change how the engine processes air, fuel, and spent gasses. This calls for adjustments to fuel and spark curves, which can only be performed by a professional tuner. You can purchase off-the-shelf tune packages, which will get you started. When it's time to lay down rubber, you need a professional tune. Here are the numbers: 526.2 hp at 7,000 rpm and 402.92 ft-lbs at 5,700 rpm.

Ford Performance Parts Boss 302 Intake with 90-mm Throttle Body, Boss 302 Cam Swap, BBK Shorty Headers and Full Throttle Kustomz Tune

We learned quickly that without a professional tune I had gone as far as I could go with the JGM Coyote. We installed a quartet of Ford Performance Boss 302 cams and moved on to the next phase of testing. Ray McClelland arrived and promptly went to work on the Coyote's PCM and dialed in a custom tune. He made adjustments to fuel and spark curve and here's what happened: With a custom tune and Boss 302 cams, it gained 25.3 hp and 19.85 ft-lbs of torque. Here are the numbers: 551.5 hp at 7,000 rpm and 422.77 ft-lbs at 4,400 rpm.

Ford Performance Parts Cobra Jet Intake with Twin 65-mm Throttle Body, Comp Cams 191160 and BBK Shorty Headers

Ford Performance sent both the Boss 302 and Cobra Jet induction packages for an opportunity to show you how power is made via two induction systems with different missions. The Boss 302 intake with 90-mm throttle body is a great street and track manifold. It delivers a broader torque curve because it is engineered for both street and track performance. You get the benefit of high-RPM breathing when the throttle is pinned; you get good low- to mid-range torque for raw power coming out of the turns. And this is what

Ray McClelland of Full Throttle Kustomz joined us for dyno tuning. He made the difference between success and failure. Ray took the JGM Coyote from 529 hp to 551 with professional tuning technique. Ultimately, it was at 591 hp.

To act on the Coyote's greater potential, we looked to Trent Goodwin at Comp Cams for advice about where to go next. He and his tech staff set me up with the 191160 cam package and stiffer valve-springs, which is when this engine really came alive. This cam is just right for street and strip; not too radical for street but with plenty of lung for track use. It moves the power band higher.

the Boss 302 manifold is all about. As you can see, the Boss 302 delivered excellent mid-range torque at 4,400 rpm during the previous pull and came on strong at 7,000 rpm.

The Ford Performance Cobra Jet manifold is a high-RPM racing manifold designed primarily for drag racing. When we fired the Coyote with this manifold it immediately went into "limp-home" mode, which called for extensive tune time and reprogramming before Ray could get it running smoothly. This shows how vital a professional tune is to induction, cam, and exhaust modifications.

Between dyno sessions, we decided to swap in the Comp Cams 191160, which is a maximum-performance street cam designed to increase high-RPM horsepower. The 191160 cam package moves the power band higher, where the Cobra Jet manifold lives. While ordering the 191160 cams, I opted for stiffer valvesprings from Comp to keep the valvetrain stable at the expected higher RPM.

Ray went back into the PCM and made finite adjustments to fuel and spark curves. He also raised the rev limit to 7,600 rpm. Ray understood that the Coyote had more lungpower in it. Here is the result in three consecutive dyno pulls: 567.3 hp at 7,500 rpm and 399.63 ft-lbs at 5,700 rpm; 587.5 hp at 7,600 rpm and 400.27 ft-lbs at 6,500 rpm; 585.5 hp at 7,600 rpm and 401.09 ft-lbs at 6,500 rpm.

Ray took these numbers and

Although valves-prings could have been swapped on the engine, we decided to pull the heads and do it on a bench. Stiffer springs from Comp Cams were the key to getting the Coyote to 7,600 rpm, where power lives in this engine.

Comp Cams' 191160 cams were installed along with phaser limiters to limit the amount of valve timing advance.

went to work tuning for the fourth and final pull. It turns out that leaner is better, but it's risky. This is why Ray likes to find a happy medium between lean and risky lean. He made adjustments to fuel and spark curve and we wound up with the following numbers: 591.5 hp at 7,600 rpm and 406.52 ft-lbs at 5,400 rpm.

You learn from Ray McClelland how important professional engine tuning is to performance. Finite adjustments to fuel and spark curve are what the professional engine tuner understands and most of us don't. Building performance into the Coyote via bolt-on parts is all well and good but you must couple this effort with tuning.

Ford Performance's Cobra Jet manifold with a dual-blade throttle body, coupled with the Comp 191160 bumpsticks, and a Ray McClelland tune took the Ford Coyote to 591 hp. (Photo Courtesy Ford Performance Parts)

Because we didn't want to keep replacing the torque-to-yield factory cam journal bolts I opted for these fasteners from ARP.

These are Comp Cams phaser limiters, with one for each cam phaser. (Photo Courtesy Comp Cams)

You can also lock in valve timing with these phaser locks from Comp Cams. (Photo Courtesy Comp Cams)

191160 Specifications

RPM range: 1,900 to 7,200
Valve timing: .006
Lobe separation: 126 degrees
Intake centerline: 129 degrees
Valve lash: Hydraulic; no adjustment
Duration (degrees): Intake, 276; exhaust, 283
Duration at .050 inch (degrees): Intake, 236; exhaust, 239
Valve lift (inch): Intake, .459; exhaust, .453
Lobe lift (inch): Intake, .2440; exhaust, .2660

Dyno time with Ford's 5.0L Ti-VCT Coyote has shown something about how power is made and what it takes to get there. Simple bolt-on mods such as short- and long-tube headers show how important exhaust scavenging is to horsepower and torque. Shorty headers prove they're a good choice for street and weekend strip. Long-tubes cater more to high RPM and horsepower. I'm convinced that the Ford Performance crate Coyote would have gone over 600 hp with long-tube headers and more of Ray's engine tuning capability.

The two Ford Performance induction systems show how different they are when it comes to the torque and horsepower power band. Stock Coyote induction operates where it was designed to on the street with good low- to mid-range torque, and its CMCV system with variable runner length (2015–2016) comes on strong at high RPM.

The Boss 302 manifold raises the power band where torque comes on stronger in a higher-RPM range than you see with stock induction. Torque begins to arrive around 4,500 rpm with the Boss manifold and cams, giving this thing a nice broad torque curve between 4,500 and 6,500 rpm.

The Cobra Jet manifold coupled with the 191160 aggressive Comp grind leaves low-end torque behind, yielding to high-RPM horsepower, which is what the Cobra Jet manifold was designed for. Ford Performance has provided a foundation on which to build power in its 5.0L and 5.2L Coyote engines. It is the most rugged member of the Modular engine family. This means that you can take the Coyote's bones and get into power adders without concern for durability. And if you're planning more than 600 hp you can order up an Aluminator crate engine from Ford Performance and go to more than 1,000 hp.

Comp Cams 191160

This is a aax-effort street/strip cam set. It has strong power gains above 5,500 to 7,200 rpm, benefitting from full-length headers and 3.73 gears. It requires a phaser limiter kit and custom PCM/ECU programming. XFI NSR Ford 5.0L Modular 4V hydraulic roller swinging/finger follower camshafts (no springs required). Stiffer springs are suggested.

SOURCE GUIDE

Addiction Motorsports
818-313-8863
addictionmotorsports.net

American Muscle
877-890-4785
americanmuscle.com

ARP Bolts
800-826-3045
805-339-2200
arp-bolts.com

BBK Performance
951-296-1771
bbkperformance.com

Comp Cams
901-795-2400
compcams.com

Crane Cams
866-388-5120
386-310-4875
cranecams.com

CJ Pony Parts
717-657-9252
cjponyparts.com

Federal Mogul/Speed Pro
federalmogul.com

Ford Performance Parts
800-367-3788
fordperformance.com

Full Throttle Kustomz
805-200-5500
fullthrottlekustomz.com

Holcomb Motorsports
800-475-7223
holcombmotorsports.com

JBA Performance Exhaust
909-599-5955
jbaheaders.com

JGM Performance Engineering
661-257-0101

Justin's Performance Center
410-729-0005
jpcracing.com

Late Model Restoration
866-507-3786
lmr.com

Livernois Motorsports & Performance
313-561-5500
livernoismotorsports.com

Modular Motorsports Racing
805-383-4130
modularmotorsportsracing.com

MSD Ignition
888-258-3835
msdignition.com

National Parts Depot, California
800-235-3445
805-654-0468
npdlink.com

National Parts Depot, Florida
800-874-7595
352-861-8700
npdlink.com

National Parts Depot, Michigan
800-521-6104
npdlink.com

National Parts Depot, North Carolina
800-368-6451
704-331-0900
npdlink.com

Roush Performance
800-597-6874
roushperformance.com

Stage 3 Motorsports
877-578-2433
stage3motorsports.com

Summit Racing Equipment
800-230-3030
330-630-3030
summitracing.com